Manhood Is a Mindset

PRAISE FOR *MANHOOD IS A MINDSET*

"How do you teach your son God's wisdom, intentionally? This book is the answer. I cannot speak highly enough about *Manhood Is a Mindset*. It follows the approach of the wisest man who ever lived, taking a young man through the foundational principles of Solomon's wisdom and making them real to him. I plan to use the book with my own son. There is no other resource like it."

—CODY LIBOLT, CO-FOUNDER,
FOR THE NEW CHRISTIAN INTELLECTUAL

"Colin Trisler has provided a valuable resource for family ministry. In *Manhood Is a Mindset*, Trisler highlights the importance of mentoring in the father-son relationship. His conversational approach is perfect for encouraging and equipping dads for their most important mission in life."

—CHRIS SHIRLEY, PROFESSOR OF EDUCATIONAL MINISTRIES,
SOUTHWESTERN BAPTIST THEOLOGICAL SEMINARY

"What is manhood at its finest? In *Manhood Is a Mindset*, after wide research and deep meditations, J. Colin Trisler answers the question in ten letters to his son, and Solomon's ancient wisdom ascends in modern style. Brace yourself and hear the startling voice of God. Recommended!"

—D. SCOTT MEADOWS, PASTOR,
CALVARY BAPTIST CHURCH (REFORMED), EXETER, NEW HAMPSHIRE

"Amid the shifting sands of our world's ideas about morality and manhood, J. Colin Trisler has provided solid ground for fathers to stand on as they endeavor to raise their sons to be great men. Using an engaging writing style full of pop culture references and modern illustrations, he expounds on the ancient wisdom of the book of Proverbs with clarity and logical precision."

—BILLY FORD, LEAD PASTOR, BOUQUET CANYON CHURCH,
SANTA CLARITA, CALIFORNIA

"Every good father knows the importance of instructing their children but cannot teach what they do not know. *Manhood Is a Mindset* is a thorough, well-considered work on wisdom for fathers who have been raised in an age of folly. Fathers, Trisler's book is a tool that can help you build wise men out of the boys sacredly entrusted to you by the Lord."

—MATTHEW L. NOWLIN, DIRECTOR,
CONSERVATIVE CHRISTIANS OF TENNESSEE

"I highly recommend *Manhood Is a Mindset*. It is a book that I wish I could have read when I was a teenaged boy and when I was raising my own son. J. Colin Trisler has written a book that will hook young readers with pop culture references while it teaches and inspires them from God's wisdom in Proverbs. I will heartily share it with the boys that I work with."

—KYLE AMBROSE, PRINCIPAL OF LONGVIEW CHRISTIAN SCHOOL,
LONGVIEW, TEXAS

"Trisler's *Manhood Is a Mindset* is an engaging work relaying truths for young men to help them navigate life's often grey areas without resorting to the maudlin or milquetoast tone of much of current literature. The message proved beneficial, notably his warnings of the perils found with worthless men and forbidden women. I recommend this book to any father, no matter their son's age, and even just for their own edification and application."

—CAMERON BROWN, TEACHER, WRITER, AND FATHER OF TWO SONS

"In preparation for fatherhood, Colin Trisler's book fuels my motivation. He is skilled in demonstrating that the mental aspects of manhood are practical for daily life. Also, it is with certainty that I would introduce my son to the lady mentioned in letter number four. In all of the letters, wisdom is not just a lofty concept; instead, it is about the nuts and bolts of living as a good man."

—ANTHONY RAMOS PETERSON, TEACHER, CHICAGO, ILLINOIS

"Trisler has written a book that is much more than an enjoyable read or interesting subject. It is a practical tool that gives priceless advice for both young men and fathers navigating true and biblical manhood. The decision to write the book in the context of letters to his son proved to be a valuable roadmap for understanding how we should really be speaking and thinking about manhood and masculinity in our current society. The book is refreshing and unique in its approach in a way that feels closest to the actual truth about a subject that has been horribly misconstrued in today's world. What Trisler has written will actually help Christian men understand manhood more than almost any other book on the subject, because it is spoken on the basis of 'truth' and 'reality' as its core for the foundation of what is required of men. I could simply not agree more with Trisler, and I am thankful for the blueprint it has given me as a father to my own son."

—Justin Wilson, Founder, Studium Sapientiae

"By walking through the wisdom found in Proverbs, Trisler pulls out, with great clarity, valuable biblical truths that not only our sons need but the fathers teaching them as well. As Trisler mentions early on, manhood is not merely a 'random acquisition' but a mindset to be learned. *Manhood Is a Mindset* is a great resource for the church and I warmly recommend this book to fathers and sons everywhere."

—Scott Hutson, Ratio Christi Chapter Director, Dallas Baptist University

"*Manhood Is a Mindset* strikes to the heart, from the introduction and throughout each practical example of truth riveted in biblical and life examples. God's word reaches into every aspect of humanity in the psychology of the Psalms, yet Colin Trisler brings the life principles of wisdom into the lives of sons via Proverbs. As Sam Adams, the last Puritan, constantly wrote, our youth should be inculcated in 'piety, religion and morality.' *Manhood Is a Mindset* is a superb guide for dads to develop godly men."

—Tom Niewulis, author and founder of
www.samueladamsreturns.com

"Colin Trisler offers a tender yet strong look at biblical manhood in the form of these letters to his son. Well-read and wise, every dad should read this book. I was challenged and encouraged as I seek to raise my own two boys into men."

—Jesse Van Der Molen, high school English teacher

"Mining ancient wisdom, affirming it as divine truth, and framing it creatively with contemporary, easy-to-understand illustrations, pastor J. Colin Trisler draws on the initial chapters of Proverbs to convey to his son—and to all fathers and sons—what manhood is from a biblical perspective. The high adventure of godly manhood is richly rewarding. It is fulfilling and exhilarating as is nothing else to a man; yet it also is challenging and demanding. With God's help and with his father's guidance, every boy can achieve biblical manhood. Here is a great place for both fathers and sons to begin!"

—B. Nathaniel Sullivan, writer and blogger at wordfoundations.com

Manhood Is a Mindset

Fatherly Instruction from the Wisest Man Who Ever Lived

J. COLIN TRISLER

RESOURCE *Publications* • Eugene, Oregon

MANHOOD IS A MINDSET
Fatherly Instruction from the Wisest Man Who Ever Lived

Copyright © 2020 J. Colin Trisler. All rights reserved. Except for brief quotations in critical publications or reviews, no part of this book may be reproduced in any manner without prior written permission from the publisher. Write: Permissions, Wipf and Stock Publishers, 199 W. 8th Ave., Suite 3, Eugene, OR 97401.

Unless otherwise noted, Scripture quotations are from the New American Standard Bible ® (NASB), Copyright © 1960, 1962, 1963, 1968, 1971, 1972, 1973, 1975, 1977, 1995 by The Lockman Foundation. Used by permission.

Scripture quotations marked CSB have been taken from the Christian Standard Bible ®, Copyright © 2017 by Holman Bible Publishers. Used by permission. Christian Standard Bible® and CSB® are federally registered trademarks of Holman Bible Publishers.

Scripture quotations marked ESV are taken from The ESV® Bible (The Holy Bible, English Standard Version ®), copyright © 2001 by Crossway, a publishing ministry of Good News Publishers. Used by permission. All rights reserved.

Scripture quotations marked KJV are taken from the King James Version (KJV). Scripture quotations marked RSV are taken from the Revised Standard Version of the Bible, copyright © 1946, 1952, and 1971 National Council of the Churches of Christ in the United States of America. Used by permission. All rights reserved.

Apocrypha quotations marked RSV are taken from the Revised Standard Version of the Bible, Apocrypha, copyright © 1957; The Third and Fourth Books of the Maccabees and Psalm 151, copyright © 1977 National Council of the Churches of Christ in the United States of America. Used by permission. All rights reserved worldwide.

Resource Publications
An Imprint of Wipf and Stock Publishers
199 W. 8th Ave., Suite 3
Eugene, OR 97401

www.wipfandstock.com

PAPERBACK ISBN: 978-1-7252-6226-3
HARDCOVER ISBN: 978-1-7252-6227-0
EBOOK ISBN: 978-1-7252-6228-7

Manufactured in the U.S.A.   08/11/20

To Brooks

"Your eyes will see your Teacher,
and whenever you turn to the right or to the left,
your ears will hear this command behind you:
'This is the way. Walk in it.'"

—Isa 30:20–21 CSB

Contents

Acknowledgments		xiii
Introduction		xv
Letter 1	Today is a Good Day to Make Wise Decisions	1
Letter 2	Factor Fear into Your Way of Thinking	16
Letter 3	Take Home with You When You Leave the House	30
Letter 4	There's a Lady Calling for You	42
Letter 5	Listen to Your Two Most Trusted Sources of Wisdom	56
Letter 6	The Everyday Hero	70
Letter 7	Two Hard Truths About Happiness	92
Letter 8	Walk in Your Father's Footsteps	111
Letter 9	Let's Have A Rational Talk About Sex	130
Letter 10	Earn Your Own Self-Respect on a Daily Basis	153
Bibliography		175

Acknowledgments

Clear and meaningful thanks are in order:

To God. I know from personal experience that you are a hands-on Father because only a loving and active God could have blessed me with the family that I have. My wife and children are shining examples of your direct involvement in my life. They testify to the depths of your love and forgiveness. I do not deserve my family, yet you have seen fit to smile on me with this most perfect earthly gift—and for that I am forever grateful. This book is my effort to make the most of the blessing you've given me.

To Cody Libolt. I have two versions of this book: a pre-Cody version and a post-Cody version. The post-Cody version is the one you're holding right now. Your editorial comments ranged from insightful to vicious—but they were always valuable. This book wouldn't be what it is without you. Thanks for believing in this project. You are a good man and a good friend.

To my son, Brooks, and my daughters, Alexis, Scarlett, and Juliette. Each of you, in your own way, has taught me so much about life and how to live it. You've helped me understand what it means to be a man. And you've shown me what true love looks like in real life. You are living, breathing proof not just of God's existence, but of his goodness and his grace. Thanks so much for all your prayers and your encouragement (and a special thanks to you, Lex, for donating your proofreading skills for free). Even if no one else reads this book I know you all will. And based on that fact alone, I consider this work a job well done.

To my wife, Amanda. If I were to thank you for all that you do, I would end up writing a whole other series of letters. So for the sake of space, I'll keep my words concise yet sincere. Thank you for your constant support. Writing this book is one of the hardest jobs God has ever given me to do.

Oftentimes, it felt more like a boxing match than a creative process. I went many painful rounds with discouragement. But no matter how many times frustration knocked me to my knees, you were always in my corner, pounding the mat, encouraging me to get up and keep moving forward. Your words of wisdom gave me the motivation I needed to stand up like a man and keep on punching. I went the distance with this book because of you. I love you so much. You are the wife of my youth. My Adrian Balboa. My Abigail Adams. My Lady Wisdom. And I will hold tight to you for as long as God sees fit to keep us together. Oh, and by the way—thanks for encouraging our children, particularly our son, to read Daddy's book.

Introduction

A Letter to the Fathers Who Will Read This Book

When I was three years old, my father told me Santa Claus wasn't real.

About three years later, he told me professional wrestling was staged.[1] To be honest, the truth about Santa wasn't anywhere near as shocking as the truth about pro wrestling.

My six-year-old brain didn't know what to make of my dad's mind-blowing assertion. I was so taken aback at first that I rejected him outright. I didn't believe him when he told me that Hacksaw Jim Duggan and Kamala the Ugandan Giant weren't really fighting. I didn't believe him when he said all the punches, the body slams, the chops, the tackles, and the big splash were all an act. I didn't believe him when he told me the ending of their match was predetermined, or when he said the wrestlers weren't really trying to hurt each other and were probably friends in real life.

My shock quickly turned into anger, and I accused my dad of trying to play a nasty trick on me. But my dad, to his credit, didn't get mad. He simply said, "Son, you're old enough to know the truth. Just watch it close and you'll see for yourself."

As much as it pained me, I listened to my father. I took his advice and watched the next wrestling match closely. For myself. With open eyes and an open mind. And as I did, the truth floored me like a missile dropkick off the top rope. I saw with my own eyes what he was talking about—and I was stunned when I discovered that *he was right the whole time.* The wrestlers weren't really fighting. The harder I focused, the more I could see that their

---

1. *Fake* was the word he used, but I refuse to use that word because it's insulting. There's nothing fake about a pro wrestler's toughness and athleticism. Although their art involves a certain degree of showmanship, even the most casual fan can see the pain that accompanies many of the choreographed bumps and blows is very real.

moves were choreographed—and I realized that their match was less of a brawl and more like a rough-and-tumble dance routine.

The mental grenade my father had tossed my way blew my mind wide open. After the smoke cleared, I saw the world in a completely different way, and I realized for the first time in my young life that pro wrestlers pull their punches—but the truth does not.

It took me about a week to fully wrap my mind around this newfound reality. After much soul searching, I finally came around and swallowed the red pill in totality. I discovered the truth for myself. I put my preconceived notions aside and saw professional wrestling for what it actually is: a TV show, just like any other—a cool TV show, but a show nonetheless.

My days of blissful childish ignorance were over and there was no going back. I had taken my first step toward real-world manhood. All thanks to my dad, who used this experience to teach me two valuable, life-changing truths.

He taught me that a man can't negotiate with reality. The facts of reality don't bend to my preferences. Nor do they take my feelings into consideration. Reality is what it is and there's no getting around it. As my father pointed out, the reality of the situation was this: No matter how badly I wanted the fight to be real, Hacksaw Duggan and Kamala weren't really fighting. They were athletic actors putting on a show; and if I wanted to enjoy the show, I would be wise to accept that reality on its own terms.

I also learned that my father actually knew what he was talking about. No matter how much I didn't want to hear what he had to say, what he said proved true. And I realized that I would be wise to take his words more seriously from now on.

DADS, THIS BOOK IS FOR YOU, TOO

Nearly four decades later, my father's lessons still ring true.

Now that I'm a father myself, I want to follow his lead and teach my children the truth about life, no matter how uncomfortable it may be. One thing I've learned about being a father is that telling the truth isn't always easy. The truth can make you unpopular, especially with your children. But fatherhood is not a popularity contest. It's a responsibility. And a responsible father stands firm in the truth, even when it's inconvenient. Even when his children don't appreciate it. He stands firm because he loves his children. He wants what's *best* for them. And he knows it's his job to give his children what they *need*—and not always what they *want*.

Any hands-on father will tell you that one of his biggest responsibilities is to provide for his children.[2] We want to give our children good lives, so we buy them clothes and food, toys and games, computers and cars. But as every responsible father understands, material *things* don't make for a good life—and the greatest gift any man can ever give his children is *the truth*.

And that's why I've written this collection of letters to my son: to better instruct him in the truth he needs to grow into a self-respecting man, one who's prepared to go out into the real world and build a good life for himself. I've chosen to go public with these letters because I want to help other hard-working fathers do the same for their sons. I want to support them as they take on the tough responsibility of molding their young and inexperienced boys into strong and godly men.

So to all the fathers (and father-figures) who are reading this right now, I want to make one thing clear: I may have written these letters to my son, but I've written them from a father's perspective. With a father's heart. That means I've designed this book to not only help teenage to twenty-something guys grow into manhood, but also to support *you*—the dads and mentors who are helping them get there.

I've written these letters with *you* in mind. This book is for the men who are working hard every day to guide their sons in the right direction. Those proactive fathers who want to be something more meaningful to their sons than just a reactive disciplinarian or a human ATM. My hope is that this book will give all you hands-on dads the support you need to teach your sons how to apply practical biblical principles to the everyday life situations most young men face. My aim is to help you create a respectful and educational home environment, one in which your sons will grow into capable men who are ready to go out into the real world and meet their responsibilities to God, their families, their neighbors, and themselves.

I want these letters to facilitate meaningful interactions between you and your sons, with the hope that it will inspire the two of you to work together as a team and put God's word to work in your daily lives. Then, hopefully, you'll see for yourselves how something as profound and as simple as *the truth* can make a lifetime of difference in the life of a family.

The truth is, any ol' dude can bark at a boy and tell him to *Grow up and act like a man!* (as if becoming a man is as simple as flipping on a mental switch).

But *authentic* manhood is not some random acquisition. It's a mindset that must be learned. And it takes a special kind of man to be a good

---

2. I discuss the responsibilities of a hands-on father in detail in letter 8.

father—one who's willing to put in the work necessary to help his young and inexperienced son learn how to be a successful man of God.

So, naturally, the question arises: How exactly does a father help his immature boy transform into a mature and self-respecting man?

As we'll see in my first letter, I answer that question with just one word: Wisdom.

Sincerely,
A fellow father

Letter 1

Today is a Good Day to Make Wise Decisions

Proverbs 1:1

*"Every day you will have decisions to make.
Real-world decisions that your life depends on."*

Son, think of all the decisions you've made so far today.

Based on your own independent judgment, you chose what you were going to eat for breakfast (if you ate breakfast). You chose to take a shower (if you took a shower). You chose to brush your teeth (if you brushed your teeth). You chose the clothes you're wearing (if you're wearing clothes). And on and on and on.

People face a multitude of choices and make hundreds of decisions every day of their lives. Some are too insignificant to even register as self-conscious thought. For example, those routine decisions that you hardly even know you're making—like whether to open the carton of milk with your left or right hand, or in what order to put your socks on when you're getting dressed. Those sorts of mundane choices tend to be inconsequential, and I don't want to waste precious time micromanaging your microdecisions.

Instead, I want us to concentrate on those everyday choices that can have real-world significance. The ones that have the potential to impact the trajectory of your entire life.

Daily decisions, like:

- Will you choose to pursue God today? Or will you choose to stand in opposition to him?
- Will you walk in the upright way of wisdom? Or will you take the easy route like a fool and walk on the path of the wicked?
- Will you focus your romantic interests toward the right woman? Or will you blur the lines of your integrity with forbidden lusts?
- Will you make the effort to earn self-respect? Or will you waste your time chasing worthless pursuits?

These are everyday choices that every man must make. And believe it or not, your overall success or failure in life depends on how you handle these daily decisions.

A lifestyle that emphasizes good choices can lead to real success, while a series of bad choices can lead to untimely ruin. I learned this lesson early in life when I saw the movie *Indiana Jones and the Last Crusade*. I was an eleven-year-old boy when this movie came to theaters in the summer of 1989. And to this day, the climactic scene involving Indy, the Nazi stooge, the beautiful-but-untrustworthy Austrian, the seven-hundred-year-old knight, and the Holy Grail still plays a role in my decision-making philosophy as a man in my forties. After all, the notion that the wrong choice could cause a man's flesh to rot off, his eyeballs to sink into his skull, and his skeleton to disintegrate into dust all within a matter of seconds is the kind of idea that can (and probably *should*) recalibrate anybody's understanding of the concept of *consequences*.

Let's consider the scene. Donovan, the Nazi stooge, had one decision to make upon entering the ancient Grail chamber: choose the one true Holy Grail.[1] But there was a twist. The true Grail was mixed in with dozens of other false grails. And anyone who sought to claim the Grail had but one chance to choose wisely. Drinking from the true Grail "will bring you life," the guardian knight said. Drinking from the false grail, however, "will take

---

1. The Holy Grail is an artifact of lore. It is the chalice Christ used at the Last Supper and, according to legend, possesses supernatural powers. In the cinematic universe of Indiana Jones, the Grail has the power to grant eternal life and healing to anyone who drinks from it.

it from you." With the stakes set, Donovan scanned row after row of chalices and goblets with a gun in his hand and a blank stare of bewilderment in his eye. "I'm not a historian," he said. "I have no idea what it looks like. Which one is it?"

The multitude of choices overwhelmed him. The pressure of having only one shot to choose the one true Grail from an excess of options paralyzed his mind. So instead of choosing for himself, he deferred to the judgment of a supposed expert: the beautiful-but-untrustworthy Austrian professor. He allowed her to make his choice for him. This, of course, resulted in Donovan's aforementioned destruction.

"He chose poorly," as the knight put it when Donovan drank from a false grail and melted away.

Donovan was a ruthless and self-absorbed man with a bad habit of making bad choices. That one short sip from the false grail was the bad decision that cost him his life. But it was hardly the first poor choice he had made in this story. A slew of bad choices got him to that point in the first place and contributed his demise.

These bad choices included:

- Lusting after the power of the Grail and attempting to manipulate the mighty hand of God to fulfill his own corrupt ends.
- Aligning himself with bad influences. In his case, the Nazis—or the *armies of darkness*, as Indy's father aptly labeled them.
- Compromising his integrity by lying and cheating his way into the Grail chamber.
- Failing to possess the proper knowledge, especially regarding the character of Christ. As a result, he failed to make a wise decision as to which cup was the true Grail and which ones were deadly imposters.
- And in his final act of foolishness, surrendering the authority of his own mind to someone else—that is, letting the beautiful-but-untrustworthy Austrian professor make up his mind for him. This foolishness cost him his life.

Donovan's pursuit of the Grail proved to be a quest of self-destruction because his decision-making skills were inept (to put it mildly). Indiana Jones, however, won the day by making a series of wise choices, proving yet again why he's the most industrious swashbuckling hero this side of Han Solo.

Indy's wise choices included:

- Fearing the power of God and respecting the power of the Holy Grail.

- Partnering with his wise father, Henry Jones Sr., and utilizing his guidance to succeed in his mission.

- Drawing upon his own vast knowledge of facts and employing a strong sense of reason to make informed choices. Examples include: using his father's instructions to successfully navigate the lethal challenges in the Grail temple, and properly understanding the character of Jesus ("That's the cup of a carpenter," Indy said as he grabbed the cup of Christ) to discern the true Grail from the false ones.

- Backing up his decisions with action. Indiana Jones as a character is a rare breed of alpha male who is both intelligent and courageous. He's smart enough to develop a plan and skilled enough to carry it out. He thinks quickly on his feet and never allows opposition stop him from achieving his goals.

- Being mentally strong enough to think for himself. Unlike Donovan, Indy didn't need to rely on someone else to do his thinking for him. In the Grail chamber, he took responsibility for his own mind and made his own decision. And as a result, he chose wisely, as the knight said.

Son, as Indiana Jones proved, reality forces every man to make choices. Every day you will have decisions to make. Real-world decisions that your life depends on. If you want to find true success, a Donovan-esque evasion of this responsibility is out of the question.

The only question is: *Day in and day out, will you make good choices or bad choices?*

Wise decisions lay the groundwork for a life of meaning and productivity. A life worth living. And while not all bad choices immediately result in your face melting off, every bad choice does plague your life with wasted time and lost opportunities and long-term suffering.

The real world, as it turns out, has a lot more in common with that ancient Grail chamber than we realize. Every day the world is going to present you with a multitude of choices to make. The right choice can lead to abundant life, while any one of the wrong choices can result in certain failure. This overabundance of options has the power to overwhelm your thought process. It can paralyze your mind and make the truth seem ambiguous or even impossible to discover. Thus making the wise choice and finding that one right answer in any given situation can be difficult because there are often multiple answers that look and feel like the right answer.

If such everyday decisions have the potential to impact a man's entire life, how then is he supposed to choose? How can anyone discern that one grail of truth from among life's many falsehoods?

Well, as the knight said in the Grail chamber, any man who desires to go forth and lay claim to the gift of life must first take on the responsibility of making wise choices.

THE WISDOM EQUATION

Since wisdom is the dividing line between life and death, let's take a moment to sharpen our understanding of *wisdom* as a biblical concept.

The Hebrew notion of wisdom denotes both intellectual aptitude and physical skill.[2] According to Old Testament scholars Andrew Hill and John Walton, "wisdom is basically the very practical art of being prudent, sensible, and skillfully insightful so that one might prosper and have good success in life." Hill and Walton point out that wisdom involves "the ability to discern and achieve order" in the world, in political and social relations, and within one's own heart. "Wisdom taps the life experience of accumulated years and harnesses that knowledge and understanding for the purpose of safety, long life, right behavior, sound moral character, happiness, material prosperity, and integrity." They conclude: "Ultimately, wisdom results in the ability to steer through life in a way that wins favor and a good name in the sight of both humanity and God."[3]

With this broader biblical context in mind, I will now give you my own refined definition of *wisdom*. In its most basic sense, wisdom is making *knowledgeable*, *moral* life choices and acting on those choices with an effective degree of *rationality* and *skill*.

Think of this four-part definition as a mathematical equation:

Knowledge + Morality + Rationality + Skill = Wisdom

Each constant within this equation is valuable in its own right. But a wise man will utilize all four in conjunction to find the correct answers to his everyday problems. To better understand how wisdom works as a life solution, let's take a closer look at the value of each constant.

Knowledge. A man kickstarts his quest for wisdom by seeking out the cold, hard facts of reality. Knowledge enables a man to make informed decisions. Knowledge, therefore, is the cornerstone of the wisdom equation. After all, you can't do the right thing if you don't first know on an intellectual level what the right thing is.

The man who has a handle on the facts is a man who's well on his way to getting a handle on his life. To be clear: an astronomical IQ score

---

2. Mounce, *Complete Expository Dictionary*, 793.
3. Hill and Walton, *A Survey of the Old Testament*, 390.

doesn't make a man wise. But knowledge is a foundational aspect of a wise mind. Take Indiana Jones for example. He had knowledge not only of the Grail itself, but also the cup's Owner. As a result, when the time came to make a decision, he chose wisely. Donovan, by his own admission, lacked the knowledge he needed and paid for his ignorance with his life.

Son, as these men proved, a working knowledge of the facts kick-starts the thinking process. It leads to both mental and moral clarity, which lay the groundwork for good decision making.

Morality. And make no mistake: Morality and wisdom go hand-in-hand. Knowledge of the facts is not enough. If you want to make good decisions, then you must also be able to discern good from bad in any given situation. If knowledge is the foundation of the wisdom equation, then morality is the spinal cord—it signals your reflexes, coordinates your movements, and stabilizes your behavior. If you disregard morality in your decision-making process, you've paralyzed yourself from the get-go. The man who incorporates a strong sense of morality into his thinking, however, acts on noble motivations. He stands firm in his convictions and walks tall in his integrity. His attention to virtue facilitates self-respect and allows him to take genuine pride in his choices.

Morality facilitates wisdom by simplifying your choices. Making tough decisions is never easy. But an absolute sense of morality streamlines the process by dividing your options into two mutually exclusive categories: good or evil. With every decision you make, you're either accomplishing righteousness or perpetrating wickedness. Like Indy and Donovan, you're either drinking eternal life from the true cup of Christ, or you're sipping death from a fatal pretender. There is no morally neutral middle ground. There is only morality and immorality—life and death—and everything you choose to think and say and do falls into one of those two categories.

Son, the world will try to label you a moral zealot if you refuse to operate in subjective shades of gray. But as a wise man, you must cut through the amoral dissonance of this world and see life for what it really is: a series of binary choices. The truth is there is no gray. There is only white or black. Wisdom or wickedness. Truth or lies. Life or death.

Moral subjectivity is an empty concept that fosters sympathy for the devil. So make sure you use absolute definitions of right and wrong to govern your behavior.

Rationality. Knowledge informs your choices. Morality empowers you to take genuine pride in your choices. But rational thinking enables you to make good choices in the first place. The man who thinks rationally is the man who can see the world as it truly is. He can distinguish between truth and falsehood. And he is wise not because he perceives the truth, but because he chooses to think and act in accord with the truth. This makes him a rational man.

The truth is that which corresponds to reality—that which is real. Reality itself is an objective and absolute fact. Existence is what it is, and it exists independent of our opinions or wishes or imaginations. Reality is absolute and firm. The truth, therefore, is absolute and firm. This means the truth is always true. Neither the passage of time nor the cycle of culture can change it. Rationality is the recognition of and the submission to reality. And the rational man is the one who lives in uncompromised harmony with that reality. With the truth. Rational thinking is an essential aspect of the wisdom equation because it grounds your decisions in the truth. A wise man doesn't have to be brilliant. But he must think reasonably. He must be *rational*.

For an example of rational thinking in practice, look once again to the example of Indiana Jones in the Grail chamber. Indy knew Jesus was a modest carpenter and not a man of worldly means. Based on this fact, he deduced that the cup of Christ would not be some lavish royal vessel (as Donovan thought it should be). It would instead match the humble personality of a King who came not to be served but to serve (Mark 10:45). Unlike Donovan, Indy didn't base his choice on what he thought the Grail *should* look like. He instead chose a cup that was battered and worn and humble in outward appearance, like its true Owner.[4] Indy committed himself to a rational thought process which followed the facts rather than his personal preferences. And his success in choosing the one true Grail testifies to my point: The man who thinks rationally is a man destined to make wise decisions.

Son, God has blessed you with a miraculous, one-of-a-kind mind that is like nothing else on this earth. He has equipped you with the ability to think: to know, analyze, understand, discern, prioritize, and decide. A man of true wisdom is a man who knows not simply *what* to think, but *how* to think. He knows how to distinguish good from evil. Right from wrong. Truth from lies. Wisdom from foolishness. A wise man never stops thinking. He uses *his mind* to discover the truth. And he exercises wisdom when he strives to live a rational life—that is, in harmony with the God-given truth that governs reality.

Skill. Thinking, however, is time wasted unless it is a precursor to *action*. Knowledge is worthless, morality is ineffective, and rationality is pointless until they are brought to life by skillful action in real-world situations. A

---

4. Regarding the Messiah's physical appearance, the prophet Isaiah said the Christ would have "no stately form or majesty that we should look upon Him, nor appearance that we should be attracted to Him" (Isa 53:2).

man of true wisdom is serious about his life and the choices he makes. He is wise because he carries out his knowledgeable, moral, and rational decisions with an effective degree of skill. Thus he is productive in achieving his goals. In short, he is both a thinker and a doer—for as Jesus said, true wisdom is vindicated by her *deeds* (Matt 11:19; see also Jas 1:22–25).

In the Grail chamber, Indiana Jones didn't hesitate to act. He saved his father's life. He overcame the armies of darkness. And he preserved the Grail's integrity because he was confident enough to bring his decisions to life in real-world situations. Son, as Indy proved, personal values are worthless unless you have the grit to act on them. Even in the face of extreme danger. The man who has the will to act is the man who achieves real-world success with the choices he makes.

On paper, the wisdom equation is straightforward and simple. But real life doesn't exist on a wrinkle-free piece of two-dimensional paper. Nor does it unfold within the safe confines of a movie screen. It unfolds in the chaotic four-dimensional space of the here-and-now.

So how does the wisdom equation play out in real life? With all due respect to fictional heroes like Indiana Jones, the best way to answer that question is to observe the behavior of a living, breathing, real-world wise man.

And what better case study is there to learn from than that of the wisest man who ever lived?

WISDOM IN REAL LIFE

Son, that man is not me.

I am not the wisest man who ever lived. I am not a genius, nor do I claim to know all there is to know about life. I am, however, a thinker. I'm also a doer. That means I make great efforts to understand how the world works and I work just as hard to govern my life by the truth that governs our existence. I may not be a world-renowned action hero like Indiana Jones, but I am a wise man—and I am *your* father. And those two facts make me more qualified than any other person on this planet to provide you with the instruction you need to grow into a man of wisdom and strength.

My goal as a father is simple: I want to help you transform from a child into a man. To achieve this goal, I will do what a good father does. I will honor my God-given responsibility and train you up in the truth so you can learn how to think like a man, how to act like a man, and how to build a life worthy of a man. I will instruct you in the wisdom you need to get up off the couch, go to work in the real world, and reap the rewards of a meaningful life. I will come alongside you, not as a drill sergeant or a boss, but as your daddy—and I will teach you how to handle the responsibilities of manhood.

I will guide you every step of the way—but I will not live your life for you. I will protect you—but I will not overprotect you. I will provide for you as I teach you what it means to be self-reliant. I will tell you what you *need* to hear, not just what you *want* to hear—but you have my word: I will always speak to you with a sense of love and respect.

My hope is that together, as a team, you and I will take that unsophisticated mess of testosterone and insecurity the world calls adolescence and mold it into a chivalrous mindset of godly masculinity.

Son, I'm here to let you know that manhood starts not in the muscles, but in the mind. And *wisdom* is the key that unlocks that treasure chest of masculinity within you. We are going to unlock that treasure together. But we'll need a guide to show us how it's done. Fortunately for us, I know just the man for the job. The man God himself proclaimed to be the wisest man who ever lived.

Israel's King Solomon.

With these letters, I will guide you through the mind of the world's wisest man. We're going to go verse by verse through the first nine chapters of the biblical book of Proverbs. Solomon dedicated these chapters to instructing his son in the principles of godly wisdom and the practices of authentic masculinity.[5] He looked to God as the ultimate source of wisdom. And I will do the same.

---

5. Regarding the Solomonic authorship of Proverbs, Hill and Walton note, "The book of Proverbs represents the literary legacy of the Hebrew sages, or wise men." These wise men were generally associated with the king's royal court. The Solomonic authorship of the proverbs credited to him is in dispute among some scholars. The arguments for or against Solomonic authorship extend beyond the scope of these letters. However, the following points are worth noting. Hill and Walton do not claim a Solomonic authorship. They do point out, though, that "King Solomon's sagacity is well attested in the Old Testament." Solomon is credited with uttering some three thousand proverbs (hundreds of which are preserved in the book of Proverbs). "According to 1 Kings 4:29–34, Solomon's knowledge and understanding surpassed that of all the other sages in the academies of the ancient Near Eastern World. King Solomon stands as the 'patron of the arts' in ancient Israel. Not only did he popularize the wisdom tradition of the Hebrews, but also his example as sage and scholar served as the model for future generations" (*A Survey of the Old Testament*, 443). Raymond C. Van Leeuwen makes the following claim: "it is clear that Solomon is not the author of the book in its present form . . . though some have argued for the origin of sections of the book in the Solomonic court." He goes on to point out that for the ancients, the issue "was not authorship in the modern sense, but the authority of works written in the 'spirit' of the archetypal lawgiver, psalmist, or sage" (*Introduction to Wisdom Literature*, 20). With all this in mind, I treat "Solomon, son of David, king of Israel" (Prov 1:1)—be it in the archetypal or literal sense—as the author of Prov 1–9. For as Duane Garrett

I have followed Solomon's lead and written this book as a personalized discourse. As a series of letters to you, my son. These letters are for you because the truth of God's wisdom is the best instruction I could ever give you. Be aware, though, that the wisdom in these letters did not originate with me. I am not qualified to hand out eternal truths (I can only discover them). God, however, is very much qualified to define wisdom and truth. And it's his divinely inspired wisdom and truth that I will impart to you because *that* is my highest responsibility as your earthly father.

I have used Solomon's proverbial discourse as the basis for these letters because even though Solomon and his son lived thousands of years ago, they were regular people just like you and me: a father and his son, men created in the image of God, seeking to live wise and meaningful lives in a world filled with foolishness and confusion.

We are going to learn by example. By observing a wise and insightful man. Let's begin our study by looking to the good example of Solomon to understand what wisdom looks like in real life.

SOLOMON, THE WISEST MAN

Prov 1:1

In the time of the Old Testament, God raised up Israel as his special people to receive and proclaim the wisdom of his word.

God blessed Israel with many wise and mighty leaders, beginning with Abraham and continuing with other wise men like Moses, Joshua, and Solomon's father, King David. David was so devoted to walking in the wisdom of the Lord that the Bible calls him a man after God's own heart (1 Sam 13:14; Acts 13:22). He was a brave warrior, a wise king, and a godly but imperfect man who, like every human being who has ever lived, had moments in his life when he abandoned God's wisdom and lapsed into foolishness. Although his sins rendered real consequences, the Lord brought David to repentance. And through his forgiveness, God restored their fellowship.[6]

David walked closely with God in humility and wisdom, and Israel flourished under his leadership. When he grew old and died, his son Solomon succeeded him as the new king of Israel.

---

notes: "The biblical assertion that the Solomonic monarchy witnessed a great literary renaissance and that Solomon himself was the fountainhead is reasonable" (*The New American Commentary*, 52). I likewise treat his son—again, be it in the general or literal sense—as the intended audience.

6. David's most notable sins were murder and adultery. Read about David, his temptation, his sin, the Lord's discipline, and his restoration in 2 Sam 11–12.

Solomon was young and inexperienced when God put him on the throne. By his own estimation, he was not ready to lead. He even went so far to describe himself as a *little child* who didn't know if he was coming or going in life (1 Kgs 3:7). Ready or not, however, the throne was his. And the legacy of an entire nation now rested upon his fledgling shoulders. Needless to say, the inexperienced Solomon felt overwhelmed by the weight of his newfound responsibility.

The Bible tells us that "Solomon loved the LORD, walking in the statutes of his father David, except he sacrificed and burned incense on the high places" (1 Kgs 3:3)—meaning, in a very basic sense, that up to this point in his life, Solomon was inconsistent in his walk with God. He loved his Heavenly Father, and he followed in the wise footsteps of his earthly father. Yet Solomon had not committed himself to walking *full-time* in the wisdom of the Lord. His indecisiveness—his failure to take on the full responsibility of manhood—rocked his youthful spirit back and forth like a tiny paper boat struggling to stay upright in an angry sea of insecurity.

Reality, however, waits for no man; and like it or not, the throne was his responsibility. In that moment of high anxiety and self-doubt, reality forced Solomon to make a choice. Would he allow his insecurity to master him? Or would he *man up* and master his insecurity?

By this time, David, his earthly father, had died. But Solomon still had a Heavenly Father who recognized his dilemma. One night, God appeared to Solomon and offered his support.

"Ask what you wish me to give you," was how God began the conversation (1 Kgs 3:5).

Solomon had a genuine heart for God. He loved the Lord because he had seen with his own eyes how loyal God was to his wise father, who had walked full-time in the principles of God's wisdom. So Solomon took God up on his offer.

This was his prayer:

> "You have shown great lovingkindness to Your servant David my father, according as he walked before You in truth and righteousness and uprightness of heart toward You; and You have reserved for him this great lovingkindness, that You have given him a son to sit on his throne, as it is this day. Now, O LORD my God, You have made Your servant king in place of my father David, yet I am but a little child; I do not know how to go out or come in. Your servant is in the midst of Your people which You have chosen, a great people who are too many to be numbered or counted.... Give me now wisdom and knowledge, that I may

> go out and come in before this people, for who can rule this great people of Yours?" (1 Kgs 3:6–8; 2 Chr 1:10).

Notice that Solomon did not back down from his responsibility as the king. Nor did he look to abuse his newfound authority by asking God for worldly glory or tyrannical power. Instead he asked for something of real value. Something only God can give: true wisdom.

Solomon's mature choice pleased God. And he responded to Solomon's request in this way:

> "Because you had this in mind," God said, "and did not ask for riches, wealth or honor, or the life of those who hate you, nor have you even asked for long life, but you have asked for yourself wisdom and knowledge that you may rule My people over whom I have made you king, wisdom and knowledge have been granted to you . . . behold, I have done according to your words. Behold, I have given you a wise and discerning heart, so that there has been no one like you before you, nor shall one like you arise after you." (2 Chr 1:11–12; 1 Kgs 3:12)

Solomon could have asked God for anything. But instead of wealth or fame or power, he asked for what he decided was his highest value: to know the ways of God's wisdom in full.

When reality called on him to make a decision, Solomon put the wisdom equation into effect:

Knowledge. Solomon *knew* what he needed from God. Israel was God's covenant people and he was their king. He was young and inexperienced, but the responsibility of the throne was his nonetheless and there was no getting around that. His firm grasp of these facts put his situation in context and informed his next move.

Morality. Solomon made the *moral* choice in asking for wisdom. He could have asked God for something easy and cheap. But he instead took the more responsible route. He sought the wisdom he needed to govern with justice and righteousness and integrity. Solomon pleased God with his maturity, when he proved his heart was virtuous like his father David.

Rationality. Solomon made the *rational* choice in asking for wisdom. Solomon was inexperienced and scared. But he refused to surrender to his fear. He stood strong and accepted his responsibility like a man. He allowed his mind to rise above his emotions, and he made a good choice when he decided that long-term wisdom, not some easy or shortsighted scheme, was the solution to his inexperience.

Skill. Solomon put his God-given gifts into action; and with God's wisdom as his guide, he led Israel into a golden age of prosperity.

Notice, though, that Solomon didn't face his challenges on his own. When reality forced him to make a choice, he turned to two reliable sources for support.

- He looked up to God, his Heavenly Father, as the singular source of all that is right and true.
- He also looked back on the godly example of his earthly father to see what wisdom looked like in real-world everyday life.

Solomon saw with his own eyes that David was a man who walked before God with integrity. He saw how God rewarded his father's wisdom with great and faithful love (1 Kgs 3:6). He acquired the wisdom he needed to be a successful king by focusing his attention on both his Heavenly Father and his earthly father. He took what they taught him, all those things that are proven to be good and right, and governed his life by those truths day in and day out.

And he found great success along the way.

Solomon understood the insecurity that comes along with raw youth. But he also understood that God's wisdom was the answer to solving the problems that inexperience and immaturity can bring about.

The truth never changes

Like Solomon, we all have a choice to make. In our daily decisions, we can choose to think long-term and act with wisdom. Or we can choose to pursue some short-sighted scheme and get tripped up by our own foolishness.

The reason foolishness continues to thrive in our world is because, as sinners, we would rather trade knowledge, morality, rationality, and skill for their opposites: ignorance, immorality, irrationality, and incompetence.

Even wise men like Solomon are not immune to the temptation to indulge in foolish behavior. As Israel's king, Solomon developed a worldwide reputation for unparalleled wisdom. But later in his life, he shifted his focus away from God and lapsed into severe disobedience. This does not mean that he stopped loving God or that God stopped loving him. It means that Solomon made a series of bad choices that caused him to stumble in his personal life and in his relationship with God. He chose to reject God's wisdom for the sake of sinful distractions; and for a time, he sought fulfillment in the pleasures and possessions of this world. But after he considered all his foolish behavior, he realized such empty pursuits were "vanity and striving after wind and there was no profit under the sun" (Eccl 2:11). Solomon knew well the rewards of wisdom. But he also experienced firsthand the painful consequences of folly.[7]

Before we pass too harsh of a judgment upon Solomon, however, let's keep this fact in mind: The Bible tells us he was a *wise* man, not a perfect man. Since the beginning of time, the world has been full of people just like him: men who possess the capacity to be wise yet still choose to do foolish things. Even today, the wisest among us stumble over our own foolish choices because foolishness is easy. Acting like a fool requires no real effort. Living like a wise man, however, requires much effort. It demands self-control, rational sacrifice, and long-term thinking. The straight and upright path of wisdom is a challenging path to walk. But the wise man remains devoted to this way of life because he understands this simple fact: the *rewards* of living wisely make all the work more than worthwhile.

God created us to live wisely because there is true happiness in it. Like any good father, he wants his children to do well. But to achieve the success God has in store for us, we must make the choice to put his wisdom into action in every area of our everyday lives. That's why God inspired Solomon to share these words with us in the book of Proverbs: to instill wisdom in God's people so that we may live meaningful lives and walk in a covenant relationship with our Lord forever.

"The proverbs of Solomon the son of David, king of Israel" (1:1) are just as applicable to us today as they were to the people of ancient Israel because God's absolute truth never changes. It stands the test of time because God has woven his truth into the very fabric of our reality. Wise living is living in harmony with reality. With God's truth. And any man who makes the day-by-day choice to live in harmony with the truth is a wise man in the making.

Son, wisdom itself is a choice—it's *your* choice.

If you choose to dedicate yourself to a life of wisdom, you will quickly mature beyond your youthful inexperience and grow into a strong man of good judgment.

---

7. The final two verses of Ecclesiastes indicate that Solomon learned his lesson and repented of his wayward actions: "The conclusion, when all has been heard, is: fear God and keep His commandments, because this applies to every person. For God will bring every act to judgment, everything which is hidden, whether good or evil" (Eccl 12:13-14). Although the human author of Ecclesiastes is technically anonymous, as the author simply refers to himself as "the Preacher," he also refers to himself as "the son of David, king in Jerusalem" (Eccl 1:1). Solomon was indeed the son of David and king in Jerusalem (compare with Prov 1:1). Therefore, Solomon is the probable author. Traditional scholarship also credits Solomon as the author.

Throughout the course of these letters, I will use Solomon's words of wisdom to teach you how to think, speak, and act like a man of true wisdom. I will impose upon you the highest standards of behavior so that you can grow into a man of personal excellence. That excellence includes these features: a strong mind, solid values, powerful principles, righteous confidence, and a healthy sense of self-respect.

I invite you to follow Solomon's example—to join with your Heavenly Father and with me, your earthly father, as we work together to train you in the wisdom of the truth and help you mature you into the man God has fearfully and wonderfully made you to be.

Love,
Dad

Letter 2

Factor Fear into Your Way of Thinking

Prov 1:2–7; 9:10

"Fear is healthy when you use it according to its purpose."

I opened the previous letter with the tale of a brave hero, dark enemies, and perilous heroics.

These kinds of stories are helpful because they bring ideas to life using images that are relevant and striking (and thus easy to remember). C. S. Lewis, a man who understood the power of narrative, agreed with me on this point: "If it is so likely that children will meet cruel enemies, let them at least have heard of brave knights and heroic courage. Otherwise you are making their destiny not brighter but darker."[1]

That being said, the visuals from Indiana Jones and stories like his can be rather ferocious at times, and I'd prefer to open this letter with a brighter, more heartwarming illustration. The image I have in mind is from one of your favorite movies: Disney's animated version of *The Lion King*.

This film has a deeper sense of symbolism than your standard children's movie. The story itself is rich with character and meaning and is

---

1. Lewis, *On Stories*, 39.

worthy of much consideration. Especially for young men, as it serves as an astute visual representation of a boy's difficult journey into manhood.

The story begins with the birth of Simba, a lion cub who is destined to rule the kingdom of the African Pride Lands. Early one morning Simba and his father—the present king, a wise and mighty lion named Mufasa—ascended to the summit of a large stone formation named Pride Rock. There the father and his son, the king and his heir, sat side-by-side and observed the glory of their kingdom entire. And as the Pride Lands sparkled in the light of the rising sun, the two lions marveled at the radiance of their realm.

"Look, Simba," Mufasa said. "Everything the light touches is our kingdom."

"Everything the light touches . . . " repeated young Simba with wide-eyed wonder. Simba then stood to his feet and strolled away from the presence of his father. His eyes moved across the vast African plain until they settled on a strange patch of darkness out in the distance. The cub walked to the edge of the rock and asked, "What about that shadowy place?"

Mufasa moved closer to his son. His answer and his voice were firm. "That's beyond our borders. You must never go there, Simba."

"But I thought a king can do whatever he wants."

"Oh, there's more to being king than getting your way all the time," Mufasa said with a smile as he casually moved back toward an area of more solid footing. Young Simba, as if by instinct, followed his father away from the edge of the rock and asked "There's *more*?"

Mufasa chuckled at his son's natural curiosity. And with great thoughtfulness he instructed him on the importance of living with wisdom. In *harmony* with the circle of life that surrounds him.

When Disney originally released *The Lion King* in theaters in 1994, I was in my mid-teens. So watching it today with my own family in my middle-aged years conjures up a fond sense of nostalgia. As a teenager, I identified more with the character of Simba, the impulsive lion cub who embodies the carefree joy and adventurous potential of a young man who has his whole life ahead of him. These days, as a husband and a father and a pastor, I identify more with king Mufasa, the responsible patriarch who dedicates his life not only to governing his kingdom with justice and righteousness, but also to leading his family with strength and love.

The scene at Pride Rock especially resonates with me. The visual of the wise father sitting high and mighty alongside his young son, who is much smaller but sitting just as upright, is an image as powerful as any scene of heroic battle. It reminds me that a man doesn't have to use his fists to be a hero. A hero isn't the man who can hit the hardest or run the fastest. A hero is the man who does the right thing in the right way and for the right reasons. By this definition, any man can be a hero. Even the one who does something as simple as relating to his family with a sense of respect and responsibility. The father who invests time and effort into his relationship with his son is just as heroic as any mighty king. And the son who honors his father's effort with his attentiveness is just as heroic as any brave knight.

Son, with this letter, you and I will follow Solomon's lead and take the first step on our very own hero's journey. I will establish myself as your instructor and you will be my student. As Henry Jones Sr. did with Henry "Indiana" Jones Jr., I will give you the truth you need to succeed in your journey toward manhood. And as Mufasa did with Simba, I will equip you with the understanding you need to avoid the shadowy fringes of life—those formless voids that lie beyond the borders of truth, goodness, and beauty—and teach you to set your mind on everything the light touches.

That is my job as your father. Your job as my son and my student is to take hold of my words and utilize them to illuminate your mind and let the light of God's wisdom radiate within you like a majestic sunrise.

But in order to accomplish your job, you must first honor my effort with your utmost respect and attention.

FATHER TO SON

Prov 1:2–6

After introducing himself as the author in v. 1, Solomon opens his discourse by asserting his God-given parental authority over his son.[2]

Notice how he doesn't hunch down to the boy's level and present himself as his buddy. He stands tall and upright as the boy's father, forcing his son to turn his gaze upward and approach him with veneration. When he speaks, he speaks with authority and commands the respect that comes with the title of *daddy*.

God had appointed Solomon as the boy's father. That made it *his* job to provide his son with the influence and instruction necessary to live a meaningful life. Notice how Solomon doesn't use his authority to intimidate his son. Nor does he seek to tear him down or provoke discouragement. Instead, his goal is to build him up in his image. As a man of wisdom. A man of integrity. A man of God.

He establishes this as his intention from the outset by introducing the discourse in this way:

---

2. Although Solomon doesn't explicitly identify his son as his intended audience in these opening verses, he goes on to single him out as his primary reader in v. 8 (letter 3).

"²To *know* wisdom and instruction, to discern the sayings of *understanding,* ³to *receive* instruction in wise behavior, righteousness, justice and equity; ⁴to give prudence to the naive, to the youth knowledge and discretion, ⁵a wise man will hear and increase in learning, and a man of understanding will acquire wise counsel, ⁶to understand a proverb and a figure, the words of the wise and their riddles." (1:2–6, emphasis added)

From the outset, Solomon establishes a relational hierarchy between him and his son. He, the father, takes on the authoritative role of *instructor,* while the son adopts a subordinate role as his *student.*

As the student, the son's job is to meet three specific responsibilities:

1. *To know wisdom and instruction.* Learning is a cooperative process, not a passive one. Solomon's job is to teach, and his son's job is to learn. He calls on his son to *know* wisdom and instruction—that is, to memorize his words, get a handle on his instructions, and absorb them into his consciousness. As the student, the boy is responsible for taking an active role in the learning process. He is to pay attention to his father, observe his behavior, and acquire from him the knowledge he lacks as a young man just starting his journey into manhood.
2. *To discern the sayings of understanding.* Wisdom, however, is more than memorized facts. Memorization is an essential part of learning. But true learning also requires an active mind that grapples with ideas and develops those memorized facts into rational concepts. The student who thinks on a conceptual level understands how things work. He gains *understanding* when he's able to answer the two primary questions of any idea: *How?* and *Why?* He then gains insight when he's able to recognize, to *discern,* the logic that underlies his teacher's instructions. Such understanding and discernment provide a solid foundation for authentic learning.
3. *To receive instruction in wise behavior, righteousness, justice, and equity.*³ The purpose of this instruction is the application of wisdom in

---

3. The word *equity* as it is used here denotes personal *integrity* and is not to be confused with *equality* (particularly some impossible collectivized notion of equal distribution of outcomes). The Hebrew word *ūmêšārîm* (from *meshar,* translated here as *equity*) derives its meaning from the root word *yāšār* which, according to Mounce, "usually denotes appropriate human conduct with respect to ethical norms and religious values. . . . This word also describes the straight, level pathway that believers are to walk, in contrast to the crooked and uneven pathway that the wicked follow" (*Complete Expository Dictionary,* 760–61). In their commentary on the book of Proverbs, scholars Carl F. Keil and Franz Delitzsch translate *meshar* as *integrity* to emphasize the word's moral connotation, which involves "a way of thought and of conduct that is straight,

day-to-day living. That means the son is to *receive* his father's instructions and *integrate* them into his way of life. He is to use this knowledge to live with a sense of integrity—that is, to deal with others in a way that is wise, righteous, just, and equitable.[4]

By opening the discourse in this way, Solomon shows that he's embraced the responsibility of being a wise father. He doesn't step aside and farm out his parental responsibilities to someone else. He steps up, like a man, and asserts himself as his son's chief source of wise counsel. He knows it's his job to *give prudence to his naive and youthful son* who lacks life experience.

The son's lack of experience doesn't make him immoral. It simply makes him a young man in need of guidance. By describing him as *young* and *naive*, Solomon isn't insulting his son—he's *relating* to him. Remember, Solomon too was once an inexperienced young man. He understood all too well the insecurity that comes with raw youthfulness because, as we covered in letter 1, he experienced that same fear as an untested king.

Here, Solomon acknowledges that young people especially have a great need for wisdom. Teenage years are a precarious time in every man's life. In those years more than any other, a young man needs to develop a good sense of wisdom and discretion. Ever the wise father, Solomon takes the time to give his son the anchor he needs to navigate the chaotic waters of youth culture. His goal is for his son to *obtain the guidance necessary* to *increase in learning* and adopt the *mindset of a wise man*. That fact is why he aims this entire discourse directly at his son.

And that's why I'm writing these letters to you, *my* son.

Like Solomon, I have resolved to honor the sacred responsibility of being a father. I will take on the responsibility of being your instructor. In response, I expect you, as my student, to do *your* job and meet the same three responsibilities Solomon expected of his son.

Again, those responsibilities are:

1. to *know* the wisdom and instruction I am teaching you,
2. to make the effort to *understand* my words of insight and obtain the knowledge necessary for success,
3. and to *receive* my words and live out God's standards of wisdom, righteousness, justice, and integrity in your everyday life.

---

i.e., according to what is right, true, i.e., without concealment, honest, i.e., true to duty and faithful to one's word." (*Proverbs, Ecclesiastes, Song of Songs*, 39). Also see https://biblehub.com/hebrew/4339.htm.

4. We'll discuss in more specific detail how to accomplish this in your day-to-day relationships in letter 7.

Son, if we're going to succeed in this venture, you and I need to *respect* each other. You must respect me as your father and your instructor. I must respect you as my son and my student. And we must both respect God and embrace the individual responsibilities he has given us.

Throughout the course of these next two letters, we will explore the concept of *respect*. In letter 3, we'll discuss the hierarchical nature of our relationship as father and son and the respect you owe me and your mother as your parents.

I will spend the remainder of this letter, however, instructing you in the importance of respecting God as your Heavenly Father. My goal here is to help you realize the essential role *respect* plays in every successful relationship. Mutual respect—that is, respect both given and received—is mandatory if we want to achieve success in meeting our sacred responsibilities, both to God and each other.

And as Solomon will explain, if a young man wants to know how to give respect where it's due, he must first learn to factor *fear* into his way of thinking.

FEAR IS A HEALTHY FACTOR IN THE LIFE OF A WISE MAN

Prov 1:7

Fear is not a bad thing.

It is a natural human instinct. An unconscious impulse of the spirit. Thus it is neither good nor evil. Like any other inanimate object or emotion (weapons, the internet, anger, etc.), the morality of fear lies not with the object itself, but within the heart and mind of the human who wields it. Take a gun for example. The crook who uses a gun to rob a store is evil. The hero who uses a gun to thwart the crook is righteous. The gun itself is amoral. It is merely an object, a tool a man uses—like a car, a fire, or a pen—to accomplish a specific goal.

Son, the same rationale applies to fear. The fear you experience at any given point is neither good nor evil. It's what you choose to do with your fear that gives it a sense of morality. Fear is sinful when you use it as an excuse to compromise your integrity. Fear is healthy when you use it according to its purpose: as a God-given warning system designed to pull you away from harm and push you toward *the good*.[5] Fear becomes righteous when you use

---

5. As I will touch on in letter 6, the fear of God is rational, but the fear of men is irrational. The persecution of this world is shallow and fleeting, so never submit to the

it as motivation to think faster than possible, to love more than you knew you were able, and to stand up stronger than ever before as you preserve your integrity and achieve your values.

Fear can be a powerful tool of motivation in the arsenal of a wise man. Solomon understood this to be true.

That's why he tells his son:

> "⁷The fear of the LORD is the beginning of knowledge; fools despise wisdom and instruction." (1:7)

Son, a healthy and righteous fear of God is the starting point in a man's quest for wisdom. But again, don't be thrown off by Solomon's use of the word *fear*. To understand *fear* in its entirety as a concept, you must move beyond the superficial perception of *fear* as mere feelings of danger, dread, and terror. Indeed, the ancient Hebrew definition of *fear* does involve a healthy sense of trepidation. But it also includes a sense of awe and respect and worship. Especially in regard to the Lord.[6]

The fear Solomon speaks of in Prov 1:7 is a righteous fear designed to facilitate a deep respect for God, who, as your Heavenly Father, possesses a rightful authority over you.

His authority stems from these three absolute truths:

1. He is the sovereign Lord of everything he has created.
2. You exist as a part of his creation.
   Therefore:
3. He possesses a legitimate authority over you.

The Bible tells us that God created humanity in his own image, according to his likeness (Gen 1:26–27; 9:6). This status confers upon us the unique responsibility of living as God's standard bearers on earth. That means in everything we think, say, and do, we are to reflect the character of our wise and righteous Father.

Son, keep this fact in mind as you make your daily decisions: You exist to reflect God's image. He does not exist to reflect yours. As a child of God, you have a responsibility to submit to your Heavenly Father's sovereign authority and do the job he put you on earth to do. We'll discuss the biblical concept of *submission* in the next letter. But for now, I'll use the

---

threats of bullies. Jesus called on his disciples to stand strong on the rock of their convictions, even in times of intense persecution. He warned them to fear not "those who kill the body but are unable to kill the soul; but rather fear Him who is able to destroy both soul and body in hell" (Matt 10:28).

6. Mounce, *Complete Expository Dictionary*, 244.

example of a guitar and a guitar player to help you get a handle on the scope of God's authority.

A guitar exists to make music. But the guitar cannot play itself. It is an instrument that necessarily requires a musician in order to accomplish its created purpose. It's the guitarist, not the guitar, who arranges the music. His mind develops the melody. His fingers strum the strings and glide over the frets to produce harmonious tones. The guitarist makes the guitar *work*. A guitar is productive as an instrument when it follows the guitarist's lead and stays on key and produces the right sounds in the right moments.

But what if the instrument refuses to cooperate? What if the guitarist plays the right notes but the guitar produces off-key sounds? At this point, the guitarist has a series of options. He can give the guitar a chance to correct its mistakes by tuning and re-tuning the strings until the guitar produces the harmony he desires. If the guitar remains consistently off key, he can go through the difficult process of removing the old strings and re-stringing the guitar with a brand new set. Or, if the guitar's structural integrity is compromised beyond repair, he can trash that guitar and start strumming a new one. These are his sovereign rights as the guitar's owner.

In the real world, God is the musician and you are the instrument. Like a guitar in the hands of a skilled guitarist, your life rests in the wise hands of the Almighty God. He is the divine luthier who created you to live in harmony with him. He is the sovereign musician who strums your heart strings and moves his fingers over the frets of your mind to orchestrate an elegant melody of rationality and righteousness.

Just as the guitar exists to accomplish the guitarist's purposes, so we exist to accomplish God's purposes. He holds the entirety of our lives in his hands. A wise man will respect the reality of God's authority. He will submit to his direction and live in melodious concert with him.

The stubborn fool, however, refuses to cooperate with God because he *despises wisdom and instruction* as Solomon says. The fool's disobedience produces disharmony. As a result, he lives his life perpetually off key; and like a deformed or unplayable guitar, he runs the risk of being condemned to the trash heap.[7]

Son, once you realize the scope of God's authority over you and your life, you will understand the role rational fear plays in your relationship with

---

7. This analogy is appropriate, as the biblical image for hell comes from a deep narrow gorge southeast of Jerusalem called the Valley of Ben Hinnom, which was used as a garbage dump. The Valley of Ben Hinnom "became known as a garbage dump, the place of destruction by fire in Jewish tradition. The Greek word *gehenna*, 'hell,' commonly used in the NT for the place of final punishment, is derived from the Hebrew name for this valley." Ryken et al., *Dictionary of Biblical Imagery*, 376.

him. A healthy sense of trepidation is a reasonable response to the ultimate authority that by right belongs to the Lord of all existence.

Fear motivates you to keep your priorities in order

A rational sense of fear helps you develop the right attitude when it comes to knowing your place in God's world. A proper *attitude* toward God fosters proper *behavior* toward God. A healthy fear is a necessary aspect of your quest for wisdom because it motivates you to live in obedience to your Heavenly Father's established commands.

At this point I will caution you to avoid applying a displaced and legalistic connotation to the concept of *obedience*. If you misunderstand the purpose of obedience, you will misunderstand the purpose of wisdom.

Obedience in and of itself is not the goal of wisdom. God did not create humanity just so he could have a group of employees to boss around. Nor did he establish his commands on a whim just to watch us jump through a series of arbitrary hoops. Obedience as an end unto itself is cold and robotic and compulsive. As theologian John Calvin once said, God does not desire *a slavish, forced fear* by which he can extort through the threat of judgment insincere behavior from us as his unwilling captives.[8]

God's desire is for us to relate to him as a Heavenly Father. Not as a cosmic tyrant. The difference between the two is this: A tyrant abuses his authority and uses force to oppress his subjects. A tyrant is a worthless man who isn't skilled enough to build himself up. So he exploits his position of power to tear others down.

Son, this is not the God we serve. God is not a divine despot. He did not create humanity to subjugate or exploit us. He does not need to hold us down in order to feel better about himself. Nor does he desire an emotionally vacant association with us, one akin to a taskmaster's association with his slaves. Such an insincere existence would be one of drudgery for everyone involved. Including God.

A good father, on the other hand, uses his authority to elevate his children, not to hold them down. In everything he does, he is motivated by steadfast love and affection. And the boundaries he establishes are set in place to protect his children—to steer them in the right direction, not to torment them. He corrects his children when they ignore those rational borders. In the same way, he rewards them when they act with wisdom and avoid those pockets of darkness that lie outside the boundaries of the light.

---

8. Calvin, *Institutes*, 50.

In every way, a good father works for his children's benefit, to help them reach their full potential and achieve the mantle of adulthood.

God is indeed a good Father. And living in a covenant relationship with him is a privilege, not an obligation. But like every relationship, there are rules by which you must abide in order to maintain proper fellowship.

With God, the two greatest rules are these:

1. Love the Lord your God with all your heart, soul, mind, and strength.
2. Love your neighbor just as you love yourself.

If a man keeps these two commands in their proper order, he keeps the entirety of God's word (Mark 12:28–31; Matt 22:37–40). A healthy fear of the Lord motivates you to abide by these rules on a daily basis.

The concept of *rules* rubs some people the wrong way. If you're one of those people, then replace the word *rules* with the word *promises*. Every relationship is defined by certain promises. Take my marriage to your mother as an example. On our wedding day, she and I exchanged specific vows. I gave your mother my word when I promised to love and cherish only her, forsaking all others. I promised I would never harm her and that I would always treat her with respect and dignity as my wife—for richer or poorer, in sickness and in health, until death do us part. She made the same promises to me as her husband.

We gave each other our *word*. The promises we made, the *rules* that we follow, they *define* our sacred union. Your mother and I value our relationship. We abide by these rules not out of obligation, but to nurture our shared love and preserve the sanctity of our marriage. These rules are in place not to oppress, but to *protect*. They establish healthy boundaries to ensure that we avoid those pockets of darkness that lie beyond the sparkling borders of our well-lit kingdom. They foster intimacy and promote happiness and establish a healthy home environment for our children. We follow these rules with gladness because we cherish our love *and* because we fear the far-reaching consequences of a failed marriage.

The same philosophy applies to your relationship with God. Jesus said, "If you love Me you will keep My commandments" (John 14:15). God has put his commands in place for your benefit—to define and protect the sanctity of your shared union. Your obedience to his commands keeps your relationship healthy and productive. It brings your affection for God to life and enables you to express your love in a real way in the real world.

Love is indeed the foundation of your relationship with God. But fear plays an active role in keeping that love intact. Because your love for God is true, you should fear the consequences of failing to honor the covenant you share with him. Let the thought of existing apart from him terrify you. Fear the depression of a meaningless existence. Fear the weakness of your flesh and the damage sin can cause. Fear your own capacity for evil. Fear the hungry shadows that lurk within the dark corners of your own mind—those rebellious urges that have the potential to rob you of your life and ruin your relationship with God, your family, and the other people you care for. Fear the consequences of losing the battle for your own soul and shudder at the thought of drinking from the cup of God's wrath. Embrace that fear. Breathe it in. Let it circulate within the depths of your spirit. Face it. Understand it. And use it as motivation to obey God's commands and make good on the promises that define your relationship with him.

In everything he does, including the boundaries he has established by his own righteous authority, God acts with wisdom. His twofold goal is to achieve his own glory and to work for your benefit. He values you as his son. He wants you to succeed. He takes his role as your Heavenly Father seriously. In turn, he expects you to take your relational responsibilities as his son and his student just as seriously. As the psalmist wrote, God has given his precepts with the intention that you will walk in them. He has established his commands for your benefit, so that you would keep his commands with diligence and receive the blessings that come from living in harmony with him as your Heavenly Father (Ps 119:1–4).

But son, you can't keep God's commands if you don't know what his commands are. As Solomon and I will explain in the next section, the only way to acquire a proper knowledge of God's commands is to crack open a Bible and start reading.

GOD HAS GIVEN YOU HIS WORD—NOW USE IT!

Prov 9:10

Solomon's call to fear the Lord is the call to develop a deeper knowledge of him as your Heavenly Father.

He makes that point clear when he says:

> "[10]The fear of the LORD is the beginning of wisdom, and the *knowledge* of the Holy One is understanding." (9:10, emphasis added)

Solomon once again cites the *fear of the LORD* as the starting point in a man's quest for wisdom. Notice how he frames this fear as a healthy fear that motivates a man not to run away from God in terror, but to draw closer to God by pursuing a deeper *knowledge* of him as the ultimate example of true wisdom in action.

God exercises wisdom in everything he does. He is supremely rational by nature—and God *must* act in accord with his nature. He is identical with it. He cannot separate himself from it. Nor can he act inconsistently with who he is as a perfectly simple Being.[9] Just as God *is* love, and Jesus *is* the way, the truth, and the life, so he also *is* wisdom. In all things, God thinks and speaks and behaves with perfect knowledge, morality, rationality, and skill.[10] He is never ignorant or immoral. Nor does he ever act on a whim or with incompetence. He is an eternal and unchanging God. He is eternally wise. And son, he expects you to exercise that same devotion to wisdom in your life. As a man who bears his image, God expects you to reflect his character and to act in harmony with the values and principles he has established for his household. And the best place to gain *knowledge* of the Holy One and *insight* into the specifics of his wisdom is the Bible.

This *knowledge of the Holy One* that Solomon speaks of goes far beyond facts and information. To truly know God is to be engaged in a working and active relationship with him. If your desire to attain knowledge of God's commands is authentic—if you really want to understand the character of God, if you want to gain insight into his values and live in harmony with his principles—then get into the daily habit of studying his word.

The Bible is the very word of God. It contains all you need to know to live a wise life. But let's be honest: Sometimes people get intimidated when they think of reading the Bible. Some people find its size and scope overwhelming and get confused as to where to even begin. Some people also have a hard time acclimating themselves to the cadence of the text and the style of writing.

Son, you may at times experience these same struggles when you sit down with your Bible. Don't worry. These are normal reactions for younger disciples. But you must never use them as excuses to avoid carving out time for Bible study.

---

9. God is immutable—that is, unchanging—by nature: "For I, the LORD, do not change" (Mal 3:6). Regarding God's relationship to his nature, the philosopher Anselm pointed out that God does not possess his nature. Rather, he *is* his nature (*Monologion and Proslogion*, 30).

10. Job said God is "Wise in heart and mighty in strength," that he possesses "wisdom and might," and "to Him belong counsel and understanding" (Job 9:4; 12:13). The prophet Jeremiah said of God: "It is He who made the earth by His power, who established the world by His wisdom; and by His understanding He has stretched out the heavens" (Jer 10:12). Paul called God "the only wise God" (Rom 16:27), and David marveled at God's intellect, proclaiming God's thoughts to be intimate, timeless, and precious; and he glorified God's knowledge as beyond definition (Ps 139:1–6).

Let me give you some words of encouragement that will alleviate any intimidation you may feel when it comes to the word of God. Yes, the Bible is thick and contains a lot of information. Yes, sometimes parts of the Bible require multiple readings and an *acute attention to context* to gain a fuller understanding of its meaning. Yes, some of the biblical names are hard to pronounce and some of the ancient customs can seem a little strange. But son, do not let these things stop you from spending time in the word. These are superficial hurdles that any rational man of the Spirit can overcome with study and perseverance.

God gave mankind his perfect word so that we may learn the way and the truth of life. He gave his disciples his Holy Spirit to steer us away from the world's conventional foolishness and guide us into all that is true and wise.[11] And he gave you an elegant mind that is more than capable of reading and understanding his word.

I have never heard the audible voice of God. But the God of all existence speaks directly to me every day through the light of nature and in the text of the Bible. He has breathed out the truth of his word over the span of hundreds of years and through the inspired hands of many wise men. He preserved his words and canonized them as Scripture. The Bible is perfect and without error and is therefore *profitable* for every man who takes the time to study it (2 Tim 3:16–17).

Son, the best way to get to know God is through his word. Through disciplined and thorough Bible study, you will gain deeper insight into the character of God and you will develop a more intimate knowledge of him as your Heavenly Father. The more you study, the more you will grow in wisdom. And as you mature in your faith, you will come to know what it means to truly fear the Lord—and the more certain you will be of his unique involvement in your life.

Sinful fear stifles a man.

It freezes his mind and numbs his senses and renders him an ineffectual coward. Rational fear, however, is a righteous motivation that lights a spark within the wise man's spirit. That spark kindles action, not cowardice. The man who lives with a rational fear of the Lord is the man who gives real-life proof of his *respect* for God at all times. He honors his Heavenly Father by thinking and acting within the well-lit borders of all that is righteous and good.

---

11. Brunton, "The Wisdom of the World."

Son, you can likewise honor the image of God when you live in accord with the commandments of his word. He has put his statutes in place to protect his relationship with you. He is a good Father who values his relationship with you as his child. And his commands are proof of his love.

You can in turn prove your love for him by obeying those commands and respecting his authority.

But the call to obedience doesn't stop with God. As Solomon and I will explain in the next letter, God expects you to take that same spirit of respect you have for him and extend it toward me, toward your mother, and toward the rules we've set in place to govern our home.

Love,
Dad

Letter 3

Take Home with You When You Leave the House

Prov 1:8–19

"Son, the people you allow to influence you can make or break your life."

Son, Solomon and I explained in my previous letter why you would be wise to fear God and respect the authority he possesses over you as your Heavenly Father.

With this letter, we will explain why you should take that same sense of respect and apply it to your two biggest earthly sources of authority: your parents.

I think it would be helpful if I paused for a moment to remind you that as your father, I rank second only to God himself when it comes to authority figures in your life. God has appointed me and *me alone* as your daddy. By his own sovereign authority, your Heavenly Father has put you in my home and under my care. That means it is my job—not the government's job, not society's job, not the church's job, but *my* job—to be your primary teacher. I am the man God has made most responsible for providing you with the guidance and support you need to go out into the world and achieve your God-given destiny.

I do not take my job lightly nor do I ever take a day off. But I hope by now you've come to realize that being your father is more than just a job to me. Fatherhood is one of the greatest privileges God could ever give a man. And being the father of a son as *all boy* as yourself is a special kind of reward. Your presence in my life is a testimony to the graciousness of Almighty God, and I plan to make the most of this blessing he's given me.

But as is always the case with God, with great blessings come great responsibilities.

Son, if I were standing there with you right now, I'd reach out and give your shoulder one of those dad squeezes that's as firm as it is sincere. Then I'd look you in the eye and give you my word: I will never use my God-given authority to hold you back or treat you with disrespect. I will always give you the respect you deserve as my son who shares my blood and bears my image. And I promise to do my best to honor my fatherly responsibilities and be an active part of your life for as long as God sees fit to keep us together.

But as I said in my previous letter, in order for us to make the most of the time God has given us, we must trade respect like the men that we are. That means you must likewise promise to respect me as your father—to submit to my leadership and honor my God-given authority over you.

As Solomon points out in Prov 1:8, one of the main ways you can do that is to honor the rules your mother and I have put in place to govern our home.

Allow me to pause once again to explain in a little more detail about what I mean by home. *Home* is an intellectual concept that extends beyond the bricks and wood that form our physical house. Home is also a state of mind you can take with you wherever you go. It's a stabilizing mentality hewn not of axe and hammer, but of the Bible-based code of morals your mother and I have taught you. These homegrown values and principles serve as the foundation of your character. They're designed to keep you grounded in every stage of your life; and no matter where you go, you will always take the stability of home with you when you live your life by the fundamental convictions your mother and I have worked so hard to instill within you.

Solomon likewise wove this concept of *home* into the fabric of his son's consciousness. After his introductory remarks in the first seven verses, Solomon goes on to issue two specific commands to his son.

Those first commands are:

1. Honor the good influence of your parents (and earn the rewards that come with a respectful attitude).
2. Steer clear of the bad influences that can destroy your life.

His goal with these commands is twofold:

1. To push his son toward *the good* by promoting a healthy relational dynamic at home.
2. To pull his son away from harm by warning him against falling in with the wrong crowd.

Son, the people you allow to influence you can make or break your life. Good influences (like your mother and me) are easy to spot because they're the people who actually care about you. Whether they're blood relatives or personal friends, they love you like family and they work hard to bring out the best in you. They are good sources of support and stability. But they also challenge you with wise counsel when necessary. Their positive influence keeps you grounded in those homegrown values that will preserve your integrity no matter where you go in the world.

In the previous letter, Solomon and I explained the importance of fearing God as your Heavenly Father and respecting the rules he has put in place to govern his creation. With this letter, Solomon and I will explain why you should apply that same sense of respect to me, your earthly father. And we'll explain the benefits that come with respecting your parents and honoring the rules that govern our home.

Like Solomon, two of the main rules your mother and I have set in place are:

1. Take the positive influence of home with you every time you leave the house.
2. Stay far away from bad influences.

Your homegrown convictions will protect you from the bad influences you are sure to encounter out there in the world. And by bad influences, I mean those phony friends who promise fun and companionship, but in the end will only serve to bring you down. These bad influences often run in numbers, like a gang of outlaw dogs. And like the predatory pack hunters that they are, their main goal is not to build you up, but to hunt you down and chew you up and spit you out.

No matter if a young man lives in ancient Israel or the present-day United States, bad influences are always bad news. But as Solomon and I will explain, one of the best ways to ward them off is to honor your mother and me and respect the rules that govern our home.

HONOR YOUR FATHER AND MOTHER

Prov 1:8-9

Son, I want to make something very clear: Your mother and I are not your friends, nor are we your peers, and you are never to treat us as such.

Instead, God has blessed us with the greater privilege of being your *parents*. That means you are to treat us in a special way that is reserved only for us. The call to honor your parents is not a suggestion. It's an imperative. God *commands* you to respect your mother and me. He *requires* you to honor the authority we have over you. Not because we are perfect or infallible (because we are neither), but because obeying your parents will yield great rewards for your life. Your faithfulness to this command will result in many blessings, not least of which is a sustained relational peace with God and with your family.[1]

Solomon understood the foundational nature of this command in the life of a child. So it's of little surprise that his first command is for his son to honor the wisdom and authority of his parents.

> "⁸Hear, my son, your father's instruction and do not forsake your mother's teaching; ⁹indeed, they are a graceful wreath to your head and ornaments about your neck." (1:8-9)

In these verses, Solomon reaffirms a command that appears throughout both the Old and New Testaments. That command is: *Honor your father and your mother* (Exod 20:12; Eph 6:1-4). A young man *honors* his parents by holding them in the highest esteem and relating to them with the respect they deserve as his primary earthly caretakers. Of the Ten Commandments, this is the only one that comes with a specific reward. Those children who honor their parents will receive the prize of *long days in the land of God* (Exod 20:12). As we'll discuss more thoroughly in letters 6 and 7, Solomon's reference to *long days in the land of God* is not necessarily a promise of a long lifespan (although a good long life can be one of the results of living wisely). More specifically, it's a guarantee that those children who keep this command will enjoy the sustained peace and stability that comes from living in harmony with God and their parents.[2]

---

1. I'll talk more specifically about how to achieve peace in your home in letter 6.

2. *The land* that Solomon mentioned here is a reference to the promised land, which, in a general sense, is the physical symbol of a peaceful and productive life of fellowship with God. That peace, productivity, and fellowship are rooted in a man's obedience to God's statutes. David, Solomon's father, used *the land* in this context in Ps 37:3-4: "Trust in the LORD and do good; dwell in the land and cultivate faithfulness. Delight yourself in the LORD; and He will give you the desires of your heart."

Son, to honor your parents is to honor God.[3] In contrast, to dishonor your parents—that is, to disrespect us with contemptible attitudes and actions—is to dishonor God. A family with children who honor their parents is a family that lives in peace and stability. A family filled with dishonor and disrespect, however, is doomed to self-destruction.[4]

Your mother and I are not perfect. No matter how hard we try, we will not always do the right thing by God or by you. But we are still your parents. And God expects you to honor us by showing us the proper respect at all times. Even if you feel we don't deserve it.

You may not always understand every decision we make. That's normal. But even if you don't understand why we do the things we do, you have to respect our decisions and our authority. You *must* relate to us with honor—and never with an attitude of disrespect. As I explained in the previous letter, Jesus said we show our love for him by obeying his commandments (John 14:15). Similarly, one way you show your love for us as your parents is by respectfully obeying the rules that we've established to govern our home.

Son, your mother and I love you. We want you to be safe and well-adjusted as you go out into the world and create a beautiful life for yourself. That means we are going to set some boundaries and make some decisions that are unpopular with you. We'll set curfews. We won't permit you to go to certain places or hang out with certain people. We'll restrict your internet and media usage. We'll make you responsible for doing certain jobs around the house. Whatever the case may be, as a young person who's inexperienced in life, you must learn to trust in our wisdom and trust that we have set those boundaries with your best interest at heart.

My primary ministry on this earth is to my family. God has commissioned me not just as a pastor but as a father to ensure that my children have submissive hearts that honor the word of God (1 Tim 3:4).

I plan to make good on that commission.

At this point, though, I want to caution you against confusing *submission* with *weakness*. The biblical concept of *submission*, like the biblical concept of *fear*, is a multi-layered notion that goes much deeper than our

---

3. Theologian Andreas Köestenberger notes that "words denoting respect for parents are elsewhere used with reference to reverence for God himself" (*God, Marriage, and Family*, 100).

4. Sometimes good parents make mistakes and behave in such a way so as to annoy or discourage their children. Even in those moments of frustration, children must still honor their authority and address them with respect. Some parents, however, are worthless and act with malice toward their children. In such a case, a child may find it morally impossible to honor them and their godlessness. Unfortunately, such circumstances do exist. However, they definitely are not applicable in your case. Your mother and I might be unusual at times, but we are never malicious.

modern interpretation of the word. When some people hear the word *submit*, they conjure up an image of domination. Admittedly, my first instinct when I think of submission is to imagine a professional wrestler squeezing and twisting his opponent with enough brute force to cause him to tap out in agonizing defeat.

Needless to say, this is not the biblical definition of submission.

Son, you are an individual who bears the image of God. That means you possess the same unalienable rights as anyone else (adult or child). When you submit to your mother and me, you are not giving in to defeat, nor are you admitting that you are inferior to us on a basic human level. Instead, you are acting in accord with your God-given family *role* as a child who is still dependent upon his parents.

Understand that you and I and your mother and your sisters are all equal in *value*. But we each serve in *different roles* within our family unit. For example, my role as a husband is to love my wife as Christ loved the church. That means I give all of myself for her benefit. Even to the point of death if necessary. And I live with her not to be served, but to shepherd her in love and leadership. I honor my role when I respect her as I would my own body, when I love her as if she were bone of my bone and flesh of my flesh. Because, by God's design, that's what she is (Gen 2:23–24; Eph 5:28–33).[5]

My role as a father is to raise up my children in the discipline and instruction of the Lord. But in so doing, I must never provoke my children to anger or discouragement (Eph 6:4; Col 3:21). That's my God-given job as your father. As my son, God has called on you to do your job and "be obedient to your parents in all things, for this is well-pleasing to the Lord . . . for this is *right*" (Col 3:20; Eph 6:1–2, emphasis added).

Ideally, a father and mother will serve as the primary good influences in the lives of their children. God instituted the family structure the way he did—one husband/father, one wife/mother, and children—because children need the guidance of a father and a mother in order to grow into well-rounded adults.[6] Just as you are commanded to honor your father and mother, so also parents, specifically fathers, are instructed to avoid acting in a disrespectful or tyrannical manner toward their children. God did not put your mother and me in place to be dominating or discouraging. God expects dads and moms to love their children and to exert godly influence over them, more so than any other person or group of people on this

---

5. We'll talk in greater detail about how a husband and wife become one flesh in letters 4, 9, and 10.

6. I'm not saying a child needs both a father and a mother to come to know Jesus or to be a wise and successful person. I'm saying the biblical formulation of the family unit is the *best* way to achieve these goals.

planet. That means I will never intentionally provoke you to anger. Nor will I ever abuse my authority in an effort to dishearten you. I will communicate respectfully with you as I bring you up in the discipline and instruction of the Lord.

Your job, in return, is to integrate the lessons of my instruction into your day-to-day thinking. To take my words of wisdom and install them within the very core of your consciousness. Do this and you will take the safety and support of *home* with you every time you walk out the front door.

My goal in fostering this concept of home is to help you understand that your mother and I are not trying to keep you tied up on a leash. Our job is to arm you with the wisdom and the strength you need to run free and take on the world. Solomon said the godly counsel of your parents will prove to be a *graceful wreath for your head* and *ornaments for your neck*. The wreath and ornaments are signs of victory. Of success. They symbolize the rewards that God and parents give their children for acting with maturity and wisdom. To receive the rewards God has in store for you presently and down the road, you must be sure to take the wisdom of home with you everywhere you go. You have a responsibility to your Heavenly Father and to yourself to make the most of the opportunities he's given you. Those opportunities are yours by right, so go out and make the best of them. You can start your journey toward destiny on the right foot by staying true to the wisdom of home.

Trust me: The good influence of your parents will come in handy every time you walk out the front door.[7]

And as we'll discuss in the next section, our words will prove especially useful when it comes time to avoid those roaming packs of bad influences you're sure to encounter as you make your way in the world.

HOW TO IDENTIFY (AND AVOID) BAD INFLUENCES

Prov 1:10-19

Son, the first thing you need to recognize about bad influences is this: They like to operate in groups.

They prey on the insecurities of weak-minded fools by offering promises of companionship, fun, and power. This is not a modern phenomenon. Bad influences operated this way in the ages before us just as they do today. As Solomon once wisely (or perhaps cynically) noted, "What has been is

---

7. Solomon and I will discuss the wisdom of listening to your parents in greater detail in letter 5.

what will be, and what has been done is what will be done, and there is nothing new under the sun" (Eccl 1:9 ESV). That means no matter where you go, you'll always come across dangerous men and women who make empty promises of friendship.

That's why with his second command, Solomon warns his son to avoid the worthless company of bad influences:

> "¹⁰My son, if sinners entice you, do not consent. ¹¹If they say, 'Come with us, let us lie in wait for blood, let us ambush the innocent without cause; ¹²let us swallow them alive like Sheol, even whole, as those who go down to the pit; ¹³we will find all kinds of precious wealth, we will fill our houses with spoil; ¹⁴throw in your lot with us, we shall all have one purse,' ¹⁵my son, do not walk in the way with them. Keep your feet from their path, ¹⁶for their feet run to evil and they hasten to shed blood. ¹⁷Indeed, it is useless to spread the baited net in the sight of any bird; ¹⁸but they lie in wait for their own blood; they ambush their own lives. ¹⁹So are the ways of everyone who gains by violence; it takes away the life of its possessors." (1:10–19)

In these verses, Solomon warns his son to guard himself against having the wrong friends. As a father, he understood the danger a gang of bad influences posed toward young men like his son. This particular gang he describes were *thieves* looking to *draw blood* and *ambush* innocent victims without cause. They wanted Solomon's son to join them as they committed these random acts of savagery. Notice, though, that this gang had no plans to do anything productive. Nor were they interested in authentic friendship. Their main goal was violence. And they only cared about the young man so long as they could use him to further their own nasty agenda.

Solomon was able to spot these bad guys a mile away. And like a good father, he gives his son the tools he needs to likewise see them for the fake friends they really are.

The four characteristics of a bad influence

Son, when you leave the house and go out into the world, you too will encounter dangerous people who make phony offers of friendship. But you must stand strong against anyone who uses sin and violence to entice you. Like the gang Solomon spoke of above, such people only want you around so long as you can serve their purposes; then once they've gotten what they need from you, they'll cast you off like a fleck of garbage. Their promises of brotherhood will prove empty because to them you're not a friend or a brother. You're nothing but an object, a tool they can use to carry out their destructive desires. And when a time of reckoning comes, when guilt can be neither fled nor hidden from, they'll make sure you're the flunky who gets stuck with the blame while they turn tail and make their getaway.

The world hasn't changed very much in this respect. Just as Solomon had to warn his son, so I too need to warn you to fear the consequences of running with the wrong crowd. Bad people make for bad friends. And like I said earlier, bad friends will only bring you down.

The best way to steer clear of bad influences is to measure your friends by the standards your mother and I have instilled within you. Solomon and I will explain in further detail in letters 5, 9, and 10 how wisdom is a young man's best weapon in his battle against bad influences. But for now, we'll simply outline the four specific characteristics of a bad influence so you can more easily identify and avoid them.

According to Solomon, these are the four characteristics of a bad influence:

1. A bad influence is attracted to trouble

You can tell if a person is a good guy or a bad guy by taking note of the things he's attracted to. A bad influence is fairly easy to spot because he is attracted to rebellion. To *trouble*. He likes to break the rules. He likes to lie. He likes to cheat. He likes to stir up drama and turmoil. His feet *run to evil*, as Solomon says in the first half of v. 16.[8] He is a troublemaker who refuses to respect the authority of God or his parents or even his own common sense. He's the kind of guy Solomon will go on to describe as a *worthless* man, and his juvenile attraction to trouble will cause God's wrath to reverberate through his life like a blast of apocalyptic thunder.[9]

A good influence, in contrast, is a man of maturity who works hard to avoid trouble. He isn't perfect and his life isn't free of problems. But his life is stable because he governs himself with a sense of responsibility; and as a result, he lives in harmony with God, himself, his family, and his friends. His structured and respectable lifestyle is the hard-earned reward of a dedication to wise decision making.

---

8. These four characteristics apply to both males and females. However, since Solomon and I will discuss the characteristics of the forbidden woman in deeper detail in letter 9, I will limit this discussion to the negative male influences you're sure to come across.

9. We'll discuss in more detail the characteristics of a worthless man in letter 10.

2. A bad influence is excited by violence

The bad influence's unhealthy attraction to trouble naturally motivates him to commit actual, real-world damage. Solomon points out in the second half of v. 16 that bad influences aren't content with mere mischief. They like to make people *bleed*. They have a hunger for carnage that makes them *hasten to shed blood*. The Apostle Peter was tracking on this same idea when he pointed out that Satan prowls around seeking someone to devour (1 Pet 5:8).[10] He described the devil as a bloodthirsty predatory beast who savors the gritty taste of destruction. And those bad influences who embrace that kind of devilish character stoke that same sense of bloodlust within themselves. Like the functional sociopaths they are, they celebrate pain, and they don't think twice about hurting other people.

A good influence, however, acts on the godly motivation to build up, not tear down. With his words and actions, he cultivates positivity and respect and honor. And in the process, he not only creates a noble life for himself, but he also serves as a positive influence in the lives of his family, his friends, and the people he comes into contact with.

3. A bad influence doesn't think things through

In v. 17, Solomon uses the analogy of an incompetent hunter to highlight the bad influence's failure to think things through. According to Solomon, a bad influence is like a foolish fowler who acts with no forethought as he sets his trap out in the open, without disguise, *in the sight of any bird*. Such short-sighted ineptitude is always doomed to failure.

A smart hunter, on the other hand, will think ahead. He'll put consideration and effort into his snare. For example, when a man goes duck hunting, he camouflages himself and the duck blind so that they blend in with their surroundings. That way, when the ducks approach, they never suspect that they're flying into a trap. Good influences are like a good hunter, in that they put that same kind of forethought into their actions. Bad influences, on the other hand, don't think ahead. And it's this particular character flaw that makes them act less like a skilled huntsman and more like a dumb dog chasing a car. The dog has no idea why he's running after the car, nor does he consider the danger involved in nipping at the tire of a speeding multi-ton

---

10. Keil and Delitzsch note that in his admonition of Cain, God likened sin to a "wild beast, lurking at the door of the human heart, and eagerly desiring to devour [Cain's] soul" (*The Pentateuch*, 70, emphasis added).

vehicle. Bad influences operate in a similar way. They're all reckless action and no forethought.

A good influence, in contrast, thinks ahead. He is a sensible man who chooses his words carefully and as a result speaks with meaning and clarity. He applies that same sense of forethought to his actions. He thinks before he acts. Thus he is able to anticipate potential outcomes and avoid harmful consequences. He is patient and thoughtful. He does not live *for* the moment. But when the time comes, he's able to *seize* the moment because he lives in a constant state of mental focus.[11]

4. A bad influence is self-destructive

Solomon explicitly warns his son in vv. 18 and 19 that sinful behavior always results in painful consequences. He says men who toy around with sin are unwittingly *lying in wait for their own blood*. Bad guys may think they're having fun, but what they don't realize is that they're *ambushing their own lives*—they're only hurting themselves with their rebellious, violent, and reckless antics.

I'll be honest with you, son: Bad people cause a lot of trouble and sometimes they even seem to get away with it. But rest assured: God will never let wicked men go unpunished. He will always in his sovereign way and in his sovereign time give bad men their just due—just as he will always reward the honest work of a righteous man.[12] A life of trouble is of no use to a child of God. Self-harming behavior is irrational because it has only one outcome: early demise. "So are the ways of everyone who gains by violence," concludes Solomon. "It takes away the life of its possessors" (1:19).

Solomon most likely learned this lesson from his father David, who spoke of God's promise of happiness for the man who *takes delight* in his instruction. David said the man who lives in harmony with God's wisdom is "like a tree firmly planted by streams of water, which yields its fruit in its season and its leaf does not wither; and in whatever he does, he prospers. The wicked are not so, but they are like chaff which the wind drives away. Therefore the wicked will not stand in the judgment, nor sinners in the

---

11. We'll talk more about the benefits of maintaining your focus in letter 8.

12. David praised God for the rewards he bestows upon those who keep their integrity intact: "The LORD dealt with me according to my righteousness; according to the cleanness of my hands *he rewarded me*. For I have kept the ways of the LORD and have not wickedly departed from my God. For all his rules were before me, and from his statutes I did not turn aside. I was blameless before him, and I kept myself from guilt. *And the LORD has rewarded me according to my righteousness, according to my cleanness in his sight*" (2 Sam 22:21–25 ESV, emphasis added).

assembly of the righteous. For the LORD knows the way of the righteous, but the way of the wicked will perish" (Ps 1:3–6).

Son, being a troublemaker is like being a wise man—it's a personal choice.

A man chooses to be a troublemaker when he lives under the delusion that breaking the rules is cool or funny. But he doesn't realize that bad decision making is no laughing matter. Remember a lesson from letter 1: Making bad choices can melt the flesh off your face.

And there's nothing funny about that.

Son, God's word is clear: "Bad company corrupts good morals" (1 Cor 15:33). Don't make friends with people who live like dumb animals. Act like the man we've trained you to be—after all, you were raised in a home and not a barn.

Your mother and I have worked hard to bring you up in the ways of God's wisdom. When you go out into the world, be sure to take your home-grown convictions with you everywhere you go. Honor our instructions and choose your influences wisely. If you want to create a fun, successful, and (relatively) drama-free social life both inside and outside the house, then make the wise choice to surround yourself with good people who love you like family.

Love,
Dad

Letter 4

There's a Lady Calling for You

Prov 1:20–33; 8:1–9

"It has long been my belief that the sight of a good-looking woman lowers a man's IQ by at least twenty points."

Son, a smart man named Thomas Sowell once made a brilliant observation about the effect an attractive woman can have on a man's mind.

"It has long been my belief that the sight of a good-looking woman lowers a man's IQ by at least twenty points," Mr. Sowell said. "A man who doesn't happen to have twenty points to spare can be in big trouble."

From a man's perspective, I can say that statement is often true. But with all due respect to Mr. Sowell, his point is valid yet unfinished. Allow me to make a slight addition to his insight. But to do so, we must go back to the first marriage ceremony in the history of the world.

In the garden of Eden, when Adam was a single man working the ground and naming the animals, he made a startling discovery. He recognized that among the majesty of God's creation, there was no creature fit to be his physical and spiritual complement. He stood in the midst of paradise alone and incomplete as the world's only human being.

Obviously, it was never God's intention for the man to be alone. But like the wise Father he is, God knew Adam needed to come to grips with the truth of his own limitations before he could appreciate the blessings of sincere companionship. Once Adam came to this realization, God caused a deep sleep to come upon him. And during his nap, God took one of his ribs and fashioned that rib into a woman, a human being made of spirit and skin and likewise bearing the image of God. When Adam awoke, God presented the woman in all her feminine glory to the man in marriage.

Adam's reaction to his lovely bride was one of both spiritual *and* physical excitement: "*This one, at last,* is bone of my bones and flesh of my flesh; this one will be called 'woman,' for she was taken from man. This is why a man leaves his father and mother and bonds with his wife, and *they become one flesh*" (Gen 2:23–24 CSB, emphasis added).

In short, this was Adam's way of saying: *Now this is what I'm talkin' about!!!*

Imagine the expression of excitement that came across Adam's face when he first caught sight of Eve. Her eyes. Her smile. Her hair. Her skin. The woman and her feminine presence hovered high above the rest of physical creation as a living work of art. There she stood, a being rich with elegance and beauty, designed by the hand of God himself to be the man's spiritual and physical complement. In *every* way Adam appreciated Eve. So great was his appreciation, in fact, that the man immediately started talking about becoming *one flesh* with his new bride (if you know what I mean).[1]

Son, since the beginning of time women have wielded great influence over the minds and bodies of men. And this fact brings me back to Mr. Sowell's point. What he said is true. A good-looking woman has the power to completely re-route a man's internal circuitry and hinder the rational function of his male brain. In other words, a pretty woman has the power to make even the smartest of men act like a bumbling bozo. Therefore, son, I will stress to you, as Solomon did to his son, the importance of surrounding yourself with the right kind of woman.

A good-looking woman can only stimulate a man's body in the short term. But to add to Mr. Sowell's point, a beautiful and godly woman will actually *increase* a man's thinking with the positive influence of her long-term presence. Her righteous femininity will stimulate his *body* and his *mind* and thus forge a spiritual connection that transcends the physical limits of looks.[2]

---

1. I use the example of Adam and Eve to further discuss the pleasure and purpose of sex in letters 9 and 10.
2. More on this topic of the godly wife in letter 10.

Realize now that Solomon knew a thing or two about women. He understood the qualities of a good woman and appreciated the positive influence such a woman can have on a man (read Song of Solomon). But he also knew all too well of the pitfalls that can occur when a man surrounds himself with the wrong types of women (read 1 Kgs 11).

Son, at a certain point in your life, you too will have developed a keen interest in the ladies. Don't worry. God designed you that way. Adam was attracted to Eve. Men are attracted to women. That attraction is healthy and natural. I will, however, encourage you to be wise in how you manage your attractions and your affections. And I'll warn you to never underestimate the impact a woman can have in your life. A good woman will lift you up closer to the throne of God, while a bad woman can drag you down to the depths of Sheol.[3] Solomon knew this to be true. That's why he wasted little time in introducing his son to a very important woman: Lady Wisdom.

When I was a teenager in the communication dark ages, before smartphones and social media, I would get so excited when a girl would call our house on an old school landline and ask to speak to me. It really didn't matter why she was calling. The very idea that some girl thought I was appealing enough to give me a call would spin me up with all kinds of excitement. Needless to say, I would waste no time in answering her call (yes, even dear ol' Dad struggled with teenage angst).

With this letter and the next, we'll explore the important role *listening* plays in the acquisition of wisdom. In letter 5, Solomon and I will explain *why* you should listen to your father. But with this letter, we're here to let you know that a lovely lady by the name of Wisdom is calling—and she wants to talk to you. I suggest you answer her call and listen to what she has to say because, like the good woman that she is, she can help you avoid that mental stupor men are prone to fall victim to from time to time. She will smooth out the rough edges of your male brain and make sure your mind controls your body (and not vice versa).

Like Solomon, I will encourage you again and again to answer her call. Because, son, if there's one relational absolute you should live by, it's this one: When a good woman wants to talk to you, do the wise thing and listen carefully.

---

3. Sheol is the biblical realm of the dead. Solomon and I will explain with great detail in letter 9 the harm that comes from surrounding yourself with a forbidden woman.

THE ONE LADY EVERY MAN NEEDS TO KNOW

Prov 1:20–22; 8:1–9

In writing to his son, Solomon frequently characterizes wisdom as a woman.

To be clear, Lady Wisdom is not a goddess or an actual person. She is a symbol. A literary device. An archetype.[4] Solomon concretized wisdom as a concept by personifying it as a woman. Maybe he did this to give his son a better mental image of how God proclaims the truth to all humanity in a clear and authoritative way. Or maybe Solomon portrays wisdom as an appealing woman in an effort to keep his son's attention—hey, a father will do what he has to do to get his message across. Whatever the reason, Solomon wanted his son to picture God's wisdom as a beautiful and elegant woman who is working not to lower his intelligence, but to elevate him into a higher way of thinking.

He also portrays her as easy to find. In Prov 1 and 8, Solomon says Lady Wisdom extends her presence all across the city. She speaks loud enough for everyone to hear. Her words resonate high upon the commanding heights, down among the city's streets, across the public squares, and over to the city's main entrance.

Her message is straightforward and simple. And she makes it available to anyone who is smart enough to *listen*.

> "[20]Wisdom shouts in the street, she lifts her voice in the square; [21]at the head of the noisy streets she cries out; at the entrance of the gates in the city she utters her sayings.... [1]Does not wisdom call, and understanding lift up her voice? [2]On top of the heights beside the way, where the paths meet, she takes her stand; [3]beside the gates, at the opening to the city, at the entrance of the doors, she cries out: [4]"To you, O men, I call, and my voice is to the sons of men." (1:20–21; 8:1–4)

Solomon says Lady Wisdom doesn't just call—she *lifts up her voice* and *cries out* above the commotion of the masses to make her voice heard. She makes her presence known by standing firm in public places where there is plenty of human traffic. That's because God does not operate in secret. A man doesn't need a secret decoder ring to interpret God's attempts to

---

4. The Hebrew word for wisdom, *ḥokmâ*, is grammatically feminine, thus explaining the personification of Wisdom as a woman. The personage of Wisdom is often used to represent Jesus Christ, God the Son, especially regarding Wisdom's role as the agent of creation as Solomon described in Prov 8:22–31 (letter 7). Heiser, "Jesus and Wisdom."

communicate to us through the general revelation of creation and through the special revelation of his word.

God proclaims his wisdom in a clear and direct manner because his stated desire is for all people to be saved and come to understand the knowledge of the truth (1 Tim 2:3-4). He personally calls out to everyone. But he does not force himself or his wisdom upon anyone. He desires a sincere relationship with humanity. Not coercion or oppression.

God is love. And love is true only if a person has the ability to say *No*.

Son, when I asked your mother to marry me, I didn't propose to her with a ring in one hand and a weapon in the other. I didn't threaten her with injury if she refused my proposal. Instead, I gave her a choice: She could say *No* and reject my affections. Or she could say *Yes* and take my hand in marriage.

You may not realize this, but your mother is a beautiful woman. She would've had no problem attracting the attention of any man she so desired. But she didn't desire any other man. She desired me. And she chose me above all others because she decided for herself that I was the man God tailor-made to be her spiritual and physical complement.

God operates in a similar way. He has designed humanity to be in a relationship with him. Not because he needs a complement as we do, but because the God of all creation has chosen to share his glorious image with us his children. He created humanity with the intent that each one of us would freely choose to live a life that reflects the *spiritual character* of our Heavenly Father.

Our rational reaction should be to welcome such a relationship. To embrace him as our Heavenly Father. Yet in order for love to be true, it must be both freely given *and* freely received.

God has initiated the conversation by his own choice. But in order for the relationship to be real, he has given every man the freedom to decide for himself:

- Will I ignore God's call and remain estranged from him?

Or:

- Will I answer the call and accept his invitation to fellowship?

By personifying God's wisdom as a beautiful woman who delivers this divine choice to the masses, Solomon has crafted a striking dramatization of the communication process between God and man.

He follows this up by doing what my dad did for me in high school. When my dad would answer the house phone and hear a girl's voice on the other end, he would let me know (in a manner that I can only describe as *less than subtle*) that a lady was calling and that she wanted to talk to me.

Here, Solomon is doing the same thing for his son. He's letting him know that a lady is calling. A Lady by the name of Wisdom. And she wants to talk *to him*.

He then gives his son a choice. The young man could:

- Do the smart thing and answer the call and listen to what she has to say.
- Or snub her call like an idiot and suffer the consequences.

Only a fool would say *No*

Son, realize that only a man of profound absurdity would reject Lady Wisdom's call. Yet such men do exist. And, ironically, it's these types of men who make up Lady Wisdom's target audience.

During his ministry on earth, Jesus often associated with sinners, tax collectors, and the like. People the so-called elites viewed as the dregs of humanity. When the scribes and the Pharisees asked why he associated with such people, Jesus said to them: "It is not those who are healthy who need a physician, but those who are sick; I did not come to call the righteous, but sinners" (Mark 2:17).

In the same way, while Lady Wisdom's message is good for everyone, it's those men who are morally and intellectually ill who most need to hear what she has to say.

Son, you must understand this fact about the human condition: Humanity has an unhealthy infatuation with spiritual depravity that is hard to rationalize. Sin at its core is a self-inflicted disease of the soul brought about by our rejection of God. Jesus Christ offers the only antidote to the disease of sin. Yet many people choose to ignore his call and reject his offer of salvation. They would rather remain confined in the murk of their trespasses, as if they get some kind of perverse pleasure out of their spiritual malaise.

Lady Wisdom is a no-nonsense kind of gal. She is candid and clear in her speech. And rather than treat these men with kid gloves, she addresses them like the adults they are—with a couple of straightforward questions: *How long will you continue to live in this self-destructive way? Why do you choose to waste away in your sin when the solution to all your problems is staring you in the face?*

"[22]How long, O naive ones, will you love being simple-minded?" she asks. "And scoffers delight themselves in scoffing and fools

> hate knowledge? . . . ⁵O naive ones, understand prudence; and, O fools, understand wisdom. ⁶Listen, for I will speak noble things; and the opening of my lips will reveal right things. ⁷For my mouth will utter truth; and wickedness is an abomination to my lips. ⁸All the utterances of my mouth are in righteousness; there is nothing crooked or perverted in them. ⁹They are all straightforward to him who understands, and right to those who find knowledge." (1:22; 8:5–9)

In these verses, Solomon separates the spiritually infirmed into three distinct categories, each with its own symptoms and tendencies:

Immature men. The *simple-minded* men Solomon refers to are those men who refuse to grow up. They are not young men struggling with the inexperience of raw youth. Here, Solomon is describing men who are old enough to know better. Guys who are mature in body but immature in mind. These are men who refuse to man up and take on the responsibilities of adulthood. They'd rather revel in the ignorance of their immaturity. And when Lady Wisdom offers to help them grow, they use their immaturity as an excuse to snub her offer. But as Solomon will go on to point out, their rejection will come back to bite them in a big way. Their willful ignorance will prove to be no excuse. And as long as they ignore Wisdom's call, these ignoramuses will bear the full weight of their bad choice.[5]

Scoffers. These are men who hold nothing but contempt for God. Scoffers understand Lady Wisdom's message on an intellectual level. But what they don't understand is her appeal. They despise her message and respond to her invitation with ridicule. They laugh at the truth because their minds are overrun with bitterness and cynicism. They never regard God and his wisdom as values to take seriously. To them, God and his wisdom are a big joke. And they respond to Wisdom's call by ridiculing her message and mocking those who abide by it.

Fools. Solomon said fools *hate knowledge.* They despise Wisdom because they feel nothing but loathing and anger toward God. They want no part of him or his truth. In fact, so manic are they in their hatred that they willingly exchange the truth of God for the only other option: the lies of the devil. When fools make this choice, God grants them their request. He gives them over to the impure desires of their devilish minds. And although they

---

5. In his Letter to the Romans, the Apostle Paul reiterated this point: "For since the creation of the world His *[God's]* invisible attributes, His eternal power and divine nature, have been clearly seen, being understood through what has been made, so that they are without excuse." And those who exchange the truth of God for a lie will receive "in their own persons the due penalty of their error" (Rom 1:20, 27, emphasis added).

go through life seeking their own glory, these fools will only bring dishonor and destruction upon themselves.[6]

Immature men, scoffers, and fools all have one shared moral deficiency: a lack of respect. They do not fear God. They do not respect his authority. They hold his truth in contempt because none of them are man enough to take on the responsibility that comes with being a disciple of Christ.

But as Solomon will explain here at the end of Prov 1, Lady Wisdom does not compromise her message for the sake of men's personal preferences. No matter how hard these foolish men try to censor the reality of Lady Wisdom's call, they will never succeed in shutting her up.

They will only suffer the consequences of refusing to answer.

LADY WISDOM DEMANDS AN ANSWER

Prov 1:23-33

Son, every man is capable of knowing the truth.

The immature man, the scoffer, and the fool, however, fail to discover the truth not because they are blind, but because they refuse to see. They remain ignorant not because they are illiterate, but because they refuse to know. And they don't lack knowledge of God so much as they lack a desire *to know* God. In their minds, his very existence is a threat to their broad yet brittle egos. They hate the fact that he, as their Creator, has a rightful authority over them. They resent the fact that they have to answer to him for how they choose to manage the lives he's given them. So they rebel against the reality of God's authority and they respond to his message of truth with a visceral hatred.

They spend their time kicking up as much intellectual dissonance as they possibly can in an attempt to drown out Lady Wisdom's call. But their efforts prove futile as Lady Wisdom's voice rises above their ruckus. She lets nothing stop her from delivering her message with authority and power. Her aim, however, is not to destroy these men, but to unleash upon them the one thing powerful enough to spare them from the grave consequences of their rebellion.

---

6. Once again, Paul testifies to this truth: "For even though they knew God, they did not honor Him as God or give thanks, but they became futile in their speculations, and their foolish heart was darkened. Professing to be wise, they became fools, and exchanged the glory of the incorruptible God for an image in the form of corruptible man and of birds and four-footed animals and crawling creatures. Therefore God gave them over in the lusts of their hearts to impurity, so that their bodies would be dishonored among them" (Rom 1:21-24).

The truth.

Lady Wisdom offers an everlasting bond

Solomon says God will bless those men who respond to Lady Wisdom's call with his direct presence in their lives: "Turn to my reproof, behold, I will pour out my spirit on you; I will make my words known to you" (1:23).

God's promise to *pour out his Spirit* upon those who answer his call is a reference to salvation. And the Bible is very clear about the scope of God's salvation: *Everyone* who calls on the name of the Lord will be saved (Joel 2:32; Rom 10:13).

Son, I want you to understand this truth about sin and the harm that it causes. Sin results in a physical and a spiritual separation from God. This separation facilitates physical and spiritual death.[7] But in his body of flesh and by his death and resurrection, Jesus Christ, God the Son, paid the penalty for our sin. He blazed a trail of salvation that reconnects sinful men with the holy God. And any man who answers his call to salvation will receive the Spirit of God in his life.

By the power and presence of his Spirit, God himself writes the *wisdom of his word* on a man's heart and mind—and it's in this way that a man *bonds* with God's wisdom.[8] The Holy Spirit, God himself, merges with the spirit of man and sets him free to think and live with the wisdom he needs to create a meaningful life. When a man joins with God in this way, in union with his Spirit, he becomes a man in union with the very heart and mind of God. He loves the Lord. He *needs* the Lord. He elevates God as his ultimate value. He brings his love to life when he studies his Bible and lives out its wisdom. When he dedicates himself to understanding its logic and applying its principles to every area of his life. When he follows the Lord's example and crucifies unto death the irrational desires of his flesh. When he adopts a rational mind—the mind of Christ—and grounds his life in the wisdom of his word.

For the wise man, this intimate union with God's wisdom is a lifelong bond. Like a marriage. That's why Solomon likens wisdom to a godly woman full of richness and beauty. She is a companion so valuable that the

---

7. We'll discuss in greater detail the nature of sin and its impact on our lives in letter 10.

8. According to scholar John Walton, "having something written on one's heart is a metaphor of memory or intimate familiarity.... Writing on the tablet of the heart evokes the image of a scribe's practice tablet on which something is written again and again. In the same way the law is to be practiced day in and day out and be part of one's regular lessons" (*Ancient Near Eastern Thought*, 257).

cheap floozies of this world pale in comparison. Lady Wisdom's ways are faithful and true. And like a good wife, she stands beside her man, as his complement, and helps him grow in the knowledge, morality, rationality, and skill he needs to be an effective man of God.

The kind of man God created him to be.

The price of rejection is steep

Lady Wisdom sharpens a man's mind and pushes him toward maturity. But immature men, scoffers, and fools reject her call because they're too comfortable lingering in the haze of a dull and unrefined mind. They ignore her words. They reject her values. And they hate her virtue.

Solomon will describe these *worthless men* in further detail in later chapters. But odds are you already know the types of guys he's talking about.

I'm sure you've seen them around.

The *immature man* is that ridiculous and skeevy guy whose mind never graduated past high school. No matter how far removed he gets from the glory days of senior year, this dazed and confused boy is never more than one weekend away from going full-blown *woulda-been* Wooderson.[9] He may have his own place to live, a menial job, and some change in his pocket, but he is not a real man because he never thinks beyond his next beer or his next hookup. His perpetual immaturity warps the gravity in his life and traps his mind in an endless orbit of overgrown childishness.

The *scoffer* is sarcastic and rude. He resents others for their achievements because he can't or won't do the work necessary to produce anything of value in his own life. So he builds himself up by tearing others down. The demon of bitterness lives rent-free within the void of his spirit, and it bares its fangs every time the scoffer dumps his cynical filth all over someone else's accomplishment. He mocks men of integrity because he has no defined values of his own to achieve. Thus he envies the men who do. As a result, his life is one big loop of disappointment and resentment. And the only way he can cope with that fact is by making derogatory comments about men who accomplish the things he never could.

The *fool* thinks he's the smartest guy in the room. But the more he runs his mouth, the more he proves his mind to be less like an ivory tower and more like a methamphetamine lab. His goal is not to know the truth, but to quarantine himself within the echo chamber of his own poisonous

---

9. Wooderson, played to sleazy perfection by Matthew McConaughey, is the aging, mustachioed stoner jock who chases jailbait and still parties with the high schoolers in Richard Linklater's 1993 cult classic film *Dazed and Confused*.

worldview. Rather than have a discussion like an actual adult (and maybe even learn something in the process), his immediate reaction is to reject the truth and silence the people who speak it. And after he's blacklisted those people, he tries to kick them in the teeth for good measure. Anger is his default setting. He operates without any consideration for emotional restraint because he never learned how to take a deep breath, calm down, and think rationally—like a grownup. His life is nothing more than a series of extended childish conniptions. And he never stops pitching his fits long enough to ask himself this one simple question: *Am I acting like a man, or am I acting more like a whiny child in constant need of mommy's intervention?*[10]

Son, these three types of men never achieve anything of real value. They never have successful relationships. They are miserable because their lives are empty and meaningless. They reject Lady Wisdom and instead surround themselves with bad influences who fill their heads with the wrong ideas. And as a result, their lives are overcome with calamity, terror, trouble, and stress—the rancid fruit of a Spirit-less existence.

Lady Wisdom issues a stern warning to men such as these:

> "[24]Because I called and you refused, I stretched out my hand and no one paid attention; [25]and you neglected all my counsel and did not want my reproof; [26]I will also laugh at your calamity; I will mock when your dread comes, [27]when your dread comes like a storm and your calamity comes like a whirlwind, when distress and anguish come upon you." (1:24–27)

These men and their shameful rejection of reality remind me of something the philosopher Ayn Rand once wrote. Every man, she said, needs to know the difference between truth and falsehood, good and evil, in order to live properly—because man "is not exempt from the laws of reality, he is a specific organism of a specific nature that requires specific actions to sustain his life . . .

> "He cannot achieve his survival by arbitrary means nor by random motions nor by blind urges nor by chance nor by whim. That which his survival requires is set by his nature and is not open to his choice. What *is* open to his choice is only whether he

---

10. I took this question from a blog I read daily, *Ace of Spades HQ*. The chief blogger, named Ace, wrote a post titled "An Observance of the Decay of Learned Restraint." His thesis was this: Emotional restraint was once looked upon as a virtue. Calmness and rationality were seen as signs of maturity and masculinity. But these days, rational masculinity is demonized. Childishness is glorified. And flying into a rage is preferable to reasoned discussion because it virtue-signals a moral superiority over those who are calm and rational. Language warning: the blog post contains a few crude words and expressions that I do not condone.

will discover it or not, whether he will choose the right goals and values or not. *He is free to make the wrong choice, but not free to succeed with it.* He is free to evade reality, he is free to unfocus his mind and stumble blindly down any road he pleases, but not free to avoid the abyss he refuses to see. Knowledge, for any conscious organism, is the means of survival; to a living consciousness, every 'is' implies an 'ought.' *Man is free to choose not to be conscious, but not free to escape the penalty of unconsciousness: destruction.* Man is the only living species that has the power to act as his own destroyer—and that is the way he has acted through most of history" (emphasis added).[11]

God has set reality as it is. And the men who reject Lady Wisdom's call to live in harmony with reality and the truth that governs it will never achieve any real success in life. They are guaranteed only failure and torment. And in those moments of self-imposed anguish, their cries for help will ring hollow because their cries are for relief from discomfort, not in repentance to God. They don't love the truth. They don't want to submit to reality. They're only crying out because they want the pain to go away.

But as Solomon says, the only response unremorseful men will receive is a deep silence, as Lady Wisdom sees through their phony pleas and makes the choice to ignore them.

"[28]Then they will call on me, but I will not answer; they will seek me diligently but they will not find me, [29]because they hated

---

11. Rand, *The Virtue of Selfishness*, 24. Despite her commitment to reason and the truth, Rand was (ironically) an atheist. But as Cody Libolt points out, "that doesn't mean that she has nothing to offer the contemporary Christian intellectual." To learn more about how Ayn Rand got a lot of things really, really right and some things really, really wrong, see Libolt, "Ayn Rand and Christianity?" Throughout these letters, I have cited a variety of sources, most of whom are Christian thinkers. Some of the people I cite, however—people like Ayn Rand and Richard Taylor, for instance—are not. But that doesn't mean their ideas can't make a meaningful contribution to our discussion. The fact is, God has revealed himself both *in* and *out* of Scripture—that is, within the text of the Bible (special revelation), and also within the general created order, in the light of nature (general revelation, or, *natural* theology). As Jacob Brunton put it, "General Revelation is *general*, primarily in respect to its audience (everyone) and its content (knowledge about God's existence, essence and attributes). Specific Revelation is likewise *specific*, primarily in respect to *its* audience (the Church) and its content (many particular details about God's relationship to His people and His dealings with the world). Notice that *both* are revelation." See Brunton, "Athens & Jerusalem," and "Revelation and Responsibility." God has revealed his truth through *all* of his revelation. Thus non-Christian philosophers like Rand and Taylor can discern the objective truth that's woven within the fabric of reality itself, even though they reject God and the special revelation of his word. Please note: I cite a variety of thinkers, but that doesn't mean that I necessarily agree with the full spectrum of their personal philosophies.

knowledge and did not choose the fear of the LORD. ³⁰They would not accept my counsel, they spurned all my reproof. ³¹So they shall eat of the fruit of their own way and be satiated with their own devices. ³²For the waywardness of the naive will kill them, and the complacency of fools will destroy them. ³³But he who listens to me shall live securely and will be at ease from the dread of evil." (1:28–33)

God's intention is clear: He will become one in spirit with those men who pursue the knowledge of him and his truth with a sincere heart. Jesus certified this promise when he said, "All that the Father gives Me will come to Me, and the one who comes to Me I will certainly not cast out" (John 6:37).

But immature men, scoffers, and fools have zero desire to connect with God in any way. Their insincerity is obvious because they never open their Bibles. They never get connected to the church. They never develop a system of rational (i.e., biblical) values to live by. They reject reality and instead choose to go their own way—and, as Solomon says, they destroy themselves in the process. They may call out to God every now and then when the pain gets too much to bear, but they have no hope of ever finding refuge in him as long as they refuse to repent of their sin and embrace the truth of his wisdom.

The fact is, as long as they refuse to turn away from their foolish behavior—as long as they ignore God's message of salvation—the only thing they will ever achieve is a lifetime of setbacks. They will never achieve any real level of self-respect. Contentment will elude them. Their relationships will self-destruct. They'll continue to marinate in hatred and anger and no one will ever take them seriously. And like shortsighted nitwits are prone to do, they will bend over backwards to evade their own culpability. Instead, they'll rush to blame God or others for their own failures.

Solomon's message is clear: The young man who listens to Lady Wisdom and lives by her principles will live in security. Free from the fear of evil and the threat of calamity. But those men who choose to remain hidebound in their rebellion against reality can never hope to experience the real-world success that only Lady Wisdom can offer.

All they will ever do on this earth is take up space and wait to die as they grapple with the futility of a purposeless existence—one devoid of God's warm and nourishing presence.

❖ ❖ ❖

Son, the curse of depravity lingers heavily over our world.

Immature men, scoffers, and fools run rampant in our society (anyone who's spent even a moderate amount of time on the internet can testify to this). But take heart, my son, because you do not share the same destiny as them. Unlike these unbelievers, you share an intimate bond with Lady Wisdom. You would be wise to honor that bond, like a husband to his wife. Be faithful to her, and she will forever walk alongside you as your intellectual complement. Hold her close, and she will do for you what Eve did for Adam: She will give you every reason not to hang your head in gloom, but to shout for joy as God fills your life with meaning and productivity.

That being said, I am your father and I know you very well. You are a perceptive guy. And I bet I can guess what you're thinking at this point: *Wow Dad. That all sounds well and good. I sure would love to talk to this Lady Wisdom. But if she's an archetype that exists in the conceptual realm, how can I, a man of flesh and blood who lives in the physical realm, listen to her message? I mean, if she doesn't produce actual soundwaves, how can I physically listen to what she has to say?*

Son, that's an excellent observation and an even more excellent question. Fortunately for us, Solomon's got the answer—and it's sure to blow your mind wide open.

He and I will discuss that mind-blowing answer in full in my next letter.

Love,
Dad

Letter 5

Listen to Your Two Most Trusted Sources of Wisdom

Prov 2:1–22

*"I don't want to see you make the same dumb mistakes
I made when I was your age."*

Son, if you're sincerely interested in listening to Lady Wisdom, then, according to Solomon, you need to open your ears and your mind to your two most trusted real-world sources of wisdom.

Before we explain who those two sources are, let me first take a moment to make you aware of the stark difference between *hearing* and *listening*. Hearing is a passive activity, an instinctive bodily function that requires no real mental energy at all. A noise sounds. Your ears hear it. Your brain registers it as a noise. And that's it. There is no conscious effort involved in the mere act of hearing.

Listening, however, is an active exercise that extends beyond the ears and into the mind.

It's a conscious and analytical process that looks something like this:

- You receive some sort of intellectual input (spoken words, musical lyrics, written text, etc.).
- You then analyze that concept and measure it against the objective truth of reality. If what you've heard or read stands opposed to the truth, it's at best erroneous and at worst a lie; either way, disregard it. However, if what you've heard rings true, then make your ear attentive to that truth and incline your heart to understanding it because there is great reward in applying it to your life.

As this process makes apparent, *an open ear* and *an open mind* are the keys to acquiring wisdom. Solomon and I explained in my previous letter the benefits that come from listening to Lady Wisdom. In this letter, we'll explain *how* you can listen to her. According to Solomon, the best way to do that is to listen to your two main real-world sources of wisdom—and those two sources are: the words of your parents and the words of God himself.

Yep, you read me correctly. A man can actually listen to Lady Wisdom when he opens his ears to his parents and opens his mind to God.

Son, being a good listener involves listening to the right people. Solomon knew this to be true. As the ruler of a mighty kingdom with international influence, he was a man of great knowledge and life experience. The insights he put forth in the biblical books of Proverbs, Ecclesiastes, and Song of Solomon[1] testify to the amount of effort he put into studying the human condition. One of the many truths he observed about humanity was that no matter where a man goes on this earth, he will always encounter bad influences who are full of empty talk and deception. He knew these deceivers were a threat. Especially to young people. So he began Prov 2 by encouraging his son to listen to the one man he could trust above all others: *him*, his father.

I know that may sound crazy to young ears. But if you're sincere about listening to Lady Wisdom, you'll stop *hearing* me talk and start *listening* to my heartfelt words of fatherly wisdom.

OPEN YOUR EARS TO YOUR PARENTS

Prov 2:1–5

Solomon opens Prov 2 with one of his many paternal appeals.

---

1. The book Song of Solomon also goes by the name Song of Songs.

He begins this particular appeal by calling on his son to really *listen* to him. To internalize his instruction by opening his ears and his heart to his words:

> "¹My son, if you will receive *my* words and treasure *my* commandments within you, ²make your ear attentive to wisdom, incline your heart to understanding; ³for if you cry for discernment, lift your voice for understanding; ⁴if you seek her as silver and search for her as for hidden treasures; ⁵then you will discern the fear of the LORD and discover the knowledge of God." (2:1–5, emphasis added)

Notice in v. 1 that Solomon commands his son to receive and treasure up *his* commandments, to make his ear attentive to *his* words of wisdom, essentially saying: *Son, don't listen to just anybody. Incline your ear only to the people who are worth listening to. But above them all, listen to my words. Pay attention to me, your father, the one man you can trust more than any other. I want the best for you. I will always have your back. So make your ear attentive to my instruction as I train you in the truth. In the way of wisdom.*

Son, I am likewise commanding you to "receive *my* words and treasure *my* commandments within you" (2:1). Before you incline your ear to anyone else in this world, listen first to *me*, your father, as I train you up in the way you should go. Follow Solomon's instruction: *Make your ear attentive to my words of wisdom. Treasure my commands and incline your heart to understanding them.* In other words: Listen closely when I'm speaking and take my instruction to heart.

At this point, however, you may be wondering: *Dad, why should I listen to you? What makes your words more valuable than those of anyone else?*

Son, that's a fair question.

Being the kind and generous father that I am, I'm willing to share a secret that will not only answer your question, but it will also cause you to completely reconsider where you stand in our family's intellectual hierarchy.

"Why should I listen to my parents?"

As I've made clear throughout these letters, one of my main jobs as your father is to instill within you the wisdom you need to go out into the world and create a meaningful life for yourself. Your job as my son and my student is to pay attention to my words and integrate them into your day-to-day thinking so you can take those homegrown principles of wisdom with you every time you walk out the front door.

Son, you should listen to my words because whether you realize it or not, my parental wisdom is a valuable and God-given resource that will serve you well as you make your way in the world. Your mother and I are the two people on this earth who care about you the most. We love you more than anyone else and we're working harder than anyone else to help you grow into the man God designed you to be. You'd be wise to honor Solomon's instruction and open your ears to our words of wisdom. Especially right now, at this moment, because I'm about to let you in on a well-kept secret that every boy your age needs to know.

Are you ready to know why you should listen to me and your mother above every other person? Here's the secret answer: *Because parents are much smarter than their children give them credit for.*

Now, if you're like me when I was your age, you've probably responded to this red pill of truth with a deep sense of disbelief. Perhaps even the same level of disbelief Luke Skywalker experienced when he learned Vader was his real father in *The Empire Strikes Back*. "No," young Luke said with a soul-crushing groan. "That's not true. That's *impossible!!!*"

Oh, it's definitely possible. In fact, it's the God's-honest truth. Believe me. I *know*. I learned this lesson the hard way during a family vacation back when I was an awkward yet know-it-all pre-teen.

I was riding down a long escalator in a shopping mall with my mother. In a moment of immature stupidity, I decided to be cute and sit down on the escalator step as it was descending. My mother looked down at me and said, "You better stand up because you won't be able to get to your feet once we reach the bottom." I smirked one of those *Mom, you don't know what you're talking about* smirks and said with a smug arrogance, "*I'll* be able to get up." I then went on to describe, with no small degree of condescension, my plan to utilize the escalator's momentum to propel me to my feet once we got to the bottom. From there I would leap into the air and dismount the escalator with the precision of a Greek Olympian. I explained to her that this maneuver, as I had envisioned it, would testify to the power of human acrobatic capabilities. Its beauty would be such that the people lined up behind us would stand amazed at my tween-age athletic prowess.

To her credit my mother listened patiently and kept her comments to herself, responding instead by casually arching her eyebrows and tilting her head as if to say *Okay, have it your way, bud*. Mistaking her silence for approval, I sat poised and ready to impress the world. I planted my dumb butt firmly on the escalator step and rode the rest of the way down with this idiotic grin plastered across my face, totally unaware that I was descending toward a harsh encounter with the steel jaws of reality.

When we reached the bottom, my mother stepped off the escalator as any normal person would. But much to my shock, my glorious dismount did not go as planned, mainly because I wasn't able to stand upright—just as my mother had predicted. I couldn't get to my feet because the steps kept unfolding underneath me and rolling me backward and trapping me in a perpetual seated position. I tried pushing myself up with my hands, but I abandoned that strategy when my fingers were nearly mangled in the interlocking steel teeth of the escalator's collapsing steps. I couldn't use the handrails to pull myself up because my lack of balance conspired with my childishly short arms to keep the rails *just* out of reach.

As for the people behind me—well, they were hardly impressed. In fact, I found them to be quite rude and unsympathetic as they snickered and stepped over my flailing body without offering so much as a helping hand.

With nowhere else to turn, I looked up at my mother, who stood by and watched as my confident smirk gave way to a twisted expression of helpless panic. She let me flop around on my backside for another second or two before she offered me her hand. I summoned the last reserves of my strength and lunged toward her with all the graceless desperation of a midnight dry-heave. Our hands locked on the first try, thank God, and she pulled me up off the escalator to my feet. We stood there for a moment eye to eye. No words were exchanged. Just knowing gazes. My face was flush with embarrassment while hers was unflinching. Again, to her credit, she kept any and all reprimands to herself. There was nothing left for her to say or do, after all. The situation itself served as lesson enough. But her eyes said *I told you so.*

As we walked away in silence, a profound and humbling thought crossed my mind. I realized that maybe I *wasn't* as smart or as athletic as I thought I was. I then realized that maybe my mother was smarter than I gave her credit for, maybe even smarter than me (!)—and that maybe, *just maybe*, if I had listened to her from the outset, I could have avoided the *embarrassment on the escalator* altogether.

Take advantage of the wisdom your parents have to offer

This story highlights a valuable lesson: Any kid who chooses to ignore the wise instruction of his parents will get himself stuck at the bottom of life's downward escalator of failure. On the other hand, the youngster who's willing to open his ears to his parents' words of wisdom is destined to walk tall as he moves smoothly from one level of life to the next.

Son, God didn't create parents just so they could embarrass their children with old movie references or corny dad-jokes (although the God-given authority to embarrass is definitely one of the more entertaining perks that comes with being a parent). He put parents in place primarily to provide a stable foundation for their children. To instruct them in the ways of wisdom. To reward them when they do well. To help them to their feet when they stumble. And to keep them moving forward along the right path in life.

A parent's wisdom is not something to ignore. It is a precious resource that every young man should make the most of. Solomon understood this. That's why he encouraged his son to *cry out* and *raise his voice* and ask his father to share the insight and understanding he had to offer.

One of the hallmarks of a wise man is his willingness to learn from other wise people. If you want to grow in wisdom, you must never be afraid to ask good questions. And never be too proud to admit you don't know something.

Keep in mind that you're still a young man and that you are inexperienced in many of the ways of life. But don't let your inexperience discourage you. And don't try to mask it by acting like a smart-aleck poser know-it-all. Instead, own up to it and use it as motivation to call out for the insight you lack. Make good use of the resources God has made available to you, namely your parents. And you'll learn soon enough how to handle those tricky escalators that life throws your way.

Son, you have my word: I will always make myself available to help you in your quest for wisdom. Believe it or not, I understand where you're coming from far better than you might think.

Yes, I am much older than you. But I was your age once upon a time. And yes, as a young man there were times when I thought I knew everything there was to know about life. I thought my parents were clueless and out of touch with the real world. I ignored them from time to time just like any other punk kid. And do you know where my own limited punk-kid knowledge got me? It got my behind scuffed up and stuck at the bottom of a moving escalator. Later on in high school, it caused me to drive a car into a ditch on a date because I was certain I didn't need dorky eye glasses. At various other points, my youthful naivete prompted me to ignore good advice and miss many opportunities because I was too much of a knucklehead to admit to my own inexperience. This stubborn refusal to listen forced me to learn a few too many lessons the hard way. I gained plenty of real-world experience during that time; but if I had been less cocky and more willing to listen, I could have avoided some of the painful emotional scars that instigated those lessons.

I've grown much in wisdom and maturity since that time because I (finally) learned the value of listening. I figured out that a man can learn a lot when he resolves to close his mouth and open his ears. I'm humble enough now to admit that even after forty-plus years on God's earth I'm still a far cry from the world's wisest man.

That being said, *I am wiser than you are.* I know more than you do about the real world and the truth that governs it—*a lot more*, whether you think so or not. And you would be wise to take advantage of the hard-earned wisdom I'm willing to share.

Solomon likewise taught his son to listen to "your father's instruction and do not forsake your mother's teaching" (1:8). He instructed him to *call out*, to *raise his voice*, and to *seek out* their parental wisdom as though it were a resource of great value—because *it is*. If you will heed Solomon's instruction to respect your parents and seek out the wisdom we have to offer, then you will have taken your first step toward reaping the heavenly benefits that come along with wise living. As Solomon says, "if you seek her as silver and search for her as for hidden treasures; then you will discern the fear of the LORD and discover the knowledge of God," and you will put yourself in a prime position to receive the blessings God has in store for those who honor the wisdom of his word (2:4–5).

Just to be clear: I don't expect you to listen to me because I'm cool or because I have mastered the art of living well (because neither of those are true). You should listen to me because I'm your father. I love you. I want the best for you. And I can help you reach your potential by speaking to you with the wisdom of *life experience.*

Like Solomon, I am calling on you to make your ear attentive to my wisdom and incline your heart to my understanding. Not so I can lord my experience over you and make you feel small, but because I don't want to see you make the same dumb mistakes I made when I was your age. One of my jobs as your father is to teach you how to avoid many of the foolish blunders that tend to plague young men. If you want to learn those valuable life lessons the smart way and not the hard way, then pay attention to my words as I bring you up in the principles of your Heavenly Father—the one, single Being who is more qualified than me to instruct you in the ways of wisdom.

Son, I may be your chief source of wise counsel, but I am not the ultimate source of wisdom itself. God is. And according to Solomon, God promises certain blessings to the young man who not only lends his ears to his parents, but also gives his Heavenly Father full access to the most personal aspect of himself: *his conscious mind.*

OPEN YOUR MIND TO GOD

Prov 2:6-22

Solomon taught his son that everyone needs God's wisdom in order to achieve real success in life.

There's just one problem: No one is born wise.

So the question arises: How exactly does a man get wisdom?

Fortunately for us, the answer is simple. A rational man acquires wisdom the same way he acquires anything else he cannot produce on his own. Through *trade*. Based on Solomon's own example, any man who desires wisdom must seek out God, the ultimate source of wisdom, and acquire it from him.

God is wise by nature and he is very willing to share that aspect of himself. But he won't do it for free, primarily because his wisdom is *personal* and *valuable*, and he will only share it with a man who is willing to trade him something of *great personal value* in return.

Are you willing to trade value for value with God?

The logical question then naturally presents itself: What can a finite man give the infinite God?

The short answer is: nothing that God doesn't already rightfully own. As we discussed in letter 2, God possesses total authority over all his creation.[2] He is self-existent. He *needs* nothing from us. There is one thing, however, that he *wants* from you. He wants you to grant him total access to that most personal aspect of your life. That is, your *self*—your conscious mind, the essential *you* at the core of your being that forms the judgments and chooses the values that establish your identity and distinguish you as an individual.[3]

Son, nothing in this life is free. God's wisdom is no exception. If you want to acquire wisdom from God, you have to be prepared to make a trade. And your mind—your *identity*, your *life*—is his asking price. If you want God to give of himself to you, then you must likewise be willing to give all of your self to him.

Once again, we can look to the example of Solomon to see how a man makes this trade with God. Think back to when Solomon was a young and

---

2. Moses, David, and Paul testified to the eternal scope of God's sovereign authority in Deut 10:14; Ps 24:1; and Col. 1:16, respectively.

3. I borrowed this definition of *the self* from Ayn Rand (*Philosophy: Who Needs It*, 50). As we'll see in letter 8, Solomon also uses the term *the heart* to refer to the self.

untested king, when God approached him and said, "Ask what you wish me to give you."[4] Solomon didn't respond to God's generosity by making a bunch of self-centered, one-sided demands. Instead, he approached God with great humility. And he responded to God's offer by offering him something of great personal value in return.

In exchange for his wisdom, young Solomon granted God full access to his conscious mind. When he asked God to give him "an *understanding mind* to govern thy people, that I may *discern between good and evil*," Solomon tacitly surrendered his entire identity to God (1 Kgs 3:9 RSV, emphasis added). Solomon invited God to take up residence in his mind; and in so doing, he agreed to allow the moral principles of God's wisdom to define his life as a man and his legacy as a king.

Solomon valued God's wisdom so much that he was willing to trade value for value with God in order to acquire it. Solomon offered up his self to God. And God responded to his trade request by generously blessing Solomon with the *wise and discerning mind* he asked for, "so that there has been no one like you before you, nor shall one like you arise after you." But God didn't stop there. So pure was Solomon's desire to bond with God's wisdom that the Lord tacked on another layer of blessings. "I have also given you what you have not asked," God continued, "both riches and honor, so that there will not be any among the kings like you all your days. If you walk in My ways, keeping My statutes and commandments, as your father David walked, then I will prolong your days" (1 Kgs 3:11–14).[5]

God determined by his own sovereign authority that Solomon would be the next king of Israel. But in his grace, he allowed Solomon to choose what kind of king he would be. And Solomon, despite his youth and inexperience, made a wise choice. He fully opened his mind to God. And in exchange for God's wisdom, he agreed to abide by God's terms of the transaction. Solomon agreed to walk wholeheartedly in God's ways, to *keep his statutes and his commandments* and allow the principles of God's word to define his life just as his father David had done (1 Kgs 3:14).

Remember, the Bible describes Solomon's father David as a man *after God's own heart* (1 Sam 13:14; Acts 13:22) The Bible also tells us that Solomon walked "in the statutes of his father David," meaning that he listened to his father's words of instruction and learned from his example (1 Kgs 3:3). Young Solomon made his ear attentive to his father's wisdom and treasured

---

4. We discussed this situation in detail in letter 1.

5. See letters 3 and 7 for discussion of God's promise of long days and how it relates to wisdom.

up his commandments within his heart. By doing so, he was smart enough to seize the moment and take advantage of his Heavenly Father's generosity.

When God approached him and said, "Ask what you wish me to give you," Solomon first *admitted to his own inexperience*. He then *called out* to his Heavenly Father for insight and *raised his voice* for understanding. He sought out God's wisdom above all else because he valued it more than every earthly treasure. The throne of Israel may have been his birthright, but acquiring God's wisdom was his personal choice. Solomon, therefore, serves as living proof that wisdom does not adhere to the luck of the draw. Nor is it a trait that can be passed down through genetics.

It is a *value* that must be acquired not by chance, but by choice and by trade.

Son, understand this: A man can never be *good enough* to earn God's wisdom. But he can be *smart enough* to put himself in a position to receive it. And fortunately for us, God is a generous giver, especially when it comes to dishing out wisdom.

The Apostle James, the half-brother of Jesus, said this of his Lord's generosity: "But if any of you lacks wisdom, let him ask of God, who gives to all generously and without reproach, and it will be given to him" (Jas 1:5). Solomon echoed these sentiments in Prov 1:20–23, when he told his son that God will generously make his wisdom available to anyone determined enough to seek him out (see letter 4).

That means no matter who you are, whether you're the king of ancient Israel or a young man in rural America, God is willing to make the same trade with you as he made with Solomon. The only question is: Are you willing to take him up on his offer? Are you willing to trade value for value with God and offer the fullness of your mind—your life, your self, your very identity—to him in exchange for his invaluable wisdom?

If your answer is *Yes*, then pause for a moment and go to God in prayer. He is calling on you right now. He has approached you just as he did with Solomon and he is willing to trade value for value with you. If you're willing to take him up on his offer, then follow Solomon's example and answer God's call with a wide-open mind. Invite him to take his rightful seat on the throne at the center of your consciousness. Ask God to give you the wisdom you need to listen to his words and to allow his principles to define your life. Power your prayer with big faith. Don't let insecurity and doubt stand in your way.

Now don't be concerned if you don't immediately *feel* any wiser after praying that prayer. Your mind is not a smartphone. God's wisdom isn't an app that can be downloaded at the touch of a screen. The acquisition of wisdom is a day-by-day process. And as long as you follow through on your responsibility to keep your mind open to your Heavenly Father, you can always count on him to keep up his end of the transaction.

Solomon testifies to God's trustworthiness in Prov 2:6–8.

> "⁶For *the LORD gives wisdom*; from His mouth come knowledge and understanding. ⁷He stores up sound wisdom *for the upright*; He is a shield to *those who walk in integrity*, ⁸guarding the paths of *justice*, and He preserves the way of His *godly ones*." (emphasis added)

Solomon makes two statements of fact regarding the trustworthy character of God in these verses:

1. God alone is the ultimate source of wisdom. "For *the LORD* gives wisdom," Solomon says (2:6, emphasis added). And the primary means by which God distributes his knowledge and understanding is from *his own mouth*. That is, through his word, the Bible—every word of which proves true: "The sum of Your word is truth, and every one of Your righteous ordinances is everlasting" (Ps 119:160). *Every word of God proves true* because they are *breathed out by God* and thus profitable to anyone who's willing to acquire his wisdom (Prov 30:5; 2 Tim 3:16–17).[6]
2. God has plenty of wisdom *stored up* and ready to share. But as Solomon testifies in vv. 7 and 8, God won't share his wisdom with just anyone. And he won't give it away for free. Solomon teaches his son that God stores up his wisdom only *for the upright*, his *godly ones* who *walk in integrity* and *justice*. This proves that God will only entrust his wisdom to the young man who is sincere about surrendering control of his entire life to the moral principles of God's word.

Son, if you're serious about acquiring God's wisdom, then listen intently to Solomon's words. Pay attention to his example. Open your ears to wise people like your mother and me. Open your mind to your Heavenly Father. We want to be involved in your life to the fullest extent possible. Especially listen to God, who wants to search your thoughts and to see your

---

6. God is truth, thus his word is truth (John 14:6). David testified to the trustworthiness of God's word in Ps 19:7–11. "The law of the LORD is perfect, restoring the soul; the testimony of the LORD is sure, making wise the simple. The precepts of the LORD are right, rejoicing the heart; the commandment of the LORD is pure, enlightening the eyes. The fear of the LORD is clean, enduring forever; the judgments of the LORD are true; they are righteous altogether. They are more desirable than gold, yes, than much fine gold; sweeter also than honey and the drippings of the honeycomb. Moreover, by them Your servant is warned; in keeping them there is great reward." Also see 2 Tim 2:13; Titus 1:2; and Heb 6:18 for other scriptural references that testify to God's inability to lie.

heart—not so he can manipulate you like a puppet, but so he can know you intimately as his child. He wants nothing more than to do what a good Father does, which is to train you, his son, in the ways of his wisdom, to come alongside you and help you create a noble life. One that's grounded in the truth.

Once a man fully opens his mind to God, then God will take on the wonderful responsibility of being his Heavenly Father.

Son, the same is true for you. Just as I have made myself available to you as your earthly father, so also God has made himself available as your Heavenly Father. He is ready to give you that one-to-one parental attention every child craves. You need only to open your ears and your mind to his word and allow him to personally instruct you in the ways of wisdom. "For *the LORD* gives wisdom," Solomon says; "from *His mouth* come knowledge and understanding" (2:6, emphasis added).

Notice that God does not outsource his responsibilities. He is a hands-on Father.[7] He wants to be an active part of your life. *If* you offer him your mind, he will personally instruct you in his knowledge. *If* you receive his words, *if* you make your ear attentive to his wisdom and treasure his commandments within you, "*Then*," promises Solomon, "you will discern righteousness and justice and equity and every good course. For wisdom will enter your heart and knowledge will be pleasant to your soul" (2:9–10).

Use wisdom to defend yourself against bad influences

Son, as you can see, God is indeed generous when it comes to sharing his wisdom. But he is also extremely *discerning*, meaning that he will only entrust his wisdom to the young man who is sincere about using it to bring *good* into his life. God will share his wisdom with you only if you are sincere about using it to protect yourself against those harmful people who threaten your moral integrity.

As I mentioned in letter 3, these people come in all shapes and sizes. But according to Solomon, they will usually fall into one of two general categories: *worthless men* and *forbidden women*. You will recognize these people because they are the opposite of your parents. In fact, they are the kind of people your mother and I would label as *bad influences.*

In Prov 2:11–19, Solomon teaches his son this same valuable lesson. And he tells him that a wise mind is the best weapon to wield in his battle against these bad influences.

---

7. We'll discuss what being a hands-on father is all about in letter 8.

> "¹¹[D]iscretion will watch over you" Solomon says; "understanding will guard you, ¹²delivering you from the way of evil, from men of perverted speech, ¹³who forsake the paths of uprightness to walk in the ways of darkness, ¹⁴who rejoice in doing evil and delight in the perverseness of evil, ¹⁵men whose paths are crooked, and who are devious in their ways. ¹⁶So you will be delivered from the forbidden woman, from the adulteress with her smooth words, ¹⁷who forsakes the companion of her youth and forgets the covenant of her God; ¹⁸for her house sinks down to death, and her paths to the departed; ¹⁹none who go to her come back, nor do they regain the paths of life." (2:11–19 ESV)

Indeed, the young man who practices *discretion* and *understanding* can easily discern wise men from worthless men and wise women from forbidden women. Solomon and I will discuss these two particular bad influences in greater detail in later letters. For now, we'll introduce them by describing their basic characteristics.

The worthless man is fairly easy to spot. According to Solomon's description, he's a devious and gutter-minded man who uses his trashy mouth to speak twisted words. When he's not busy talking dirty, he spends his time pleasuring himself *in the perversity of evil* (2:14). He is an unfocused and short-sighted con-man who won't hesitate to use manipulation and even violence to advance his wicked schemes. As we'll discuss further in letters 7 and 10, the worthless man is *the* primary male bad influence you will encounter in your life. Do not admire or emulate him. His ways are detestable to the Lord. The world may celebrate his antics, but as Solomon will explain in Prov 3 and 6, the LORD despises him and will punish his rebellion with a flood of destruction and shame.

Be aware, however, that not all threats take on such a skeevy or thuggish exterior. Solomon also warns his son against *the forbidden woman*, who takes on a softer, more intoxicating form yet wields a sting as debilitating as any bare-knuckled sucker-punch. Her behavior is that of an untrustworthy adulteress. She seduces men with her smooth words. And in the process, she forsakes the companion of her youth—her husband or boyfriend—and forgets the covenant of her God. Her sultry talk is her snare and her aim is the satisfaction of her most whimsical and guttural impulses. She uses men as objects to satisfy her desires. Those wayward young men who are foolish enough to stray into the labyrinth of her seduction receive ruin rather than satisfaction. That's why Solomon is adamant that his son not follow this cunning seductress down the road to perdition. We'll talk about her at great length in letter 9. For now, let's just resolve to avoid her and the worthless man altogether.

Do the smart thing instead: Follow Solomon's direction and "walk in the way of good men and keep to the paths of the righteous. For the upright will live in the land and the blameless will remain in it; but the wicked will be cut off from the land and the treacherous will be uprooted from it" (2:20–22).[8]

Son, don't tune me out; instead, tune in and track with what I'm saying.

Take advantage of the value that is my life experience. Take God up on his offer to supply you with all the wisdom you need. You can do this by making your ears attentive to my words and taking my hard-earned fatherly wisdom to heart. My goal is to teach you what it means to be a man. You would be wise to utilize my instruction so we can work together to transform your youthful energy into a strong masculine *mentality*.

Trust me when I tell you this: One of the best ways to grow as a person is to develop healthy relationships—both friendly and romantic—with godly people. Avoid bad influences like the worthless man and the forbidden woman. They will only bring you down. Be discerning with your relationships. Make good friends. Court the right kind of girl. And utilize the wisdom of God's word to defend yourself against every moral threat.

Love,
Dad

---

8. As we discussed in letter 3, *the land* that Solomon mentioned is a reference to the promised land, which is the physical symbol of a peaceful and productive life of harmony with God.

Letter 6

The Everyday Hero

Prov 3:1–12

"A real hero is the man who meets his personal responsibilities with integrity and works hard to make his world a better place."

Son, one of the many things you and I have in common is a love of comic book heroes.

They capture our attention because they're interesting characters with fantastic abilities. As of today, your favorite hero is Batman. You like the Dark Knight for many of the more obvious reasons. You admire his mission as Gotham City's silent protector. You respect his fighting skills and think his top-of-the-line tech is pretty cool. But the main thing you like about the Batman is the way he uses his brain as well as his brawn to get over on the bad guys. You get a kick out of watching the world's greatest detective use his shrewd investigative skills to gather clues and develop strategies to stay one step ahead of his rogues gallery of villains.

All those qualities do indeed make for a great hero. I find the character of Batman compelling as well, but for more adult reasons. One Bat-fact I like to keep in mind is that unlike Superman, who is a superpowered alien—or The Flash, who can run with super speed—the Batman is just a man. He is unique among most other comic book heroes in that he has no superpowers. As comic book author Frank Miller pointed out, Batman can't bench-press cars or run faster than a speeding bullet or jump in the air and stay there.[1] He boasts no supernatural heritage nor does he wield a ring of power or a golden lasso or any other instrument of otherworldly ability. Quite simply, he is a normal human being who is not immune to the flaws and frailty of the human condition. He is a man of flesh and blood. Head and heart. Strength and weakness.

The Batman's humanity is his defining trait. As an adult and as a father in particular, I can relate to that. But perhaps his most admirable character quality is the strength of his spirit. His will is more powerful than any of his muscles. His mind is more effective than any of his weapons. And although he is a mere mortal in a world of godlike characters, the Batman doesn't let human limitation prevent him from doing his job as a hero.

Bruce Wayne (the man behind the mask) is motivated in his mission by the homegrown convictions he learned from his parents. But his drive to act on those convictions is rooted in their death. As a boy, Bruce could only watch as a petty thief murdered his parents in cold blood. That one moment of pain set the course for Bruce's entire life. That very night, on the street stained with his mother's and father's blood, young Bruce made a vow to rid the city of the evil that had taken their lives.[2]

In that moment of tragedy, the Batman was conceived.

Bruce, however, didn't become the Batman out of a lust for vengeance, but rather out of a sense of responsibility. Simply put, it was his way of preserving his father's legacy. Bruce's father, Dr. Thomas Wayne, worked hard as a physician to bring a sense of healing to Gotham City's fractured soul. Bruce watched his father use his mind, his talents, and his money to make his hometown a better place. He absorbed his father's example; and in the process, he realized this simple truth about heroism: Being a hero is not about possessing great power or wearing a mask. A real hero is the man who meets his personal responsibilities with integrity and works hard to make his world a better place.[3]

Son, I'd rather you not endure a life-altering catastrophe just to learn what being a hero is all about. In my previous letter, I taught you how to acquire wisdom. With this letter, I will use Solomon's instruction (and the

---

1. Miller, *The Dark Knight Returns*, 8–9.
2. Loeb, *Batman: Hush*, 8.
3. We learned this same lesson in letter 2.

mythic character of Batman as a paradigm) to teach you how to bring that heroic wisdom to life in your everyday life.

In the real-world city of Jerusalem, Israel's King Solomon, much like Thomas Wayne, set a powerful example for his son. He brought peace and prosperity to his country. He walked with wisdom and in close fellowship with God.

In Prov 3:1-12, Solomon outlines four everyday responsibilities a wise man should strive to accomplish.

These, my son, are the four responsibilities of an everyday hero.

THE FOUR RESPONSIBILITIES OF AN EVERYDAY HERO

Prov 3:1-12

1. An everyday hero preserves the peace at home

Solomon never missed an opportunity to remind his son to respect his parents.

He opens chapter 3 of his Proverbs true to form with yet another fatherly appeal:

> "¹My son, do not forget my teaching, but let your heart keep my commandments; ²for length of days and years of life and *peace* they will add to you." (3:1-2, emphasis added)

God promises certain blessings to the young man who treats his parents with respect. As Solomon points out in these verses, one of those rewards is a sustained *peace*—both with his family and with God.

One of a comic book hero's chief goals is to safeguard the city he calls home. Son, if you want to be a hero, you should likewise strive to preserve the peace in your home. One of the best ways to achieve that peace is to honor your mother and me and our God-given parental authority.

We've discussed the concept of parental respect and its benefits in letters 2, 3, and 5, so I won't rehash it here.[4] I will, however, take this opportunity to issue one more important reminder on this topic: Never confuse *respect* with *resignation*.

Yes, your mother and I have authority over you. But that does not mean we are your arch-enemies. I am not the Joker. Your mom is not Harley Quinn. And we are not conspiring to drive you mad. Our job is to train you

---

4. Solomon and I will discuss in fuller detail the specifics of my job as your father—and your job as my son—in letter 8.

up, not tie you down. When it comes to our relational dynamic, I would prefer you think of us as the Alfred to your Batman.

Alfred Pennyworth is technically Bruce Wayne's butler. But his responsibilities extend far beyond making Bruce's bed and washing his socks. Alfred became Bruce's legal guardian upon the deaths of Thomas and Martha Wayne. He stepped up of his own accord and became a father figure to a young man awash in despair and rage.

Even after Bruce grew up and took on the persona of Batman, Alfred remained his most ardent confidant. He didn't turn his back on Bruce, nor did he call the men in white coats to come and haul him off to Arkham Asylum. He instead agreed to work alongside both Bruce Wayne and Batman in every possible way: tactical support, mechanic, doctor, and general caretaker of the Wayne estate just to name a few.

But his most important responsibility is keeping Bruce's moral compass in check. The wise and weathered Alfred has refused to allow his surrogate son to compromise his integrity and tarnish the Wayne legacy. Thus he is quick to provide Master Bruce with the fatherly support and guidance he requires. And whether he's preparing supper or dishing out wise advice or reconfiguring a targeting system on the Batmobile, Alfred involves himself in every area of Bruce's life.

Son, that's what good parents do. They *involve* themselves in the lives of their children. Your mother and I are your closest allies. Honoring our authority does not involve resigning your individuality. You will always be your own man. But right now, you are a *young* man who still requires guidance and instruction. I may help wash your clothes and cook your food, but I am not your butler. I am your father. I will forever be an active part of your life. I will never let you go—but neither will I hold you back. I will steer you in the right direction when you're tempted to veer off course. And I will always provide you with the support you need to press forward and find success in your heroic mission.

It's our job as your parents to involve ourselves in your life—not to smother you, but to provide you with the tactical support you need to accomplish your God-given mission in life. Part of that mission is to preserve the peace at home. You can achieve real peace by embracing your mother and me as your partners rather than pitting yourself against us as if we were your enemies.

2. An everyday hero stands strong in his moral convictions

In Christopher Nolan's 2005 film *Batman Begins*, an enigmatic man named Ducard—a member of a group of assassins named the League of Shadows—rebuked a young Bruce Wayne for rejecting their corrupt definition of justice. Ducard held no regard for an individual's God-given right to rational due process.[5] And during their training, he chastised Bruce, an aspiring member of the League, for refusing to execute an alleged murderer without a proper trial.

"Your compassion is a weakness your enemies will not share," Ducard said as the League's sinister leader, Ra's al Ghul, looked on with an army of ninjas in tow.

"That's why it's so important," Bruce replied. His voice barely rose above a whisper. Yet his words were as divisive as an assassin's blade. "It separates us from them."

When Ducard put his integrity to the test, Bruce didn't compromise and take the coward's way out. He stood strong in his convictions, like a man, because he understood that *moral virtue* is the ideological line that separates a good guy like Batman from a bad guy like Ra's al Ghul.

Son, as a young man, you would be wise to understand this fact: A strong sense of conviction does not in and of itself make a man heroic. A bad guy like Ra's al Ghul can have sincere beliefs. It's the fact that his beliefs are erroneous and immoral that makes him a fool. And it's his devotion to commit evil acts in the name of his beliefs that makes him a villain.

Bruce Wayne understood this distinction. He refused to use evil tactics to fight evil men. He instead resolved to maintain his integrity. To stand on the side of the highest good. And he did so, despite the pressure of bad influences, by holding tight to the virtuous principles he learned from his father.

His conviction was remarkable, considering his predicament. There he stood, face-to-face with a terrorist mastermind, surrounded by a squadron of armed ninjas in an isolated hideaway atop a frozen mountain somewhere in the south of Asia—and yet Bruce would not compromise on the homegrown values his father had worked so hard to instill within him as a young man.

As we discussed in letter 3, Solomon likewise understood the power of homegrown conviction. He knew if a father trained his son in the ways of virtue at an early age, those bedrock principles would stick with him for a

---

5. According to God's law, an accused criminal must be legally tried for his crime. His guilt or innocence is established on the truthful and coherent testimony of two or three witnesses (Deut 19:15–21; 2 Cor 13:1).

lifetime (also see Prov 22:6). Bruce Wayne is a shining example of the kind of man Solomon had in mind.

As a child, Bruce watched his father's behavior. He learned from his example. He *listened* when his father spoke. He *remembered* his words of wisdom and took them to *heart*. And many years later, as a grown man—in a moment of high pressure, when murderous villains put Bruce's integrity to the test—he resisted their assault by holding tight to the clarity and conscience of *home*.

He refused to compromise on his convictions because he understood this truth: A commitment to *virtue*, not muscles or a mask, is the true calling card of a hero.

Solomon teaches his son this same lesson in Prov 3:3–4.

In v. 3, Solomon details the four basic virtues that define a hero's moral character. And he does so by using a single word: the Hebrew word *ḥesed*.

Here is his instruction:

> "³Do no let *ḥesed* (love/mercy/kindness/loyalty) and truth leave you; bind them around your neck, write them on the tablet of your heart. ⁴So you will find favor and good repute in the sight of God and man." (3:3–4)

The word *ḥesed* has deep meaning. Each layer of its definition sparkles with different shimmers of ethical significance.⁶ Thus it is a word that can be difficult to summarize into a single word. The ESV translates *ḥesed* in Prov 3:3 as steadfast "love." Other Bible versions translate *ḥesed* as "mercy" (KJV), "kindness" (NASB), and "loyalty" (RSV, CSB).

Since these four virtues serve as the basic foundation of an everyday hero's moral character, let's take a moment and discuss each of them in more detail.⁷

---

6. Per Mounce: "*ḥesed* is one of the richest, most theologically insightful terms in the OT. It denotes 'kindness, love, loyalty, mercy,' most poignantly employed in the context of relationship between God and humans as well as between one human and another—the former relationship using the word three times as often as the latter. *ḥesed* describes the special relationship God has with his covenantal people, and as such can be a difficult word to translate because it is so specific" (*Complete Expository Dictionary*, 426).

7. There are four specific archetypes, or ingrained patterns of behavior, that reside deep within the subconscious of every man. These are the archetypes of the King, the Warrior, the Magician, and the Lover. According to scholars Robert Moore and Douglas Gillette, these four archetypes serve as "the building blocks of the mature masculine" (*King Warrior Magician Lover*, ix). This section will draw heavily from their book *King Warrior Magician Lover*. As we'll see throughout this section, these four archetypes coincide with the four-fold definition of the Hebrew word *ḥesed*, the word Solomon used in Prov 3:3 to identify the specific virtues that should define his son's character. The

Love

A man motivated by love can find the strength to do things other weaker men can never do. Take Bruce Wayne as an example. Despite the loss of his parents, he managed to keep love, not hateful vengeance, as his primary motivation. A weaker man would've allowed this kind of tragedy to defeat him—but not Bruce Wayne. He refused to act like a victim. In spite of his loss, he refused to allow his pain to fester and poison his spirit. Through force of will, he brought order to the spiritual chaos that filled his life. He transcended his trauma by looking deep within himself, beyond his scars, to find the strength he needed to keep moving forward and create a meaningful life. He found his strength in his love for his parents and the values that defined them, as well as his love for Alfred, his friends, and his hometown of Gotham. And he forged the character of Batman not in an acid bath of hatred, but in the fire of steadfast love that burns at the core of his soul.[8] His love keeps him strong, connected, alive, enthusiastic, energized, and focused on his goals. And it's this love that gives Bruce's life and the Batman's mission a sense of moral purpose.

As Bruce Wayne proves, love—not muscles or gadgets—is the ultimate source of a hero's power. After all, only a virtue as powerful as love could motivate a man to risk his life to preserve the people and the ideas he values most.

Son, let Bruce Wayne's story serve as a lesson. Bad things are going to happen in life. Bad people are going to cross your path. But you must

---

study of these inborn archetypes is an important aspect of a young man's psychological development of the hero's mindset—which, according to Joseph Campbell, "is hidden within us all only waiting to be known and rendered into life." Campbell also notes that as the hero searches deep within himself to find the strength he needs to complete his journey, he will realize "the perilous journey was a labor not of attainment but of re-attainment, not discovery but rediscovery. The godly powers sought and dangerously won are revealed to have been within the heart of the hero all the time. He is 'the king's son' who has come to know who he is and therewith has entered into the exercise of his proper power—'God's son'" (*The Hero With A Thousand Faces*, 31). Accessing these four psychological archetypes—the King, the Warrior, the Magician, and the Lover—is the key to awakening the hero that resides in the subconscious mind of every man.

8. Per Moore and Gillette, the energy of the Lover "is the primal energy pattern of what we could call vividness, aliveness, and passion. It lives through the great primal hungers of our species for sex, food, well-being, reproduction, creative adaptation to life's hardships, and ultimately a sense of meaning, without which human beings cannot go on with their lives. The Lover's drive is to satisfy those hungers." Bruce Wayne maintains his integrity by drawing properly from the Lover energy. He lives close to the fiery power of his creative unconscious. "Being close to the unconscious means being close to the 'fire'—to the fires of life and, on the biological level, to the fires of the life-engendering metabolic processes'" (*King Warrior Magician Lover*, 120, 122, 129).

never allow the hatred they provoke to corrupt your spirit. Every hero will suffer hardship and opposition. But as Solomon's father David wrote in one of his psalms, in those moments of trial, "My God in his steadfast *love* (*ḥesed*) will meet me;" and God will use that steadfast love, not hatred or vengeance, as motivation to arouse the strength you need to press forward and, as David said, "let me look in triumph on my enemies" (Ps 59:10 ESV, emphasis added).

Mercy

Every hero should operate with a rational sense of mercy. Once again, Bruce Wayne sets a good example. Remember when Ducard pressured him to execute the alleged murderer. Bruce acted with rational mercy when he refused to condemn the man without a proper trial. He acted with *compassion* when he didn't succumb to peer pressure and kill the man on the spot. Without knowing the truth. But he also acted with *rationality* when he called for an official hearing so the facts could determine the man's fate.

An everyday hero will treat others with that same sense of rational mercy. He will act with neither cruelty nor naivete toward the people he encounters. He will follow God's command and "Execute true judgment" in every situation. But at the same time, he will "shew *mercy* (*ḥesed*) and *compassions* every man to his brother" (Zech 7:9 KJV, emphasis added). A strong respect for justice coupled with a vibrant sense of mercy are the keys to facilitating peace, calm, and order in the world.

Son, you too should strive to embody this same sense of order within your own life. You can execute true justice in your daily dealings when you judge each man according to the reality of his actualized moral character—when you praise a man's virtues and condemn his vices.[9] But at the same time, you would be wise to treat everyone with the same sense of rational mercy, of *compassion*, that God shows you on a daily basis. Remember what Jesus said: "For by your standard of measure it will be measured to you in return" (Luke 6:38).

This rational sense of mercy will bring order to your thinking and help you develop a keen sense of discernment, which will in turn allow you to

---

9. Keil and Delitzsch note this "judgment of truth (cf. Ezek 18:8), is such an administration of justice as simply fixes the eye upon the real circumstances of any dispute, without any personal considerations whatever, and decides them in accordance with the truth"—that is, with the reality of the situation. And therein lies the biblical definition of justice: giving to each person that which he has worked for; in short, giving each man his due (*Minor Prophets*, 561).

look upon yourself and the people you encounter with eyes that are both firm and kind.[10]

Kindness

A kind man is not a weak man, however. A kind man, according to psychologist Jordan Peterson, is a powerful man who is capable of inflicting great harm—yet he makes the moral choice to treat others with civility and respect. A kind man is not harmless or puny or helpless. He is a civilized monster. As Peterson put it, "a hero has to be a monster, but a *controlled* monster. Batman is like that."[11]

The Batman has a well-earned reputation as Gotham City's Dark Knight. He is a *knight*, in that he lives by a chivalrous code of ethics. He is a virtuous protector whose goal is to foster civil order and justice. But the Batman is also *dark*, in that he uses controlled and rational brutality to protect law-abiding citizens from dangerous threats. In this way, Batman is both inspiring and terrifying. He serves as a ray of hope to the innocent people of Gotham. But he also exists as a monstrous nightmare to the city's criminal element.

The Bible speaks of a man like this, of a hero who was capable of great kindness on one hand and rational ferocity on the other. His name is Joshua, and a few hundred years before Solomon, he too served as the leader of God's people.

---

10. Channeling the energy of the King is a key point in the maturation process. The King archetype is an organizing force that brings about order and healing in both the spiritual and physical world. As Moore and Gillette note, the King archetype in its fullness "brings maintenance and balance. It defends our own sense of inner order, our own integrity of being and purpose, our own central calmness about who we are, and our essential unassailability and certainty in our masculine identity. It looks upon the world with a firm but kindly eye. It sees others in all their weakness and in all their talent and worth. It honors them and promotes them. It guides them and nurtures them toward their own fullness of being" (*King Warrior Magician Lover*, 56, 58, 61–62). Bruce Wayne is a good example of how a man properly channels the King's energy. The King's function is to facilitate order *and* healing. As the Batman, Bruce not only brings order and healing—justice—to the city of Gotham, but also to his own psyche. He is the physical embodiment of the law. He embodies that sense of order in his mission and in his own life. He has successfully integrated his integrity into his masculine psyche. Thus his every action is reasonable, calculated, and rational. He stabilizes his emotions and avoids chaotic or out-of-control behaviors. He is centered and calm. He acts out of an integrity of being and purpose. The absence of the King's energy leads to disorder and chaos. This sort of negative drive defines villainous characters like the Joker. A proper channeling of the King archetype helps the Batman oppose such agents of chaos and succeed in his mission to bring order and healing to Gotham.

11. Peterson, "Maps of Meaning."

As Israel stood poised to conquer the promised land, Joshua acted with civility, as a *gentleman*, when he traded *kindness (ḥesed)* for *kindness (ḥesed)* with a virtuous woman named Rahab. But when the time came for battle, Joshua put his gentlemanly nature aside and embraced his inner warrior. Like a true gladiator, Joshua went on the offensive and led the Israelite army to total victory over the dangerous people of Jericho (Josh 2:12-14; 6:17, 22-27).

Any young man who aspires to be a hero must follow the examples of both Batman and Joshua. He too must operate as a civilized monster. Civilized in that he acts primarily with grace and respect, trading kindness for kindness with other civilized people. But dangerous as well, in that he is ready on a moment's notice to channel the warrior within and dispose of threats—and to do so severely when necessary.[12]

There exists a warrior energy within the subconscious of every person. This natural aggressive energy is rooted in genetics, not rage. And it is concerned with mental and physical skill, power, accuracy, and control. Not wanton violence or tyranny.

As Robert Moore and Douglas Gillette point out in their book *King Warrior Magician Lover*, a true warrior is a man whose mind has control over his body. "He knows through clarity of thinking, through discernment" how and when to channel his aggressive energy. "The warrior is always alert," they claim. "He is always awake. He is never sleeping through life. He knows how to focus his mind and his body. . . . This means that he has an unconquerable spirit, that he has great courage, that he is fearless, that he takes responsibility for his actions, and that he has self-discipline. Discipline means that he has the rigor to develop control and mastery over

---

12. In his novel *The Lion, the Witch, and the Wardrobe*, C. S. Lewis used this same *civilized monster* idea to describe the character of Aslan, the great Lion, who serves a literary representation of Jesus Christ. During a conversation with the Pevensie children regarding Aslan, Mr. and Mrs. Beaver described their King in this way:

"'Is—is he a man?' asked Lucy.

"'Aslan a man!' said Mr. Beaver sternly. 'Certainly not. I tell you he is the King of the wood and the son of the great Emperor-beyond-the-Sea. Don't you know who is the King of Beasts? Aslan is a lion—*the* Lion, the great Lion.'

"'Ooh!' said Susan. 'I'd thought he was a man. Is he—quite safe? I shall feel rather nervous about meeting a lion.'

"'That you will, dearie, and no mistake,' said Mrs. Beaver; 'if there's anyone who can appear before Aslan without their knees knocking, they're either braver than most or else just silly.'

"'Then he isn't safe?' said Lucy.

"'Safe?' said Mr. Beaver; 'don't you hear what Mrs. Beaver tells you? Who said anything about safe? 'Course he isn't safe. But he's good. He's the King, I tell you.'

"'I'm longing to see him,' said Peter, 'even if I do feel frightened when it comes to that point' (*The Chronicles of Narnia*, 146-47).

his mind and over his body, and that he has the capacity to withstand pain, both psychological and physical. He is willing to suffer to achieve what he wants to achieve.... Thus the psyche of the man who is adequately accessing the Warrior is organized around his central commitment.... The man who is a warrior is devoted to his cause, his God, his civilization, even unto death."[13]

The world needs this kind of man now more than ever. Bad men will always step forward as long as good men step back and do nothing. So step up, young man, and take on the responsibility of protecting all that is good and valuable in your world. Remember, every man can be a warrior. You too can be a dark knight when you act with rational aggression. Not as a milksop wimp nor as a hyper-aggressive bully. But as a true warrior—as a man with a hard edge who is capable of delivering a gentle touch.

Loyalty

Bruce Wayne is not some reckless and bloodthirsty vigilante. He is a man of moral principle who operates in his mission by a strict code of ethics. And he is doggedly loyal to his primary rule: no killing.

The Batman protects innocent people. He maintains order in Gotham by opposing evil and corruption with an aggressive physicality. He does not, however, take the lives of the villains he fights against. Remember what Bruce told Ducard on that mountaintop: "I will go back to Gotham, and I will fight (evil men), but I will not become an executioner."

Bruce understands the lingering pain of death's sting better than most. As a boy, a thief with hollow eyes and loaded gun stole the lives of his parents. As the Batman, Bruce has refused to kill for one primary reason: Murdering criminals in a spirit of vengeance would make him no better than the murderer who killed his mother and father.

As I mentioned earlier, Batman's loyalty to his chivalric code makes him an honorable man, a modern-day knight (a *dark* knight, but a knight nonetheless). Because he is honorable, the Batman serves as a ray of hope to a city that often finds itself drowning in moral darkness. In spite of his dark exterior, he is a shining symbol of strength and virtue. And in this way, he serves as a source of inspiration to the people of Gotham. As a living reminder that their city belongs to them, not to criminals and the corrupt.

Batman accomplishes his goal so long as he governs himself with absolute moral integrity. That means no matter the situation, he does not allow himself to deviate from his moral code. His loyalty to his rational

---

13. Moore and Gillette, *King Warrior Magician Lover*, 79–85.

convictions demonstrates the sincerity of his values. It guides his choices and his actions and thus keeps his mission grounded in virtue.[14]

Son, if you want to keep your integrity intact, you must follow Batman's lead and remain steadfastly loyal to that code of ethics that governs your behavior. In your case, that code is the truth of God's word. When it comes to your Christian walk, God said he prefers genuine loyalty—that is, sincere devotion to his word—as opposed to mindless religious ritual. He desires the company of a man who acts on a heartfelt love for the truth—as opposed to the presence of some heartless automaton who's just going through the motions. "For I delight in *loyalty (ḥesed)* rather than sacrifice," God said, "and in the *knowledge* of God rather than burnt offerings" (Hos 6:6, emphasis added).[15]

---

14. A man is properly channeling the energy of the Magician archetype when he acts with careful and deliberate insight. When he uses wisdom—that is, the knowledge and special training an ethical code provides—to discern "the links between the unseen world of spirits—the Divine World—and the world of human beings and nature." The Magician energy is an energy of discernment. It is "the archetype of awareness and of insight, primarily, but also of knowledge of anything that is not immediately apparent or commonsensical.... Its proper role is to stand back and observe, to scan the horizon, to monitor the data coming in from both the outside and the inside and then, out of its wisdom—its knowledge of power, within and without, and its technical skill—make the necessary life decisions." The Magician archetype is divided into two aspects: (1) the theoretical *knowing* aspect, and (2) the technological, or applied science, aspect. Despite being a mere mortal, the Batman succeeds in his mission because he properly draws from the energy of the Magician. That is, he possesses the appropriate knowledge and special training. But he is also the knower and master of technology. This knowledge helps him bring the integrity of his moral code to life. Moore and Gillette, *King Warrior Magician Lover*, 98, 99, 101.

15. According to Mounce, *knowledge (daʿat)* of God is more than a cognitive exercise. As we discussed in letter 2, to *know* God is to be involved in an intimate relationship with him, a relationship akin to the covenant of marriage. (*Complete Expository Dictionary*, 384–85). R. C. Sproul et al. point out that a man cannot properly worship God with his heart "if he has no prior mental awareness"—no intellectual knowledge—"of Him . . . the heart cannot truly embrace what the mind repudiates" (*Classical Apologetics*, 21). As we discussed in letter 2, a man manifests his love for God when he keeps his commands (John 14:15). But he cannot manufacture the will to keep those commands if he does not *know* and *understand* them on an intellectual level. God has put his commands in place to define, preserve, and protect the sanctity of our shared union with him. Our obedience to his commands keeps the relationship healthy and productive. It brings our affection for God to life. By keeping his commands, we express our love, our intimate and heartfelt *knowledge*, of God in a real way in the real world. This knowledge of God goes far beyond facts and information. To truly know God is to be engaged in a working and active relationship with him. If a man's desire to attain knowledge of God and his commands is authentic—if he wants to understand the character of God, if he wants to gain insight into his values and live in harmony with the principled and rational mind of Jesus Christ—then he will get into the daily habit of studying God's word. He will then develop a love for the word of God and make its

The man who lives with a loyalty to God's word is a man who truly loves the Lord. If you compromise on your moral code, not only will you alienate God, but you'll also undermine your own integrity. If you remain loyal to your chivalric convictions, however, you will stand tall in the power of God as a shining symbol of virtue, as a source of inspiration to others. And in that way, you will do what a hero does, which is inspire others to make the world a better place.

In order to maintain that firm sense of loyalty, a hero must utilize both his head and his heart. That is, he must not only mentally *know* the difference between good and bad, but he must also have the *heart* to apply this knowledge to his life in the real world. Notice throughout these examples how Bruce Wayne utilized his head and his heart in unison to keep his loyalty strong.

Solomon also linked the head and the heart—the mind and the will—in Prov 3:1.[16] "My son, *do not forget* my teaching, but let your heart *keep* my commandments" (emphasis added). Here, he taught his son to use his mind (to *remember* his words) in conjunction with his heart (to *keep* or *act on* his commands).[17]

A young man would be wise to keep his heart and his mind unified as he works to maintain his loyalty. Essentially, a man's mind enables him to know *how* to act. His heart, in turn, determines *why* he's acting. The mind provides the knowledge while the heart supplies the motivation, the *will*, he needs to act on his head knowledge. The unrestrained *will to act* moves a man from intention to motion and thus testifies to the sincerity of his integrity.

The Rewards of Keeping Your Integrity Intact

Son, I encourage you to follow Solomon's instruction and Bruce Wayne's example. Unify your heart *and* your head to keep your integrity intact. "Do not let love/mercy/kindness/loyalty and truth leave you; bind them around your neck, write them on the tablet of your heart." Solomon follows up this

---

statutes his personal code of ethics.

16. Solomon also links the head and the heart in Prov 4:20–27. We'll discuss these verses in detail in letter 8.

17. Sproul et al. affirm the primacy of the mind as well as the primacy of the heart in the Christian faith. This is not a paradoxical statement, as the mind and the heart are two different kinds of primacies. "The mind has a primacy of order, while the heart has a primacy of purpose. By this we mean that one can have no meaningful love or passion for that which is utterly unintelligible to the mind" (*Classical Apologetics*, ix).

command with a promise of reward: "So you will find favor and good repute in the sight of God and man" (3:3-4).

If you allow these four basic virtues to define your character, then according to Solomon, you will find favor and a good name in the sight of rational men. I say *rational* men because bad men like Ducard will never understand the benefits of virtue. As you get older, you'll discover the world is full of men like him. Men who will whisper in your ear and tell you that your integrity makes you vulnerable and weak. There's no friendship to be had with such irrational men. So pay them no mind. They will only serve to derail your focus and reduce your life to a pile of rubble. But there is *favor and a good name* to be had in forming friendships with rational people, with men and women who value their integrity and remain loyal to the same basic moral principles as you do.

As we discussed in letter 3, there is great benefit in surrounding yourself with the right kind of people (and great harm in surrounding yourself with the wrong people). If you want to achieve meaningful relationships with good people, then you need to be the kind of man good people want to be friends with. Integrity attracts integrity—and you will attract the attention of good people when you act with virtue and treat others with respect.

The man who walks proud in his integrity will also find favor and a good name *in the sight of God.* Solomon tells his son in vv. 5-8 that his Heavenly Father will reward his integrity by doing what a good father does. Namely (as we learned earlier), by involving himself in every aspect of his life and providing him with the tactical support he needs to walk tall on his hero's journey.

In these verses, Solomon instructs his son to welcome his Heavenly Father's involvement in his life and to trust in his leadership:

> "⁵Trust in the LORD with all your heart and do not lean on your own understanding. ⁶In all your ways acknowledge Him, and He will make your paths straight. ⁷Do not be wise in your own eyes; fear the LORD and turn away from evil. ⁸It will be healing to your body and refreshment to your bones." (3:5-8)

Son, every hero needs a mentor. A trusted adviser to instruct him in the ways of wisdom. A protective figure to point him in the right direction on his hero's journey.[18]

Like Solomon, I am calling on you as an everyday hero to embrace God as your ultimate mentor. *Acknowledge* his authority. *Fear* and *respect* him as your Heavenly Father. *Trust* in the wisdom of his word and he will

---

18. "What such a mentor figure represents," said Campbell, "is the benign, protecting power of destiny" (*The Hero With A Thousand Faces*, 59-60).

make your paths straight. He will guide your steps and mold your life into a meaningful and heroic narrative, all while preserving the integrity of your individual freedom. He will come alongside you, shoulder-to-shoulder as a Father to his son, and provide you with the guidance you need to move forward on the *straight and upright path* of wisdom.

Be aware, however, that his presence comes at a price.[19] Every hero must be willing to make certain sacrifices on his hero's journey. That means you must be willing to let go of a smaller piece of yourself to make room for the bigger and better things God has to offer.

Do not, however, misunderstand the meaning of *sacrifice*. A sacrifice is not a pointless offering. It's a trade: an exchange of something of lesser, short-term value for something of greater, long-term value. In this case, Solomon has called on his son to sacrifice his own short-sighted worldly perspective in order to take on God's heavenly, long-range vision for his life.

Son, in return for God's intimate involvement, you too must sacrifice that self-centered, short-term mindset that will only hold you back. The failure to sacrifice will result in a failure to advance. But if you adopt God's long-term method of thinking, you will live with complete confidence as a man who finds security in the protection of God's providential hand.

You can trust his guidance because his aim as a good Father is to bring out the best in you. He has given you natural abilities and talents. But you can only reach the fullness of your capabilities when you allow him to lead you into your potential.

If you want to move out of the realm of mediocrity and into the special realm of manhood—if you want to *strengthen your bones and rejuvenate your body*—then you too must sacrifice your own self-centered, short-sighted perspective on life and walk firm in the truth of God's word. Cooperate with him, and he will bless you with the long-term way of thinking you need to succeed in your own personal hero's journey.

I'll close out this section by charging you to remember the virtues we've discussed. Follow Solomon's instruction and store them at the forefront of your mind so you can take them with you wherever you go. Write them on the tablet of your heart so you can bring them to life at a moment's notice. That way, no matter where you find yourself on your journey—be it at home, at school, at a friend's house, on a date, or in a foreign place surrounded by a battalion of bad influences—you'll be prepared to act on your homegrown convictions and keep your integrity intact.

---

19. We discussed the necessity of trading value for value with God in letter 5.

3. An everyday hero manages his money with wisdom

As I mentioned earlier, Bruce Wayne does not have any superpowers. But he does possess one advantage the average man does not: money, and lots of it. As the owner and chairman of the multinational conglomerate known as Wayne Enterprises, Bruce Wayne has nearly unlimited financial means. He has more than enough resources to acquire whatever material pleasures tickle his fancy.

But Bruce is not interested in shallow luxuries. Sure, he lives in a mansion. Yeah, he drives on Gotham's streets in the fanciest cars and struts down her sidewalks sporting expensive clothes on his back, a fat wallet in his pocket, and a carousel of lovely ladies on his arm. But Bruce's billionaire playboy persona is merely an act, a carefully crafted alter-ego designed to conceal his true identity.

In public, Master Wayne wears many metaphorical masks. But none of the men he pretends to be—the playboy, the socialite—is the real man. It's in private, under the anonymous veil of an actual cowl, where his true spirit shines forth. Bruce Wayne has dedicated his life not to coasting on his father's name, but to preserving his father's legacy (in his own way) as the guardian of Gotham's soul.

His sense of personal responsibility motivates Bruce to be the Batman. But it's his efficient management of his wealth that *allows* him the means to carry out this mission. His high-tech Batcave. His armored Batsuit. His top-of-the-line gadgets. His Batmobile and various other vehicles. These are all made possible by the profits of his work.

Bruce can afford to be the Batman because he gives the first and the best of his mind, his body, *and his pocketbook* in service to his mission.

Like Bruce Wayne, King Solomon was a man with money to spend and a legacy to uphold. His father David was an accomplished king who solidified Israel as a nation and unified the people under his rule. When Solomon inherited the throne, he could have coasted on his father's accomplishments. But he instead chose to build upon his legacy. He honored the teachings of his father. He opened his mind to God. And as a result, Solomon led Israel into an era of unparalleled peace and prosperity.

Early on in his reign, Solomon facilitated proper worship and constructed the first permanent temple structure in Jerusalem.[20] He fortified Israel's military and renovated her infrastructure. He maintained peace by establishing trading partnerships with surrounding nations. He used

---

20. Up until the reign of Solomon, the ark of God dwelt in nothing more than "tent curtains," as David put it (2 Sam 7:2). We'll discuss Solomon's building of the temple in letter 8.

military force to subdue those nations who chose to remain hostile (2 Chron 8–9). He transformed Israel into a cultural and financial powerhouse. And as a result, "King Solomon excelled all the kings of the earth in riches and in wisdom. And all the kings of the earth sought the presence of Solomon to hear his wisdom, which God had put into his mind" (2 Chron 9:22–23 RSV).

His track record of success makes him more qualified than most to give financial advice. When the topic of money came up with his son, Solomon was quick to share his two cents of wisdom.

Here is his instruction:

> "⁹Honor the LORD from your wealth and from the first of all your produce; ¹⁰so your barns will be filled with plenty and your vats will overflow with new wine." (3:9–10)

Here, Solomon instructs his son to trust God with every aspect of his life, including the contents of his wallet. Whether you're in ancient Israel or in the twenty-first-century United States of America—that's good advice. I will follow Solomon's lead, my son, and instruct you to honor the Lord from the first of your wealth.

At this point, however, you may be thinking to yourself: *I'm not wealthy like Solomon. I'm not even fictionally rich like Bruce Wayne. How can a man like me honor God with his money?*

That's a rational question. And believe it or not, an everyman such as yourself can glorify God with his finances just as much as a wealthy man can—if not more. No matter how much money is in your bank account, you can glorify God simply by keeping your financial priorities in order.

Generally speaking, you should use the first and best of all you produce to support the two main aspects of your heroic mission: God and your family.

You honor God when you use the first of your wealth to:

- Support your church. Every church member should support the ministry and upkeep of his own church. If you benefit from it, then you should support it. To fail to do so is to mooch off the faith and hard work of other people and to steal from God (Mal 3:6–10). In the Old Testament, God required each Israelite to dedicate one-tenth (a tithe) of all his produce to the temple. If you're looking for a specific amount to give to your church, ten percent of your *total* income (before taxes) is a good starting point.[21]

---

21. Solomon told his son to honor the Lord with the first of "*all* your produce" (emphasis added). Solomon's use of the word "all" means you should give ten percent of

- Provide for yourself and your family. One of a man's most important responsibilities is to provide for his own household. The Apostle Paul said any man who does not provide for the members of his own household "has denied the faith and is *worse than an unbeliever*" (1 Tim 5:8, emphasis added). Think about those strong and sobering words for a moment: Unbelievers face an eternity of torment in the lake of fire, yet those unbelievers who abandon their own families will suffer an even deeper dimension of God's wrath. Son, when the time comes for you to get married and have children, I want you to remember this one fact: *Your* family is *your* responsibility. Strangers are not responsible for feeding your family. *You* are. Paul also said the man who isn't willing to work should not expect to eat (2 Thess 3:10–12). So if you want to put food on the table like a real man, then you have two options: (1) either do the work necessary to hunt it or grow it, or (2) go out and earn the money to pay for it.

Also remember this important fact: When it comes to finances, God is more concerned with the fullness of your heart than the fullness of your wallet.[22] Jesus himself proved that actual physical amounts are of no consequence to God. Recall the story of his feeding the crowd of more than five thousand.

The massive crowd was hungry. But no one had any food except for a little boy, who just happened to have five loaves of bread and two small fish. The doubtful disciples looked at the boy's meager portions and said, "what are these for so many people?" Indeed, the boy didn't have much. But he took what he had and handed it over to Jesus anyway. The Apostle John tells us that "Jesus then took the loaves, and having given thanks, He distributed to those who were seated; likewise also of the fish as much *as they wanted*. When *they were filled*, He said to His disciples, 'Gather up the leftover fragments so that nothing will be lost.' So they gathered them up, and *filled twelve baskets with fragments* from the five barley loaves which were left over by those who had eaten" (John 6:9, 11–13, emphasis added).

Son, if Jesus can fill thousands of bellies with five loaves of bread and two fish (and still have twelve baskets full of leftovers), he can definitely take

---

your *gross* income rather than ten percent of your *net* income to the church. God, not the government, deserves the first and the best of your paycheck.

22. See the example of the poor widow in Mark 12:41–44. While others were putting large sums of money into the temple's offering box, she put in two small copper coins, which added together equaled up to roughly one cent. Despite her meager offering, Jesus praised this poor widow because she "put in more than all the contributors to the treasury; for they all put in out of their surplus, but she, out of her poverty, put in all she owned, all she had to live on."

whatever you give him and use it to accomplish mighty things. The little boy with the loaves and the fish didn't have much. But he gave what he had to Jesus and trusted him to make something of it.

As that young boy proved, a man honors God not by the amount he gives, but by managing what he has with faith and responsibility. As Jesus also said, the way a man manages his money is a good reflector of his faith (Luke 12:34).

Like Solomon, I instruct you to honor the Lord with all you produce. Dedicate the first and the best of your money to carrying out your life's mission. Then trust in your Heavenly Father to reward your faith with the daily provisions your body needs.

Yet again, I point you to the words of Jesus, when he encouraged his disciples to trust in their Heavenly Father to live up to his own standard and provide for the members of his own household:

> "[25]For this reason I say to you, do not be worried about your life, as to what you will eat or what you will drink; nor for your body, as to what you will put on. Is not life more than food, and the body more than clothing? [26]Look at the birds of the air, that they do not sow, nor reap nor gather into barns, and yet your heavenly Father feeds them. Are you not worth much more than they? [27]And who of you by being worried can add a single hour to his life? [28]And why are you worried about clothing? Observe how the lilies of the field grow; they do not toil nor do they spin, [29]yet I say to you that not even Solomon in all his glory clothed himself like one of these. [30]But if God so clothes the grass of the field, which is alive today and tomorrow is thrown into the furnace, will He not much more clothe you? You of little faith! [31]Do not worry then, saying, 'What will we eat?' or 'What will we drink?' or 'What will we wear for clothing?' [32]For the Gentiles *[unbelievers]* eagerly seek all these things; for your heavenly Father knows that you need all these things. [33]But seek first His kingdom and His righteousness, and all these things will be added to you. [34]So do not worry about tomorrow; for tomorrow will care for itself. Each day has enough trouble of its own."
> (Matt 6:25–34, emphasis added)

4. An everyday hero understands the benefit of discipline

Bruce Wayne is indeed wealthy. But no amount of money can stop psychopaths like the Joker from acting on their evil motivations. As Alfred said in Nolan's 2008 sequel *The Dark Knight*: "Some men (like the Joker) aren't looking for anything logical like money. They can't be bought, bullied, reasoned, or negotiated with. Some men just want to watch the world burn."

The world is filled with savage men who don't respond to rational arguments. Thus good men have no choice but to respond to their savagery with brute force. And in the heat of battle, when a guardian like the Batman is nose-to-nose with the faces of evil, he needs something more persuasive than cash to overcome their relentless assault. Something the bad guys will understand—like a strong mind and a strong punch.

Bruce Wayne understands this. He may be a normal man, but he is not an average man. And he definitely is not some two-bit weakling. He is a man of tremendous mental and physical strength. Although he was born into a successful family, Bruce Wayne was not born with a strong spirit. Nor was he born with big muscles or great knowledge or combat skills. He had to acquire those capabilities on his own. And he did so by submitting himself to proper psychological and physical discipline.

Solomon likewise instructs his son to recognize the benefits of a disciplined lifestyle:

> "^{11}My son, do not reject the discipline of the LORD or loathe His reproof, ^{12}for whom the LORD loves He reproves, even as a father corrects the son in whom he delights." (3:11–12)

Son, do not misunderstand the concept of discipline. Solomon's message is clear: Regarding the discipline of his children, God's primary motivation is always *love*, and his primary goal is always *instruction*.[23]

No man can avoid discipline. Such an expectation is unrealistic. And unhealthy. You will certainly experience various trials and tribulations in your life. Some you will bring about through your own fault, and some will arise through no fault of your own. Whatever the cause, be aware of this fact: God will use the stress and hardships of this world to bring about good in your life. I know that sounds counterintuitive, but it's the truth.

God is always in control. He always has a plan. He allows resistance to come into your life with the goal of making you mentally and physically stronger. Remember: God is a good Father. His aim is never to discourage you, but to help you develop the mental and physical strength you need to be an effective everyday hero. He is always working to toughen your fortitude

---

23. Keil and Delitzsch, *Proverbs, Ecclesiastes, Song of Songs*, 64. The authors also make the following sage observation: "As God should not be forgotten in days of prosperity *[see 3:9–10, when your barns and vats are overflowing]*, so one should not suffer himself to be estranged from Him by days of adversity" (emphasis added). That is, during times of discipline.

and your faith because he wants you to be strong enough to overcome the evil forces of this world just as he did (John 16:33; 1 John 5:4).

Think of it this way: A man lifts weights to strengthen his muscles and build up his body. But the act of lifting weights initially *tears the muscles down*. Each pump, pull, and press of a weight causes little tears in the muscles to occur. This slight damage, this microtrauma, results in muscle soreness because the muscle has been torn apart to an extent. This damage, however, is a controlled damage. It's an essential part of the strength-training process. Tearing the muscle down is necessary in order to build the muscle up. After the muscle has been broken down, the weightlifter must then rebuild it with proper diet and further training. This disciplined and goal-oriented lifestyle facilitates muscle growth and over time leads to an increase in muscle size and might. That post-workout soreness is uncomfortable, for sure. But with that discomfort comes a sense of satisfaction.

The pain testifies to the development of an increased strength.

Son, you may feel like the trials and tribulations of this world are tearing you to pieces. In a way, they are. But understand this fact: God will use the microtraumas of this world to strengthen your spiritual muscles. Bruce Wayne can testify to that fact. As can Solomon. That's why Solomon encourages his son to never run from the discomfort of God's discipline: "do not reject the discipline of the LORD or loathe His reproof" (3:11). Instead, embrace it.

Yes, the spiritual strength training God puts us through is an uncomfortable process. But the resulting soreness is proof that God is tearing down the old man and raising up a new and stronger man in his place.

Son, you might as well go ahead and accept this hard truth: Life is tough. There is no doubt about it. And in those times of extreme resistance, when you think you're alone and you feel like giving up—don't. Never give up and never take the coward's way out. You can stay strong by keeping your responsibilities in mind—those people and ideas that are worth fighting for, worth *living* for: God, your family, yourself, your goals, and your integrity. Use them as motivation to make the right choices and keep moving forward on your hero's journey.

Discipline and sacrifice are essential for growth. God uses the hardships of this life to strengthen your mettle and establish your resolve. Remember, though, that heroism is like masculinity. It is found not in the frame of a man's body, but in the strength of his heart and mind.

A strong character is the key to enduring hard times. It supplies you with the fortitude you need to overcome the pain and earn the title of *hero*.

❖ ❖ ❖

Son, being a hero is, like wisdom, a choice—it's your choice.

If you choose to answer the call to adventure—to enter the realm of manhood and dedicate yourself to a life of wisdom— you will awaken the hero that lives inside you. I encourage you to let go of the child that you are and embrace the man that you were meant to be. Let go of those old concepts, ideals, and emotional patterns that no longer fit. The call to adventure is upon you. The time for the passing of a threshold is at hand.[24]

Destiny has summoned you. And it's your responsibility to answer the call. Take hold of your future. Embrace the hero's mindset and let God kick-start your transfiguration into mature and masculine manhood.

Love,
Dad

---

24. Campbell, *The Hero With A Thousand Faces*, 43, 48.

Letter 7

Two Hard Truths About Happiness

Prov 3:13–35; 8:10–11, 22–36

"Solomon didn't sugarcoat the truth for his son and I won't sugarcoat it for you."

Son, one of my main jobs is to help you understand the truth about how the world works.

Like any good father, I want you to be happy with your life. But in order to reach that point, you must first accept two fundamental truths about happiness.

Those truths are:

1. You are responsible for achieving your own happiness.
2. Your happiness depends in part upon how well you can get along with other people.

In this letter, Solomon and I will delve deeper into these truths and equip you with the wisdom you need to go out into the world and earn your own happiness.

Solomon didn't sugarcoat the truth for his son and I won't sugarcoat it for you. The sooner you learn how to live in the light of these two truths, the sooner your journey towards happiness can begin.

HARD TRUTH #1: YOUR HAPPINESS IS YOUR RESPONSIBILITY

Prov 3:13–26; 8:22–36

Son, this world doesn't owe you a thing.

It doesn't owe you physical necessities like money or food or a house. It doesn't owe you special privileges like a job or a college education. It doesn't owe you love or friendship or any other type of relational success.

And it definitely doesn't owe you happiness.

Anything of true value in this life is worth working for and happiness is no exception. When it comes to achieving true and lasting happiness, the real world gives you only two options:

1. You can waste your time sitting around with your self-entitled hands out waiting for someone to spoon-feed you the happiness you think you deserve.

Or:

2. You can go out and put your hands to good use doing something productive (like crafting a meaningful life) and earn some real happiness on your own.

Achieving happiness is not like winning the lottery. It doesn't come about by random chance. Nor is it a second-hand emotion that comes and goes based on mood or circumstance or the opinions of others. Happiness is an internal state of being you have to create for yourself. And the way a man creates happiness is by functioning properly as a human being—that is, by utilizing his rational mind and his God-given talents to build a successful life for himself.

Son, you've only got one life on this earth, so you might as well live it to win it. You'll learn soon enough that the real world doesn't give out participation trophies. It rewards competent people who *produce*. Those men and women who work hard, think creatively, and do whatever it takes to achieve success in their pursuit of life's true prize—not money or fame or power, but *meaning*.

Meaning is the key to happiness. And a man wins at life when he works hand-in-hand with God to create a life of lasting significance. A life that *matters*.

As we'll discover throughout the course of this letter, such a life is generally defined by three criteria:

- productive work,
- personal excellence,
- and rewarding relationships.

Like the good Father that he is, God is more than willing to help you meet these criteria. But he'll only work with you if you prove that you're willing to go out and do the work that he's given you to do. That means if you want to be happy, then you must learn to be self-reliant.

I need you to pay attention here. Do not misunderstand what I mean by self-reliance. Let me clarify myself by first explaining what self-reliance *isn't*. Self-reliance is not kicking God to the curb and trying to live in your own way and by your own power. Any fool who engages in that kind of behavior is self-defeating, not self-reliant. A wise man understands that apart from God he can do nothing. Yet *with* God and *through* God he can find success in every single job he was put on this earth to do. A self-reliant man understands that God has created him for his sovereign purposes. He knows that God has given him all the tools he needs to accomplish those purposes. Therefore, in every area of his life, he works *with* God, not without him, because he understands, as David did, that it is "God who accomplishes all things for me" (Ps 57:2).[1]

A wise man is self-reliant not because he works alone or makes his own way, but because *he holds himself personally responsible* for doing the jobs God has called him to do. He knows his personal limits and isn't afraid to ask for help when he really needs it. He never feels *entitled* to anyone's help, however. Nor does he ever outsource his personal responsibilities to others.[2]

---

1. Also see Exod 15:2; Deut 8:11–18; Ps 100:3; and Phil 4:13 for further elaboration on the necessity of God's presence for achieving success. Jesus, however, best synthesized this point when he said, "I am the vine, you are the branches; he who abides in Me and I in him, he bears much fruit, *for apart from Me you can do nothing*" (John 15:5, emphasis added).

2. In their book *King Warrior Magician Lover*, Robert Moore and Douglas Gillette wisely note that humility consists of two things: "the first is knowing our limitations, and the second is getting the help we need." Humility is an important characteristic of the self-reliant man because humility is the line that divides self-reliance from stubbornness (*King Warrior Magician Lover*, 145).

As I've stated throughout these letters, God has blessed me with the responsibility of being your father. I act with self-reliance when I don't farm out my fatherly responsibilities to someone else. It's not someone else's job to be your father—it's mine. It's not someone else's job to protect and provide for my family—it's mine. A self-reliant man can ask for help every now and then, but he never expects anyone else *to do his work for him*. Instead, he follows God's leadership and uses his God-given talents to do the work God has specifically called *him* to do. He works hard to meet his responsibilities. And in the process, he earns true and lasting happiness.

In the latter half of Prov 3, Solomon describes happiness as a concept that extends beyond mere positive emotions or whimsical feelings of pleasure. He teaches his son that happiness is a conscious and consistent mindset: *It's the extended sense of spiritual fulfillment a man gets from meeting his responsibilities and achieving his values and thereby creating for himself a life that really matters.*

Three steps to creating a happy life

Solomon ties happiness to self-reliance in the following verses:

> "¹³Happy is the man who *finds wisdom*, and the man who *gets understanding*, ¹⁴for the gain from it is better than gain from silver and its profit better than gold. ¹⁵She is more precious than jewels, and nothing you desire can compare with her. ¹⁶Long life is in her right hand; in her left hand are riches and honor. ¹⁷Her ways are ways of pleasantness, and all her paths are peace. ¹⁸She is a tree of life to those who lay hold of her; those who hold her fast are called happy. . . . ²¹My son, *keep sound wisdom and discretion*; let them not escape from your sight, ²²and they will be life for your soul and adornment for your neck. ²³Then you will walk on your way securely and your foot will not stumble. ²⁴If you sit down, you will not be afraid; when you lie down, your sleep will be sweet. ²⁵Do not be afraid of sudden panic, or of the ruin of the wicked, when it comes; ²⁶for the LORD will be your confidence and will keep your foot from being caught." (3:13–18, 21–26 RSV, emphasis added)

In these verses Solomon links happiness with hard work. With *action*. In fact, he goes so far as to list three specific actions a self-reliant man should take to succeed in his pursuit of happiness:

1. *find* wisdom (v. 13a),
2. *acquire* understanding (v. 13b),
3. and *maintain* a lifestyle of sound wisdom and discretion (v. 21).

Son, no one else can do this work for you. If you want to win the prize of a meaningful and happy life, then it's up to *you* to follow Solomon's instruction and take these three necessary actions:

1. *Find wisdom in everything you do*

Solomon describes happiness as a state of mind, not a state of emotion, by linking it to wisdom in Prov 3:13: "Happy is the man who *finds wisdom*" (RSV, emphasis added). Notice that Solomon also frames happiness as primarily an intellectual pursuit, not as an emotional accident, by using the action word *find* in that same verse. We can surmise, therefore, that happiness is an intellectual achievement and not an emotional fluke. That means, son, if you want to be happy, it's up to you to follow Solomon's instruction and actively seek out the wisdom that leads to happiness.

One practical way you can pursue happiness in your everyday life is to find the wisdom—that is, find the *meaning*—in all your day-to-day activities. Whether you're doing schoolwork or practicing karate or brushing your teeth or going to church—whatever part of your regular routine you're involved in, don't just go through the motions. Instead, train your mind to find the deeper *purpose* in everything that you do. You do this by not only knowing *how* to accomplish a task, but also *why* you've set out to accomplish that task in the first place. Once you understand *why* you're doing what you're doing, you'll find the motivation you need to work hard, do the job right, and earn your own happiness.

Let me give you a quick example.

You and I were mowing our yard one hot evening during the wretched Louisiana summer. We'd been working for about forty-five minutes or so when we decided to take a water break. As we drank and surveyed our work, you asked, in your boyish way, if it bothered me to know that in spite of all our effort the grass would just grow back in a few days and we'd have to do this all over again next week. You saw through the front window that your baby sisters were cool and comfortable in the living room watching a cartoon on TV. Then you asked, "Why do we even have to mow the yard in this heat when we could be doing something more fun?"

It was a genuine question from a tired and sweaty boy, and it deserved a genuine answer. First, I thanked you for helping me and I reminded you of the money you were earning for your work. Then I explained that our main goal in mowing the yard isn't just to make money or to impress other people. I told you that we mow the yard primarily because we respect ourselves and we love our family. We cut the grass, I said, because tall grass attracts snakes. And I don't want a snake to hurt one of us because I was too lazy or too tired to mow. We tough out the heat because the safety of our family is worth the work.

Our conversation lasted another couple of minutes, just long enough for us to catch our breath and slick our thirst. I explained that one of a man's main jobs is to protect his family and his property, and mowing the yard is a small but important way we keep our family safe. Plus, I added, it's hard to run or play catch or have a campout in grass that's three feet high.

My answer didn't diminish the heat. Nor did it make the job more fun. But it did give our work a sense of meaning. And it gave you enough inspiration to stop grumbling and finish the job with a good attitude. We walked back inside grimy and worn out but fulfilled nonetheless. Your mom handed us a couple of lemonades and there we stood in the kitchen: two men soaked in sweat and enjoying the genuine happiness that comes from engaging in *productive and meaningful work*.

Son, when we meet our responsibilities like the men that we are, we curate feelings of self-respect and fulfillment, the feelings of true happiness that elude many people. That hard-earned sense of happiness is as sweet as an ice-cold swallow of lemonade on a hot summer evening in the South. You can taste that sweetness on a daily basis when you learn to find the wisdom, the *meaning*, in everything you do. Then you will learn to treat everything you do like it really matters.

Because it does.

Everything done right and done well is meaningful. Even the most mundane of activities. You're not just mowing the grass. You're cultivating self-respect while providing a clean and safe living environment for your family. You're not just doing your homework. You're gaining a more solid understanding of the material so you can make a good grade in the class and move on to bigger and better opportunities in the future. You're not just washing the dishes. You're doing your part to keep our home ordered and stable. You're not just watching a movie or reading a book. You're taking inspiration or learning a moral lesson that will help you grow into a well-grounded man of conviction.

Once you find the wisdom in what you're doing, you can turn even the most routine activity into a work of art. So work hard to be the type of man philosopher Richard Taylor describes in his book *Restoring Pride*, the type of man who can find deep fulfillment in the humblest of projects. The goal of such men, according to Taylor, "is not primarily to draw applause or to enrich themselves, but just to show *themselves* that there is something quite original that they can do, and which few, if any, others can do. They do not merely laboriously assemble something, but carry out some imaginative dream. Having done it, they can note, with deep satisfaction, what they have wrought, with the realization that, but for them, it would never have been done."[3]

One last point: If there's no productive purpose—no meaning, no wisdom—in what you're doing, then stop doing it. Immediately. As I'll discuss below, there is a time and a place for beneficial leisure. But your life is far too valuable to waste on pointless (i.e., non-beneficial) distractions.[4]

Life is the greatest gift God could ever give a man. It's such a precious gift that God in His infinite wisdom and grace gave it twice: the first time upon your physical creation and the second upon your eternal salvation. He gave you life with the intention that you would use it wisely, to accomplish your created purpose and thus achieve authentic happiness. Not waste your life away chasing harmful distractions.

Which leads me to my next point.

2. Understand the difference between happiness and amusement

Solomon tells his son in v. 13 that a man must also *get understanding* in order to be happy. Son, one of the best things to understand in your pursuit of meaning is the fundamental difference between lasting *happiness* and temporary *amusement*.

Happiness is the deep and enduring sense of fulfillment that comes about through meaningful and creative work: completing a school project, playing an instrument, learning how to throw a baseball, developing good relationships, etc. As I mentioned, it's a state of being that demands an active mind that produces actual accomplishments.

Amusement, on the flip side, is that fickle and short-term feeling of shallow gratification that stems from any intellectually passive activity which serves no real purpose—that accomplishes no real goal. Today that would include basically any activity that involves staring at a screen with

---

3. Taylor, *Restoring Pride*, 59.

4. Not every diversion is pointless. Simple diversions like watching birds fly through the air or playing a game with friends or watching a TV show can be productive, even if their sole purpose is just to appreciate the beauty of God's creation, or to have some fun with people you enjoy, or to relax after a hard day of work. Such diversions are productive because they make you smile, or they recharge your spiritual batteries and stave off burnout. Diversions become *pointless*—that is, non-beneficial or even harmful—when they prevent you from meeting your responsibilities. For example: if you put off doing your homework because you decided instead to play video games or binge on Netflix all night, then those activities have officially moved beyond the realm of productive relaxation and into pointless and harmful territory.

the zoned-out eyes of an idiot.⁵ Or wasting time catering to entitled and irrational people. These kinds of meaningless time-killers provide no real challenge and require little to no creative effort. Their sole purpose is not to accomplish anything specific, just to numb the dull ache of boredom.

Son, don't misunderstand my instruction. I'm not saying you have to be a workaholic in order to be happy. You can be at leisure, at rest, and still use your time wisely. Even in your spare moments you can still be productive.

Let's discuss the concept of productive leisure for a moment. The purpose of leisure is to take a step back from the daily grind of life. Not to dawdle or goof off or escape reality, but to *think*—to recharge, reflect, self-assess, learn, and plan. Productive leisure is engaging in any constructive hobby or activity that stimulates your mind and raises your energy level and increases your overall well-being.⁶

Me, I love a good story. I read a variety of books and watch a lot of movies. One of the main purposes of artistic entertainment is to inspire personal growth, to help the reader or viewer advance on a spiritual, intellectual, and emotional level. So whether I'm reading a book or watching a movie or enjoying some other leisurely entertainment, I only engage with those works that *highlight the sublime in human nature*, as author Ayn Rand once said.⁷ My time is far too valuable to waste amusing myself to death on intellectual trash. And so is yours. I encourage you to follow my lead and be discerning with your attention. When it comes to your leisure activities, only engage with those works of art or entertainment that act as a source

---

5. Truth be told, I'm as guilty as anyone of losing time staring at a computer screen, proving that no matter your age, it's easy to get sucked into the internet's undertow of information. For example, the other day I was having lunch at my desk. In between bites I got on YouTube and watched a Guns N' Roses video. Then another one came on and I watched that one. Then I clicked on Nuno Bettencourt's face in the sidebar and proceeded to spend the rest of my lunch hour sliding down a Gary Cherone-era Van Halen rabbit hole that ended with me watching some random improvisational comedy sketch featuring Liam Neeson and Ricky Gervais. Son, that's an hour of my life I'll never get back—sixty minutes spent staring off into the virtual reality of a computer screen with nothing to show for it but this sad little footnote.

6. Kahl, "In Defense of Leisure."

7. Good stories are an effective way to bring abstract principles to life. To once again quote Ayn Rand: "I read a novel for the purpose of seeing the kind of people I would want to see in real life and living through the kind of experience I would want to live through. To those who say that this is a limited use of fiction, my answer is: No—because for any other purpose, nonfiction is better. If I want to learn something, I can learn it from nonfiction. But in the one realm where nonfiction cannot do as well—the realm of values and their concretization in human reality—nothing can take the place of art, and specifically of fiction" (*The Art of Fiction*, 176).

of insight and inspiration, and shun those that peddle meaningless amusements that serve no purpose (or worse, promote a harmful message).

My point is this: If you want to be happy, then use your time wisely. Time is a non-renewable commodity. You only have a certain amount to work with; and once you spend it, you can never get it back. Even in those moments of leisure, you can make the most of the time God has given you by pursuing only those things that are beneficial and thus lead to true happiness.

3. Maintain wisdom as a lifestyle

Finding wisdom and acquiring understanding, however, are not actions to take up only in your spare time. God didn't bless you with Lady Wisdom's presence so you could treat her casually, as if she were a hobby or an extracurricular activity.

Son, your relationship with Wisdom is not a fling. As we discussed in letter 4, it's a lifelong bond, a carefully constructed lifestyle choice that demands steadfast commitment. That means you never get to take a day off from living wisely.

Take my marriage as an example. When I married your mother, I didn't vow to remain faithful to her eighteen hours out of the day, five days out of the week. I pledged my mind and body in total fidelity to her every second of every hour for the rest of my days. You must likewise pledge your fidelity to Lady Wisdom and devote every moment to walking in her ways. This is a big commitment that requires constant self-discipline. But trust me when I tell you that the rewards are worth the work.

Solomon says as much in Prov 3:14–15. In these verses, he tells his son that Lady Wisdom's rare beauty outshines worldly treasures like silver and gold: "She is more precious than jewels, and nothing you desire can compare with her." In vv. 16–18, Solomon paints a mental portrait for his son, one of Lady Wisdom standing as firm as the heavenly tree of life, extending her arms forward like lithe branches, offering a boon in both hands to the man who commits himself to her: "Long life is in her right hand; in her left hand are riches and honor" (3:16).

Lady Wisdom's right-handed gift of *long life* is not a promise of many years. Rather, it's the guarantee of a productive and meaningful life—of a personal destiny fulfilled.[8] A wise man knows that a long lifespan isn't

---

8. The writer of the apocryphal book the Wisdom of Solomon also measured long life by productive behavior (and not by the passage of time): "Even if they *[ungodly men]* live long they will be held of no account, and finally their old age will be without honor. If they die young, they will have no hope and no consolation in the day of decision. For the end of an unrighteous generation is grievous. . . . But the righteous man, though

necessarily something to be proud of. Any coward can extend his days by running away. Any aimless fool can wander from one day to the next for a hundred years and still have nothing to show for himself. The truth is, you don't get to choose how long your life will be. That's God's decision. In his sovereign wisdom, he has ordained the number of your days (Ps 139:16). The choice he has delegated to you is this: How are you going to spend the time he's given you? Will you waste it chasing diversions and missing opportunities? Or will you *maintain wisdom as a lifestyle*? That is, will you commit yourself every day to engaging only in those activities that are in your best interest? To pursuing the fullness of your masculine potential? To acting with maturity and beauty and creativity so as to fill your life with as much meaning as possible? According to Solomon, the man who practices sound wisdom and discretion on a minute-by-minute basis won't *lose sight* of his focus. He makes the most of his time and honors God in the process. God, in turn, honors his commitment by *adorning his neck* with the divine blessings that come along with a lifestyle of wisdom: a life filled with productive work, personal excellence, and rewarding relationships. Lady Wisdom can't offer you a hundred years. But what she does offer is something much more valuable: a life packed with meaning and happiness.

Her left-handed gift of *riches and honor*, likewise, is not a promise of fortune and fame, but of physical provision and a good reputation among God and men. A wise man knows the pursuit of happiness does not involve the pursuit of material *things*. Money, recognition, and social status can be visible signs of professional excellence, but they are and always will be mere externals—that is, *things* that exist other than and apart from *the self*.[9] These things may impress others, which may in turn flatter your ego, but they cannot provide you with an authentic sense of happiness because your worth as a person comes not from without, but from within. Not from the stuff you possess or the social title you carry, but from *who you are* as a man.[10]

There's nothing wrong with making money or achieving a certain social status. But a wise man doesn't work hard just so he can stuff his bank account or puff up his ego with the applause of strangers. He works hard

---

he die early, will be at rest. For old age is not honored for length of time, nor measured by number of years; but understanding is gray hair for men, and a blameless life is ripe old age" (Wis 3:17–19; 4:7–9 RSV, emphasis added). To be clear, non-canonical apocryphal books like the Wisdom of Solomon are not inspired Scripture and should not be regarded as such. However, the author has provided an apt description of the fate of both wise and wicked men. Biblical scholar Michael Heiser made a good point when he said a book doesn't need to be canonical to be useful, or to help articulate a theological point ("The New Testament Writers").

9. Taylor, *Restoring Pride*, 118. For a fuller definition of the self, see letter 5.

10. Taylor, *Restoring Pride*, 54.

so he can earn the money he needs to meet the physical necessities of life: food on the table, a roof over his head, clothes on his back, etc. His happiness comes not in possessing these physical objects, but in knowing that he is meeting his God-given responsibilities and earning his keep as a man. Rational men and women will in turn recognize his hard work. He will earn credibility in their eyes and they will *honor* him as a man of wisdom and integrity. He does not work for their approval, but he earns it nonetheless because *personal excellence* can't help but stand out in a world chock full of mediocrity and failure.

Son, yours may be a life of downright simplicity that goes unnoticed by the world at large, save those people who matter the most to you. But that's okay because a wise man doesn't court the world's favor. He works to honor God, his family, and himself. You can rest assured, however, that God always takes notice of hard work. And as long as you remain devoted to living wisely, God will see you *safely on your way*. You will walk with *security* as you make your way in the world, and when "you sit down, you will not be afraid; when you lie down, your sleep will be sweet." You won't fear the kind of ruin that comes upon foolish men because "the LORD will be your confidence and will keep your foot from being caught" (3:24, 26).

Great people walk this earth unnoticed every day. They are men and women who live fulfilling lives like the one Solomon describes because they excel at the art of being human. They bear much fruit because they maintain wisdom as a lifestyle. And as a result, they *go safely on their way*. Their *feet do not stumble* because they live in harmony with God and work hard to stay focused and follow his lead. They are skilled and creative, thus they exhibit a level of *courage* and *confidence* few people ever achieve. They make the most of the time they have and thereby cultivate superior lives for themselves and their families. Wherever they go, they act as a positive influence on the people around them—and in that way, they make the world a better place.

Son, this same level of personal excellence is within your reach. If you maintain wisdom as a lifestyle, you will create a life to be proud of. A life of successful originality that is set apart from every other person on earth. I encourage you: Make the choice to make the most of the time, talents, and resources God has given you. Use them to create a life that is original to *you*, a life defined by productive work, personal excellence, and rewarding relationships—the kind of life that testifies to the presence and power of God inside you.

The life you create may not be spectacular by the world's standards. But as long as you're honoring God, your family, and yourself, then it's a life worth being proud of.[11]

Follow your Heavenly Father's creative example

In Prov 8:22–31, Solomon directs our attention to God himself as an example of how someone goes about earning happiness through wise thinking and creative action.

Here Solomon describes God's creation of the universe. Notice how he portrays God not as an agent of chaos, but as a divine architect who left no detail unchecked when he drew up his metaphysical blueprints and brought his cosmic building project to life. Notice too how Solomon narrates this creation account from Lady Wisdom's perspective. He does this to show his son that Wisdom was with God from the beginning of his creative work, that she serves as the founding principle of his entire creation, and that she is the common thread that ties his natural order together.[12]

> "[22]The Lord possessed me at the beginning of His way," Wisdom says, "before His works of old. [23]From everlasting I was established, from the beginning, from the earliest times of the earth. [24]When there were no depths I was brought forth, when there were no springs abounding with water. [25]Before the mountains were settled, before the hills I was brought forth; [26]while He had not yet made the earth and the fields, nor the first dust of the world. [27]When He established the heavens, I was there, when He inscribed a circle on the face of the deep, [28]when He made firm the skies above, when the springs of the deep became fixed, [29]when He set for the sea its boundary so that the water would not transgress His command, when He marked out the foundations of the earth; [30]then I was beside Him, as a master workman; and I was daily His delight, rejoicing always before Him, [31]rejoicing in the world, His earth, and having my delight in the sons of men." (8:22–31)

God *thought with wisdom* when he conceived of the heavens, when he drew a circle on the face of the deep and established his plans for the

---

11. Taylor, *Restoring Pride*, 64.

12. God possessed wisdom before he began his first acts of creation (Prov 8:22). We can rationally conclude, therefore, that wisdom itself transcends the natural order. Nature displays and communicates God's wisdom, but nature itself is not the source of wisdom. God is!

earth. With his architectural strategy in place, God performed the *creative work* of a skilled craftsman when he unfurled the sky, founded the watery depths, molded the physical landscape, brought forth the soil and the fields, and filled his creation with life. His achievement elicited *rejoicing* from his heavenly council as they marveled at his inhabited world—at this living, breathing monument that will forever testify to the depths of his wisdom (see also Job 38:7). The Lord himself even marveled at his creation, proving that even for God, an authentic sense of happiness is an achievement that demands wise thinking and hard work.

Son, I want you to take a step back for a moment and (as best you can) put yourself in God's place when he finished his work on the sixth day of creation. Picture his face when he cast his eyes upon the fruits of his labor and said, *Behold, it is very good* (Gen 1:31). Imagine his eyes wide and misty with genuine pride as he watched his created order function in synchronized communion as a living system, just as he intended. Imagine his smile of excitement on the seventh day when he claimed the heavens as his throne and the earth as his footstool and took up residence in his inhabited world. Finally, imagine the happiness of both the Creator and the creation as they rejoiced in the meaning and productivity of their shared covenant relationship.

Son, the purpose of this exercise (besides activating your imagination) is to help you understand how devoted God is to creating his own happiness. In all things, he thinks and works with wisdom. And in the process, he earns the right to smile.

In Prov 3:19-20, Solomon once again uses God as an example, this time to demonstrate how one utilizes wisdom not only to achieve his own happiness, but to also *maintain* that sense of happiness throughout his life:

> "[19]The LORD by wisdom founded the earth, by understanding He established the heavens. [20]By His knowledge the deeps were broken up and the skies drip with dew." (3:19-20)

Here Solomon makes it clear that God's relationship to Wisdom is an everlasting bond, not some on-again/off-again fling. God governs the cosmos today with that same sense of wisdom he possessed at the beginning of time. For example, whether he calls for a flood like in Noah's day ("By His knowledge the deeps were broken up"), or whether he commands the daily clouds to produce a gentle condensation ("and the skies drip with dew"), we can take confidence in knowing that God maintains wisdom as a defining character trait. He acts with a sense of purpose and meaning in *everything he does*, from the big decisions (like a destructive flood) down to even the most routine activity (like creating a gentle rain shower). He expects you, therefore, as his child who bears his image, to act with that same sense of purpose and meaning in everything you do—from the biggest decisions like choosing a wife, down to the most routine activities like mowing the grass.

God has offered you his behavior as an example with the expectation that you will follow it. According to Lady Wisdom, you can bring that same seventh-day smile to God's face when you follow his example and work hand-in-hand with her to create a life that is truly worth living:

> "32And now, my sons, listen to me: happy are those who keep my ways. 33Hear instruction and be wise, and do not neglect it. 34Happy is the man who listens to me, watching daily at my gates, waiting beside my doors. 35For he who finds me finds life and obtains favor from the LORD; 36but he who misses me injures himself; all who hate me love death." (8:32–36 RSV)

Son, as these verses make clear, the man who follows God's example, the man who thinks and acts with wisdom and a sense of creativity in everything he does, will receive God's favor. And he'll find his own happiness along the way.

True happiness is the intellectual wage you earn when you engage in productive work and achieve personal excellence. In short, it's the spiritual reward you receive when you devote yourself to living wisely: "happy are those who *keep my ways*," as Lady Wisdom says in Prov 8:32 (RSV, emphasis added). But as Solomon makes sure to point out, happiness isn't just about relating well to yourself. It also involves relating well to other people.

Remember, *successful social relationships* play a big role in your personal happiness.

And as we will discuss in the next section, the second hard truth you need to accept is this: If you want to be happy, you need to know how to get along with the people God has providentially placed around you.

HARD TRUTH #2: A HAPPY MAN KNOWS HOW TO GET ALONG WELL WITH OTHERS

Prov 3:27–35

So far, Solomon has portrayed a happy man as a man of rational pride who justifiably respects himself and loves his life.

In Prov 3:27–35, however, he informs his son that a man can't limit his respect to himself and expect to achieve lasting happiness. He points out that a wise man will balance his respect for himself with a respect for his neighbors—and not just for his closest, most immediate neighbors like his family and friends, but for *everyone*, every individual man and woman who forms the community in which he lives.

Son, no man can behave in an antisocial manner and expect to succeed in life. The truth is, your level of happiness is contingent in part upon how well you can get along with other people. Solomon of course knew this to be true. That's why he lays out in these verses three general principles his son could use to function properly in any social setting.

Those principles are:

1. Trade good for good with the people around you.
2. Do not initiate harm against your neighbor.
3. Don't copy bad behavior in an attempt to get ahead.

Since productive relationships play such a significant role in a man's acquisition of happiness, let's take a moment to examine these three principles in more detail.

1. Trade good for good with the people around you

According to Solomon, one simple way a wise man can build healthy relationships is to trade good for good with the people he comes into contact with on a daily basis:

> "[27]Do not withhold good from those to whom it is due, when it is in your power to do it. [28]Do not say to your neighbor, 'Go, and come back, and tomorrow I will give it,' when you have it with you." (3:27–28)

Son, never hesitate to give the good people in your life the honor they have earned. God will always surround you with positive influences like family, friends, teachers, mentors, and other people worthy of your affection with the expectation that you will reciprocate the good you receive from them. Trading in goodness is a sign of respect. So strive to *earn* the goodwill of others by *producing* goodwill of your own. You can create goodwill by giving your best attitude and your best effort to every person in every social interaction. Whether you're dealing with a polite stranger on the street, an effective teacher in the classroom, or with the family and friends who know you best, you can cultivate good relationships when you treat others with the respect and consideration they deserve.

Follow Solomon's instruction and never hold back on the good you have to give. Don't treat good people with contempt. Don't mooch off the goodwill of others. And don't expect goodwill when you haven't earned it. Instead, as much as it is in your power to do so, trade good for good, respect for respect, and value for value with the people around you.

2. Do not initiate harm against your neighbor

Men who trade good for good live in peace with their neighbors. Those who initiate harm against their neighbors, however, are guilty of great evil. Namely, violating the rights of others by force, fraud, or coercion.

Solomon warned his son to never initiate harm in his interactions with the people around him:

> "[29]Do not devise harm against your neighbor, while he lives securely beside you. [30]Do not contend with a man without cause, if he has done you no harm." (3:29–30)

Son, you are free to disagree with whomever you choose. In fact, I would say that you have a moral responsibility to voice your disagreement with irrational or evil men. But you are never free to *initiate* the use of force against another human being, no matter the circumstances. Regarding the use of coercive force, philosopher and novelist Ayn Rand said it best: "No man—or group or society or government—has the right to assume the role of a criminal and initiate the use of physical compulsion against any man. Men have the right to use physical force *only* in retaliation and *only* against those who initiate its use. The ethical principle involved is simple and clear-cut: it is the difference between murder and self-defense. A holdup man seeks to gain a value, wealth, by killing his victim; the victim does not grow richer by killing a holdup man. The principle is: no man may obtain any values from others by resorting to physical force."[13]

Like Solomon, I am instructing you to never initiate force in your dealings with other people. Never plot evil against your neighbor, who dwells securely, *trustingly*, beside you. Instead, be the kind of man who gets along with others, the type of man your neighbors can depend on to act with peace and civility. Such mutual respect is always earned, never given. So manage the trust and goodwill you earn with diligence. Trust breeds fellowship and fellowship leads to brotherhood. Brothers work together. They cooperate. They trade with each other. They protect one another and live in harmony. Unwarranted violence stirs up animosity. But respect, trade, and peace foster productive relationships.

---

13. Rand, *The Virtue of Selfishness*, 36.

You are well within your rights, however, to defend yourself if a man ever initiates force against you. Solomon said as much when he told his son, "Do not contend with a man *without cause*, if he has done you *no harm*" (3:30, emphasis added). If you flip this verse around, Solomon gives his son the greenlight to *contend with a man when he gives you cause, when he initiates harm against you*.

Son, no man has the right to violate the rights of another man. But every man has the right to defend his own life. Any uncivilized thug who initiates force against you *deserves* force in return—not as vengeance, but in rational self-defense. Once again I quote Ayn Rand: "The necessary consequences of man's right to life is his right to self-defense. In a civilized society, force may be used only in retaliation and only against those who initiate its use. All the reasons which make the initiation of physical force an evil, make the retaliatory use of physical force a moral imperative."[14]

3. Don't copy bad behavior in an attempt to get ahead

A self-reliant man of integrity achieves his goals through wisdom and hard work. Not by stomping on the necks of others. Only an incompetent brute needs to resort to bully tactics and harm in order to get things done.

Solomon frequently expressed contempt for violent men. In vv. 31–35, he commands his son to never admire or imitate their behavior, nor should he envy their spurious accomplishments:

> "[31]Do not envy a man of violence and do not choose any of his ways. [32]For the devious are an abomination to the Lord; but He is intimate with the upright. [33]The curse of the Lord is on the house of the wicked, but He blesses the dwelling of the righteous. [34]Though He scoffs at the scoffers, yet He gives grace to the afflicted. [35]The wise will inherit honor, but fools display dishonor." (3:31–35)

Solomon says a wicked lifestyle is not glamorous or healthy. Rather, it's impractical and self-defeating. I will admit, though, that wicked men can appear at times to get ahead in life. You may see their apparent success and wonder: *Why should I live responsibly while wicked men lie and cheat their way to more fun and more stuff?*

Son, that's a reasonable question. I wish I could tell you that life is always fair and that wicked men will never get ahead in this world. But I can't. The truth is, sometimes this unfair world seems to favor bullies and

---

14. Rand, *The Virtue of Selfishness*, 126.

cheaters. Regarding your question, the only answer I can give that might assuage your concern is this: You can never trust in life to be fair, but you can always trust in God to be just.

You can trust him to always give each man his due—that is, to reward the righteous man according to his righteousness and punish the wicked man according to his wickedness. The Apostle Paul said as much in his letter to the Galatians: "And let us not grow weary of doing good, for in due season we will reap, *if we do not give up*" (Gal 6:9 ESV, emphasis added). Here Paul said good men will definitely reap the rewards that come along with righteousness—but only if they endure in righteousness. *If they don't give up* in doing good.

God has promised to reward every man according to his integrity—or lack thereof. He will repay good for good and bad for bad in his own perfect way and in his own perfect time. So keep your head up and stand strong in your convictions, even when the going gets tough. Take comfort in knowing that any success a wicked man achieves is short-lived and worthless. His demise may not be immediate, but it is most definitely assured. That's why Solomon warned his son to never envy a man of violence or choose any of his ways: "For the devious are an abomination to the Lord; but He is intimate with the upright" (3:31–32).

Son, you don't want to be a man of violence because violent men always have to watch their backs. As Jesus said, those who live by the sword will die by the sword (Matt 26:52). Wicked men do not trade good for good. They only know how to trade in violence—it's their currency, their way of life, and, according to Solomon, their ultimate destiny: "The curse of the LORD is on the house of the wicked. . . . He scoffs at the scoffers." In contrast, Solomon said God blesses the dwelling of the righteous, and to the humble he gives favor: "The wise will inherit honor, but fools display dishonor" (3:33–35).

The success a wicked man appears to achieve is a phony success. Phony people will never experience genuine affection or happiness. Their moral short-cuts will eventually catch up with them and God will trade scorn for scorn with every last abominable one of them. Every cheater, liar, and thug will eventually find himself on the wrong side of divine justice. A con-man will eventually suffocate under the weight of his own lie. A bully will eventually push the wrong man's shoulder. A criminal will eventually find himself on the wrong side of a gun barrel. And if they somehow manage to sneak by unscathed in this life, they'll all eventually come face to face with an angry God come judgment day.

I'm going to tell you the same thing Solomon told his son. Do not envy the counterfeit success of wicked people. Never adopt their corrupt methods in order to get ahead. A compromised integrity will only result in your own destruction. Instead, endure in righteousness and give your best effort in every circumstance. Trade good for good with the people around you. Be an honest man and live in peace with your neighbors. Always do the moral thing and trust in God to administer ultimate justice. He will assuredly curse the evil man for his wickedness. And he will just as assuredly reward the upright man with the blessings of fulfillment.

So find delight in your integrity, not in immorality or revenge. And trust in God to reward your effort with the lasting happiness only a lifestyle of wisdom and hard work can provide.

Son, you will achieve happiness when you: (1) live every moment with a sense of responsibility and (2) when you work hard to maintain right relationships with the people around you.

With these two truths in mind, I want you to set a vision for your life. Visualize the kind of man you want to be and then devote every ounce of your time and energy to becoming that man. Commit yourself to living hand-in-hand with Lady Wisdom and work hard to achieve your values and earn your own happiness. As Solomon commanded his son, so I command you: Embrace her "instruction and not silver, and knowledge rather than choice gold. For wisdom is better than jewels; and all desirable things cannot compare with her" (8:10–11).

Don't allow yourself to get distracted or discouraged in your pursuit of wisdom. Instead, adopt a firm, goal-oriented mindset. Actively seek out the meaning in every activity. Understand the difference between true happiness and fleeting amusement. Devote yourself exclusively to the people and activities that advance your best interests. Be considerate of the people around you. Treat others with respect. Forge good personal and professional relationships. Trust in God and act on his truth by integrating into your life only those things that are beneficial.

Live with a sense of diligence, and your Heavenly Father will make sure you achieve your created purpose and "attain to the unity of the faith, and of the knowledge of the Son of God, to a mature man, to the measure of the stature which belongs to the fullness of Christ" (Eph 4:13).

Love,
Dad

Letter 8

Walk in Your Father's Footsteps

Prov 4:1–27; 8:17–21

"... *my job as a father provides me with the responsibility of influencing your life, not controlling it.*"

Son, one day I will have to answer to God for how I've managed the family he's given me.

On that day, when I stand before the judgment seat of Christ, I want to be able to hold my head high with honor as I look Jesus directly in the eyes and say, "Lord, I wasn't a perfect husband or a perfect father. And for that I ask your forgiveness. But I can say with all conviction that I gave my wife and my children my best effort as a man. I stumbled many times but I never stayed down. I never gave up on them and they never gave up on me. We never stopped loving each other. We built our lives on the rock of your word. We fought our way through the trials of this world. We withstood the test of time. And by your grace, we stand before you victorious. Together. As a family."

I want the Lord to honor my conviction and affirm my work as a family man. I want him to look upon my effort and say those words every man wants to hear: "Well done, good and faithful servant." I want to do a good job. I want to make him proud. So I strive every day to be the kind of husband and father he has called me to be, the kind of man my family deserves. My goal is to lead my family well. I put much effort, therefore, into studying God's word. And I work hard to bring his wisdom to life in my actions so I can set a good example for my family to follow.

That is my job as your father.

What I expect from you in return is that you do your job as my son. I want you to honor my effort and follow my lead and work just as hard to put those wise principles into action in your own life.

Solomon had the same expectation for his son. As the head of his household, Solomon used his authority to perpetuate a family tradition of wise living, one that was originally established by his father, King David, who as the Bible tells us dedicated himself to conforming his heart to the very heart of God (1 Sam 13:14; Acts 13:22). Although David frequently fell short of this ideal (as every man does), he never lost sight of his goal. He never gave up. Even in the toughest of circumstances, he remained devoted to walking in the way of wisdom. And whether he was walking along the streets of Jerusalem or through a rocky road in the wilderness or within the hallways of his home, the king of God's people strove to let wisdom guide his every step.

In Ps 101, David set forth the model behavior of an effective leader. Old Testament scholars Carl F. Keil and Franz Delitzsch refer to this psalm as "an echo out of the heart of David" in which "he gives utterance to his determination as king to give earnest heed to the sanctity of his walk, of his rule, and of his house."[1]

Son, as you read this psalm, take note of the high moral standard David set for himself. He resolved to lead, both from his throne and within his home, with the strength and integrity God expects of every man.

> "¹I will sing of steadfast love and justice; to you, O LORD, I will make music. ²I will ponder the way that is blameless. Oh when will you come to me? I will walk with integrity of heart within my house; ³I will not set before my eyes anything that is worthless. I hate the work of those who fall away; it shall not cling to me. ⁴A perverse heart shall be far from me; I will know nothing of evil. ⁵Whoever slanders his neighbor secretly I will destroy. Whoever has a haughty look and an arrogant heart I will not endure. ⁶I will look with favor on the faithful in the land, that they may dwell with me; he who walks in the way that is blameless shall minister

---

1. Keil and Delitzsch, *Psalms*, 637–38.

to me. ⁷No one who practices deceit shall dwell in my house; no one who utters lies shall continue before my eyes. ⁸Morning by morning I will destroy all the wicked in the land, cutting off all the evildoers from the city of the LORD." (Ps 101 ESV)

These verses provide good insight into David's personal code of conduct as a leader. He vowed to pursue righteousness and guard his heart against perversity (vv. 1–4). He vowed to protect his territory from the threats of bad influences (vv. 5–8). And he vowed to act with integrity, especially within the walls of his home (vv. 2, 7).

As these verses prove, David took his leadership responsibilities seriously. His aim was for his people—from the subjects of his kingdom to the members of his own household—to follow in the footsteps of his example.

Solomon wisely took note of his father's behavior. The Bible tells us that as a young man in the house of David, Solomon loved the LORD and walked in his father's footsteps. Meaning that he learned from his father's example, that he absorbed his teachings and made the conscious choice to integrate them into his life (1 Kgs 3:3).

In Prov 4 and 8, Solomon, now a father himself, continues the tradition by passing on to his son the way of life his father had passed on to him. With this letter, I will follow the examples of David and Solomon and initiate a family tradition of wise living.

Like David, I have set a high moral standard for myself. I have resolved to pursue righteousness. With the grit worthy of a man, I will guard my heart from evil. I will fight to protect my territory from every threat. I will walk in the way of wisdom, by the code of God's commands. Especially within my own home. Because those are my responsibilities as your father.

I expect you, as my son, to respond to my effort by following young Solomon's example and walking in your father's footsteps.

To show you how seriously I take my job, I will reiterate a promise I made in letter 3. Like David and Solomon, I promise to commit myself to being the best leader I can be. That doesn't mean that I will be perfect in executing my parental responsibilities. It means that I will be a hardworking, hands-on father in the way I relate to my family, not some hands-off, deadbeat dad.

And just to make sure we understand each other, let me begin by explaining what being a hands-on father is all about.

A GOOD FATHER IS A HANDS-ON FATHER

Prov 4:1–27; 8:17–21

A good father doesn't overpower his household like a tyrant, nor does he approach his family with a hands-off *laissez-faire* attitude.

Laissez-faire is a French term literally defined as *let do*. But in the modern philosophical/social/political sense of the word, the definition falls somewhere between simple *noninterference* and the less subtle *Leave us alone!*

A *hands-off* philosophy is an effective governing strategy when it comes to the state and its distinct separation from the private affairs of its citizens. But the *laissez-faire* strategy fails miserably when parents use it to govern their family.

Jennifer Roback Morse wrote an interesting book titled *Love and Economics* in which she put forth the idea that a *laissez-faire* family—that is, a family in which the husband and wife employ a hands-off approach to marriage and parenting—cannot work. "A family held together by a series of contractual understandings, even the most reasonable and elaborate," she said, "turns out to be less stable than a family held together by that vague, much misunderstood, intangible quality called love."[2]

To love is to value. And no man of integrity takes a hands-off approach to the people he values the most in this world: his family. To be clear: Love alone is not enough to teach a child all he needs to know to become a responsible adult. But love is most definitely a necessary condition for a child to grow into a well-adjusted and productive man of God. Fathers who love their children don't leave them to their own devices (both figuratively and literally). Instead, a good father will be a hands-on father. He will involve himself with his family. He will be present and active as he governs his children in ways that are good and beneficial.

In short, a good father is not a *laissez-faire* father.

Son, you have my word: I will never adopt a hands-off approach to my family. My goal as the leader of my home is to honor the ideal David set forth in Ps 101. I will pay careful attention to the way of integrity in my own life. I will protect and provide for my family, both physically and spiritually. And I will be active and involved as a husband to my wife and a father to my children. In every area of our lives, I will strive to honor the divine instruction as originally given to Moses, and I will follow the examples of David and Solomon and ultimately Jesus: I will love the Lord my God with all my

---

2. Morse, *Love and Economics*, 3, 20.

heart, soul, mind, and strength. And I will love my neighbor as I love myself (Mark 12:29–31).

My closest neighbors, my most intimate human relationships, are my family. As the leader of my household, I will work with all my heart, soul, mind, and strength to meet my God-given responsibilities—because I love my family, and my desire is for you all to live in the footsteps of my example.

Like David and Solomon and every other imperfect man, I will stumble from time to time. I will make mistakes as a leader and as a father. But son, I promise you this: I will not make stumbling a habit. I promise to never allow failure to become a way of life. And no matter how many times I stumble, I will never stay down. I will never give up. I promise to learn from my errors and to always keep striving for that Ps 101 ideal.

That means I will always be there for you. I will meet my responsibilities and lead you in the way you deserve. I will encourage you when you do well. When you trip and fall, I won't kick you when you're down; instead, I will help you up, dust you off, and set you right. I will involve myself in your activities. I will make myself available to do those daily jobs a good father does: I will help you with your schoolwork, play catch with you outside, help you practice your karate, and attend every extracurricular event you are involved in. And as you grow beyond childhood and into a young man, I will be there to teach you how to drive, to give you advice about girls (as best I can), to help you sort out what you want to do with your life, and to guide you into manhood.

I promise you: In every stage of your life, I will *do my job* as your father. I will make the second-by-second, hour-by-hour, day-by-day effort to bring you up in the way of God's wisdom. You, in return, have a moral responsibility to do your job as my son: to match my effort by learning with open ears, observant eyes, an active mind, and a sincere heart.

That's a big responsibility for you to take on. But it's not an unreasonable expectation. In fact, Solomon had the same expectation of his son. Throughout this entire Proverbial discourse, Solomon is doing the work of a hands-on father. He's instructing his son in the good precepts of God's wisdom. And in return, he rightfully expects his son to do his job—to respond to his leadership with his utmost respect and effort.

Thus he opens chapter four of his Proverbs with this direct command:

> "[1]Hear, O sons, the instruction of a father, and give attention that you may gain understanding, [2]for I give you sound teaching; do not abandon my instruction." (4:1–2)

Solomon's message here is as profound as it is sincere: *Pay attention, my son, "for I give you sound teaching." Take the good influence of home with you* wherever you go. My instruction will never abandon you, so "do not abandon my instruction" and do not ignore the example I have worked so hard to set.

Also notice how Solomon delivers his instruction with a firm yet nurturing tone. He doesn't bark at his son like a drill sergeant. Nor does he make him feel insecure about his lack of experience. He communicates his message effectively, with love and respect, because his goal is not to discourage or provoke his son, but to encourage him and lead him into manhood (Eph 6:1–4; Col 3:21).

By addressing his son in this manner, Solomon surely recalled how his father's words of wisdom helped him overcome his youthful insecurities. And even though Solomon was a grown man and a father and a king at the time he put forth his Proverbs, he could still identify with his son's raw youth.

He continues his lesson by reminding him that he too was once a young man who submitted to the tutelage of his father.

> "³When I was a son to my father, tender and the only son in the sight of my mother, ⁴then he taught me and said to me, 'Let your heart hold fast my words; keep my commandments and live.'" (4:3–4)

These verses tell us that wise behavior was a family tradition in the house of David. And when the time came, Solomon worked hard to continue with his son the same tradition his father established with him years earlier. Just as David instructed young Solomon to "Let your heart hold fast my words; keep my commandments and live" (4:4), so older Solomon instructed his son to likewise listen to "the instruction of a father, and give attention that you may gain understanding" (4:1). His aim here isn't to control his son's life, but to help him learn how to be a man—and not just any man, but *his own* man, a man responsible for achieving *his own* destiny and making *his own* decisions.

Son, being a hands-on father doesn't mean that I will act like a tyrant. I don't want to control your life. *Your* life is *your* warrant. God has given it to you. It's not mine to live—it's yours. That means it's up to you and you alone to achieve the destiny God has ordained for you. My job is to help you get there. And the best way I can do that is to train you up in the wisdom of God's word.

Along the way, I will neither abandon you like a deadbeat dad, nor will I swing the parenting pendulum in the opposite direction and hover over you like some helicopter parent. I will use a balanced, hands-on parenting strategy to create a productive learning environment for you. But I will not, I *cannot*, live your life for you. I cannot fight your battles for you. I cannot shield you from every hardship the world is sure to throw at you. As I said in letter 1, I will give my life to protect you. But I will not *overprotect* you—because I want you to be strong more than I want you to be safe.[3]

I will always be a hands-on father. But as we'll discuss in the remainder of this letter, there are two specific things a hands-on father can never do for his children:

- I cannot achieve your God-given destiny for you.
- Nor can I decide for you what kind of man you will be.

God has given *you* the responsibility of making your own decisions. If you want to live as a man of integrity and achieve the individual destiny God has ordained just for you, then it's up to you to make the right choices. I will do my job and point you in the right direction. But it's up to you to do the work—to go out into the world and create a meaningful life that is unique to you.

I'll be the first to admit: Being a hands-on father can be difficult at times. Establishing a healthy balance between too-much and too-little parenting can be a tricky dynamic to manage. For fathers *and* for sons.

Fortunately for us, we can look to the examples of David and Solomon to see how a couple of wise men achieved a good balance in a similar situation.

A hands-on father lets his son achieve his own destiny

During David's reign as king of Israel, he desired in his heart to build a permanent temple complex in Jerusalem to establish God's presence among his people. Although David's intentions were noble, God put a stop to his plans and told him explicitly: "You shall not build a house for My name because you are a man of war and have shed blood" (1 Chron 28:3).

God's outright denial may seem harsh. But upon closer inspection, it actually makes a lot of sense. God chose David, a man of both wisdom and war, to lead Israel to victory over her enemies (1 Kgs 5:3). God called on David to establish Israel as a nation and Jerusalem as her capital. He called on David to act with righteousness and justice as a godly king over Israel and to institute the house of David as a dynasty of kings to rule God's people forever. Those were the jobs God gave to David. And those were the jobs David accomplished.

---

3. This is my answer to Jordan Peterson's poignant question for parents: "do you want to make your children safe, or strong?" (*12 Rules for Life*, 47).

The task of constructing the temple, however, belonged to someone else. Someone with a different set of qualifications. God reserved that job for David's son Solomon, a man of wisdom and peace. "Behold, a son shall be born to you," God said to David; "he shall be a man of peace. I will give him peace from all his enemies round about; for his name shall be Solomon, and I will give peace and quiet to Israel in his days. He shall build a house for my name. He shall be my son, and I will be his father, and I will establish his royal throne in Israel for ever" (1 Chron 22:9–10 RSV; also see 1 Chron 28:6–7 and 1 Kgs 5:4–5).

David accepted and honored God's decree. And as he approached the end of his reign as king, he did not retire quietly into the background and abandon his successor, young Solomon, to handle this massive job all by himself. He instead responded as any hands-on father would. He involved himself in his son's activities. He stepped up and provided the young and inexperienced Solomon with the guidance he needed to help him meet his God-given responsibilities. In his final duties as king, the wise and experienced David took it upon himself to collect supplies, organize workers, divide the labor, and design building plans in order to help young Solomon get this important project up off the ground (1 Chron 22:5).

But perhaps his greatest contribution was helping his son develop a legitimate sense of self-confidence. David boosted young Solomon's spirit by charging him with these words: "As for you, my son Solomon, know the God of your father," he said, "and serve Him with a whole heart and a willing mind; for the LORD searches all hearts, and understands every intent of the thoughts. If you seek Him, He will let you find Him; but if you forsake Him, He will reject you forever. Consider now, for the LORD has chosen you to build a house for the sanctuary; be courageous and act" (1 Chron 28:9–10).

God gave Solomon a specific job to do: build a permanent temple structure in Jerusalem.[4] David saw it his responsibility as a father to help his son do his job. But for all his good intentions, David could not do Solomon's job for him. His instruction and encouragement would only go so far if Solomon did not possess the steadfast will to act on the responsibilities God had given specifically to him.

As we discussed in letter 6, *the will to act* moves a man from intention to action and thereby testifies to the strength of his character. It's a big

---

4. Prior to this time the ark of God's presence dwelt in the tent of the tabernacle. The tabernacle was a collapsible structure that served as the dwelling place of God's presence among his people. During David's reign as king, he lamented the fact that he lived in a house of cedar while the ark of God dwelt in a tent rather than a permanent house (2 Sam 7:2).

responsibility to rule over a mighty nation and build a temple to house the presence of the Almighty God. And Solomon—who if you'll remember saw himself at this time as an inexperienced youth who didn't know *if he was coming or going*—naturally felt ill-qualified to do the job (1 Kgs 3:7).

Like the hands-on father that he was, David sensed his son's insecurity (1 Chron 29:1). He continued his charge not with harsh words, but with a spirit of fatherly encouragement:

> "I am going the way of all the earth," an aging David said to young Solomon. "Be strong, therefore, and show yourself a man. Keep the charge of the LORD your God, to walk in His ways, to keep His statutes, His commandments, His ordinances, and His testimonies, according to what is written in the Law of Moses, that you may succeed in all that you do and wherever you turn, so that the LORD may carry out His promise which He spoke concerning me, saying, 'If your sons are careful of their way, to walk before Me in truth with all their heart and with all their soul, you shall not lack a man on the throne of Israel.' . . . Then David said to his son Solomon, 'Be strong and courageous, and act; do not fear nor be dismayed, for the LORD God, my God, is with you. He will not fail you or forsake you until all the work for the service of the house of the LORD is finished.'" (1 Kgs 2:2–4; 1 Chron 28:20)

Notice how David actively involved himself in Solomon's mission. But notice too that he never once offered to do his son's job for him. Instead, he struck a good balance by equipping his son with the knowledge and the encouragement he needed to carry out his own responsibilities and achieve his own destiny.

Son, I also want you to take note of young Solomon's response. He didn't blow off his father's advice like some know-it-all punk. Nor did he shrink under the pressure like a coward and beg daddy to do the work for him. He responded with wisdom—with the humble attitude of a young man who knows he still has much to learn, but also with the steely resolve of a man who knows it's time to set fear aside and get to work. He acknowledged his own youthful insufficiencies. He listened to his father's instructions and acquired the wisdom he needed to get the job done. Then he dug deep within his soul and found the strength he needed to overcome his insecurity and carry out God's command upon his life.

When destiny called upon him, Solomon stepped up and answered the call like a man. He didn't try to take an easy way out. He instead owned up to his responsibilities and completed the work in full. And in the process, he grew into the man he was meant to be.

In short, *he did his job.*

After seven years of hard work, the temple was complete.[5] And when the time of inauguration came, Solomon stood high and mighty on a platform before the Lord's altar. The new king then knelt down in the presence of all the assembly of Israel. He spread his arms toward heaven. And with a spirit of great confidence, he made the following proclamation to his nation and to his God:

> "Now the LORD has fulfilled His word which He spoke; for I have risen in the place of my father David and sit on the throne of Israel, as the LORD promised, and have built the house for the name of the LORD, the God of Israel. . . . O LORD, the God of Israel, there is no god like You in heaven or on earth, keeping covenant and showing lovingkindness to Your servants who walk before You with all their heart; who has kept with Your servant David, my father, that which You have promised him. . . . Now therefore arise, O LORD God, to Your resting place, You and the ark of Your might; let Your priests, O LORD God, be clothed with salvation and let Your godly ones rejoice in what is good. O LORD God, do not turn away the face of Your anointed; remember Your lovingkindness to Your servant David." (2 Chron 6:10, 14–15, 41–42)

After Solomon finished speaking, fire came down from heaven and the glory of the Lord filled the temple. All Israel then "bowed down with their faces to the ground on the pavement and worshiped and gave thanks to the LORD, saying, 'For he is good, for his steadfast love endures forever.' . . . Thus Solomon finished the house of the LORD and the king's house. All that Solomon had planned to do in the house of the LORD and in his own house *he successfully accomplished*" (2 Chron 7:1–3, 11 ESV, emphasis added).

Son, you and I would be wise to learn from David's and Solomon's behavior. David struck a good balance as a hands-on father. He set a good example for Solomon to follow. He encouraged his son when he needed encouragement. He gave him knowledge when he lacked knowledge. But he did not do his work for him.

Nor, son, can I do your work for you.

---

5. First Kings 6:38—7:1 says Solomon spent seven years building the temple and thirteen years building his own house. Thus, Solomon took twenty years to build "the two houses, the house of the LORD and the king's house" (1 Kgs 9:10).

My job is to train you up in the way of wisdom with my words and with my actions. Your job is to take my instructions to heart and bring them to life in *your* own way in *your* own life. As we've discussed in previous letters, it's your responsibility to seek out wisdom, primarily from your mother and me. And once you've obtained it, you are to put that wisdom to good use and fulfill the purpose God has ordained specifically for *you*.

When destiny called upon young Solomon, his father instructed him to seize the moment and embrace his God-given responsibilities. He charged him to commit himself to walking in the way of wisdom, to "know the God of your father and serve him with a whole heart and a willing mind, for the LORD searches all hearts and understands every plan and thought. If you seek him, he will be found by you, but if you forsake him, he will cast you off forever. Be careful now, for the LORD has chosen you to build a house for the sanctuary; be strong and do it" (1 Chron 28:9-10 ESV).

Son, I charge you with the same instruction. Listen to my words of wisdom. Pay attention to my example and acquire the understanding you need to carry out God's call upon your life. Just as David instructed Solomon, and Solomon instructed his son, so I instruct you: "Be strong, and show yourself a man, and keep the charge of the LORD your God, walking in his ways and keeping his statutes, his commandments, his rules, and his testimonies . . . that you may prosper in all that you do and wherever you turn" (1 Kgs 2:2-3, ESV).

Both David and Solomon are clear: The man who walks in the way of wisdom is a man who will find true success in all that he does. We can surmise, therefore, that *maintaining a wise lifestyle* is the key to fulfilling your God-given destiny.

As I explained in letter 7, you should never treat your association with wisdom as some casual, on-again/off-again fling. Treat her instead with respect. Like a lady. And relate to her with the same sense of steadfast commitment you would apply to a marriage relationship.

In Prov 4:5-9, Solomon recounts how David likewise commanded him to be aggressive and uncompromising in his commitment to Lady Wisdom.

> "⁵Acquire wisdom! Acquire understanding! Do not forget nor turn away from the words of my mouth. ⁶*Do not forsake her*,'" David said of Lady Wisdom, "'and she will guard you; *love her*, and she will *watch over you*. ⁷The beginning of wisdom is: Acquire wisdom; and with all your acquiring, get understanding. ⁸*Prize her*, and she will exalt you; she will honor you if you *embrace* her. ⁹She will place on your head a garland of grace; she will present you with a crown of beauty.'" (4:5-9, emphasis added)

Notice the romantic vibe that pulses through these verses. David and Solomon portray wisdom not as some *thing* to be taken advantage of, but as a lover to be cherished forever. By using relational concepts like *fidelity* and *protection*, as well as passionate words like *love*, *prize*, and *embrace*, Solomon calls on his son to value and nurture Lady Wisdom as a loyal groom would his lovely bride.

By her own admission, Lady Wisdom will settle for nothing less from a potential suitor. She will offer herself only to the man who pursues her with pure affections, to the man who desires commitment over conquest. "I love those who *love* me," Lady Wisdom proclaims in Prov 8:17, "and those who *diligently seek me* will find me" (emphasis added).[6]

Son, I challenge you in the same way David challenged Solomon: Step up and claim Lady Wisdom for yourself. She has made herself available to any man smart enough to seek after her with loving intentions. If you embrace her with all your heart, soul, mind, and strength, she will honor your loyalty with *riches and honor*, with *enduring wealth and righteousness*. "My fruit is better than gold, even pure gold, and my yield better than choicest silver," Lady Wisdom promises. "I walk in the way of righteousness, in the midst of the paths of justice, to endow those who love me with wealth, that I may fill their treasuries" (8:18–21).

As these verses make clear, Lady Wisdom rewards great devotion with great honor. Again, as we discussed in my previous letter, those rewards translate into the real world as a lasting sense of happiness, as well as the physical and relational blessings that come from a fidelity to wise living. She will reward the man who walks in her ways with what Solomon poetically refers to in 4:9 as a *garland of grace* and a *crown of accomplishment*.

In other words, with the rewards of a destiny fulfilled.

This is the kind of life I want for you. A life of accomplishment and happiness. But like I've said throughout this letter, my job as a father provides me with the responsibility of influencing your life, not controlling it. I can't usurp the God-given freedom of your will. Nor can I choreograph

---

6. As the author of the apocryphal Wisdom of Solomon said of Lady Wisdom: "Wisdom is radiant and unfading, and she is easily discerned by those *who love her*, and is found by *those who seek her. She hastens to make herself known to those who desire her.* He who rises early to seek her will have no difficulty, for he will find her sitting at his gates. To fix one's thought on her is perfect understanding, and *he who is vigilant on her account* will soon be free from care, because *she goes about seeking those worthy of her*, and she graciously appears to them in their paths, and meets them in every thought. The beginning of wisdom is the most sincere desire for instruction, and *concern for instruction is love of her*, and *love of her is the keeping of her laws*, and giving heed to her laws is assurance of immortality, and immortality brings one near to God; so the desire for wisdom leads to a kingdom" (Wis 6:12–20 RSV, emphasis added).

your life choices. I can introduce you to Wisdom, but I can't make you take her hand. I can point you toward the path of destiny, but I can't make you walk it.

Son, you're not a baby anymore. The age of maturity is upon you. God has tasked you and you alone with the responsibility of answering his call. And the choice he has put before you is a binary one:

- You can walk tall like a man in *the way of wisdom* and live a meaningful life.

Or:

- You can scurry around on *the path of the wicked* like a sniveling weasel and suffer a lifetime of failure.

These two paths lie in stark opposition to one another. You cannot walk on both paths simultaneously. Nor can you hopscotch back and forth from one to the other. You're going to have to choose which path you will take.

As for me, I have chosen to walk in the way of wisdom. But I can only decide for myself. I cannot make this decision for you.

The time has come, my son, for you to decide for yourself what kind of man you want to be.

A hands-on father lets his son make up his own mind

If you choose to be a wise man, then I pledge to give you the knowledge you need, to come alongside you, as David did with Solomon, and guide you toward the straight and narrow path that leads to a destiny fulfilled.

But like young Solomon, it's up to you to choose what you will do with the knowledge I give you.

Notice how an older Solomon gives his son the same option in the following verses:

> "[10]Hear, my son, and accept my sayings and the years of your life will be many. [11]I have directed you in the way of wisdom; I have led you in upright paths. [12]When you walk *[in the way of wisdom]*, your steps will not be impeded; and if you run, you will not stumble. [13]Take hold of instruction; do not let go. Guard her *[Wisdom]*, for she is your life. [14]Do not enter the path of the wicked and do not proceed in the way of evil men. [15]Avoid it, do not pass by it; turn away from it and pass on. [16]For they cannot sleep unless they do evil; and they are robbed of sleep

unless they make someone stumble. ¹⁷For they eat the bread of wickedness and drink the wine of violence. ¹⁸But *the path of the righteous is like the light of dawn, that shines brighter and brighter until the full day.* ¹⁹The way of the wicked is like darkness; they do not know over what they stumble." (4:10–19, emphasis added)

Did you see what Solomon did there? He didn't force his son to make a certain decision. He instead did what a hands-on father is supposed to do: He told his son the truth, then he gave him the freedom to think for himself and make up his own mind.

In these verses, he presents his son with an option. The young man could either walk on the life-giving path of wisdom (4:11–12). Or he could walk on the destructive path of the wicked (4:14). Solomon then explains the consequences of each choice. His son could commit himself to a wise lifestyle and achieve real-world success (4:13, 18). Or he could rebuff Lady Wisdom and stumble headlong unto failure (4:14–17).

Son, I'm here to present you with the same choice. You can be a wise man. Or you can be a fool. You can choose to walk in the upright way of wisdom and live a meaningful life. Or you can take the lazy route and waste your life stumbling down the wide *path of the wicked*.

Like Solomon, I'm warning you to *turn away* from the latter path. It's a dark and dangerous way of life, one that's full of evil people who shuffle back and forth like spiritual zombies looking to gorge themselves on *the bread of wickedness* and *the wine of violence*. Those kinds of people are bad influences who will do everything they can to sink their teeth into your soul and turn you into one of them. They won't rest, Solomon says, until they can *do evil* and *make others stumble* and bring the people around them down to their level of misery.

The *way of wisdom*, in contrast, is a sturdy path that leads *upward*—in a heavenly direction. That path is populated by stable and rational people who are worth interacting with (people like your mother and me). It's a narrow path, for sure, but as Solomon says, it's warm and *bright* and *filled with light*; and as long as you stick to it, you can avoid the cold, dark fate of the walking dead.

If you want to walk tall in this world like a real man (and not lurch around aimlessly like some mindless walking corpse), then pay attention as I lead you toward the way of wisdom. Like Solomon, I encourage you, my son, to learn from my example. *Incline your ear* to my words. *Watch me* as I bring these words to life in my everyday actions. "Do not let them depart from your sight; keep them in the midst of your heart. For they are life to those who find them and health to all their body" (4:20–22).

You can trust me to honor my responsibilities as a hands-on father. I will set a good example and lead you to the path of wisdom—but I *will not* force you to walk it. Instead, I will do what God has called me to do.

I will tell you the truth about your options and give you the freedom to decide for yourself what kind of man you want to be.

Consider the path of the wicked

Here's the truth: Of these two paths, the way of the wicked is the easier path to walk on. Think about it. It's easier to do evil than to do good—to tear something down than to create something meaningful and nurture it from the ground up. It's easier to hurt someone than to help someone—to stir up anger rather than give a gentle answer. It's easier to be a coward than it is to be a hero—to tell lies rather than speak the truth. It's easier to be miserable than to be happy—to be a hopeless cynic rather than a man of deep conviction and rational belief. It's easier to be irresponsible than to be responsible—to not care rather than to sacrifice in your pursuit of something worthwhile. It's easier to be useless than to be productive—to be lazy and mooch off of someone else rather than to work hard and make your own way.

Simply put, it's easier to waste your life than it is to make something of yourself. And if you're looking for a stagnant and worthless existence, then, son, consider the easy path of the wicked.

Consider the way of wisdom

But if your goal is to create a superior life for yourself, then I recommend the way of wisdom. Like I mentioned in my previous letter, this path will lead you into a genuine sense of happiness, one that's grounded in meaningful, real-world achievements (Solomon reiterates this point in 4:12–13).

But here's the catch: The way of wisdom is a much harder path to walk on than the way of the wicked.

Wisdom is not an easy way of life. It comes with responsibilities and challenges. Struggles and sacrifices. Solomon describes the way of wisdom as an *upright path* in v. 11. And an uphill path, by definition, is much harder to walk on than a downward slope or even an average flat road.

But keep this in mind: The fact that it's set on an incline means that it's *rising up* toward a good life. Toward meaning. Toward heaven. Toward God himself.

Son, as Lady Wisdom has made abundantly clear, the path of wisdom is open to anyone. But few people choose to walk it because it's a physically and intellectually demanding route that requires more effort than most people are willing to give. The sad truth is, many people lack the kind of fortitude—the kind of *heart*—necessary to walk the upright path of wisdom. They don't care enough about their lives to make something of themselves. They may wish for a good life, but they'll never have one because they're too lazy or too fearful to do the work necessary to go out and *earn* a good life. They'd rather settle for the status quo. So they take the easy way out. And anyone who makes a habit of taking the easy route will eventually find himself wandering among the heartless hordes that haunt the path of the wicked.

Only a person of great courage and commitment—a man with a *vibrant heart*, as Solomon put it in 4:21-22—is capable of walking in the way of wisdom and moving his life in an upward direction.

That's why he closes out chapter 4 with this command to his son:

> "²³Watch over your *heart* with all diligence, for from it flow the springs of life. ²⁴Put away from you a deceitful mouth and put devious speech far from you. ²⁵Let your eyes look directly ahead and let your gaze be fixed straight in front of you. ²⁶Watch the path of your feet and all your ways will be established. ²⁷Do not turn to the right nor to the left; turn your foot from evil."
> (4:23-27, emphasis added)

If you think you've got what it takes, my son, to walk tall on the upright path of wisdom, then step up, right now, and prove yourself a man. Show me how healthy your heart is. Prove the strength of your character and earn my trust by working hard to *keep your heart in the right place*. "Watch over your heart with all diligence," as Solomon says, "for from it flows the springs of life" (4:23).

A wise man will protect his heart above all else. Not just the physical organ, but everything the organ symbolizes: your *self*; your conscious center; the wellspring of your life; the sum total of your intellect, your emotions, and your will—that irreducible primary at the foundation of your being that defines who you are as a man.[7]

---

7. In Hebrew "the heart" (*lēb*) denotes the seat of emotion, desire, thought, and decision. According to Mounce, "Plans are made in the *lēb* . . . and it is the place where commitments are determined, kept, or broken" (*Complete Expository Dictionary*, 327). Per Keil and Delitzsch: The heart is "the instrument of the thinking, willing, perceiving

A *protected* heart is not closed off or cold. It's honest and passionate. But it's also rational and prudent. Like we discussed in letter 6, a wise man protects his heart by keeping his mind and his heart in sync. That means, son, if you want to be healthy enough to climb the upright path of wisdom, then you need to take the necessary mental precautions to keep your heart strong.

One practical way you can do that, according to Solomon in v. 24, is to keep your mouth in check. Son, whether you realize it or not, the way you speak is an effective tool for measuring the orientation of your heart.[8] Your words carry great weight. They have the power to create or to destroy. So choose them carefully. Don't go around shooting your mouth off like some thoughtless idiot. And don't let your mouth serve as a pit of negativity and nonsense. Instead, prove yourself a wise man and keep your speech productive. Think before you speak. Know what you want to say *before* you say it. Take the time to consider the ramifications of your words. Formulate your thoughts with precision and ground your words in the truth.[9]

The truth is the source of your strength. It gives you the courage and the confidence to speak directly—with clarity and conviction, not with the kind of *guile* and *deceit* that define the speech of spineless men. You can

---

life of the spirit; it is the seat of the knowledge of self . . . it is the workshop of our individual spiritual and ethical form of life brought about by self-activity" (*Proverbs, Ecclesiastes, Song of Songs*, 83). I borrowed the term *irreducible primary* from Ayn Rand, who defines it this way: "an irreducible primary is a fact which cannot be analyzed (i.e., broken into components) or derived from antecedent facts" (*Philosophy: Who Needs It*, 13).

8. A man with a vibrant heart will speak warm and lively words. A man with a rotten heart, on the other hand, will speak prickly and sour words. Every man should strive to be precise in his speech because Jesus said we will each be judged by the words we use: "Either make the tree good and its fruit good, or make the tree bad and its fruit bad; for the tree is known by its fruit. You brood of vipers, how can you, being evil, speak what is good? For the mouth speaks out of that which fills the heart. The good man brings out of his good treasure what is good; and the evil man brings out of his evil treasure what is evil. But I tell you that every careless word that people speak, they shall give an accounting for it in the day of judgment. For by your words you will be justified, and by your words you will be condemned" (Matt 12:33–37). Van Leeuwen notes that the Hebrew term for *heart* is also translated as *mind* and is used "comprehensively to indicate the inner person, the 'I' that is the locus of a person's will, thought, and feeling. Thus all of a person's actions, *especially speech*, flow from the heart, expressing its content, whether good or bad" (*Introduction to Wisdom Literature*, 60, emphasis added).

9. Psychologist Jordan Peterson articulated the importance of speaking the truth quite well when he said: "If we lived in Truth; if we spoke the Truth—then we could walk with God once again, and respect ourselves, and others, and the world. Then we might treat ourselves like people we cared for. We might strive to set the world straight. We might orient it toward Heaven *[in an upright direction]*, where we would want people we cared for to dwell, instead of Hell, where our resentment and hatred would eternally sentence everyone" (*12 Rules for Life*, 58, emphasis added).

speak with the strong heart of a wise man when you let the truth serve as the foundation of everything you say. When you resolve yourself, as David did, to "Let the words of my mouth and the meditation of my heart be acceptable in Your sight, O LORD, my rock and my Redeemer" (Ps 19:14). If you truly are a mature man who's smart enough to make his own decisions, then the way you speak will bear that out.

Another way to keep your heart healthy is to live in a constant state of mental focus (4:25–27). You will prove yourself to be a trustworthy and responsible man when you learn to keep your eyes aimed in a forward direction at all times. Don't swivel your head from side to side and allow the flashy distractions of this world to kidnap your attention. Don't fixate your gaze behind you and let yesterday's setbacks keep you stuck in the past. Instead, *keep your eyes fixed straight in front of you*, as Solomon says, *and keep putting one foot in front of the other* as you move forward on the upright path of wisdom.

Son, that ideal life I spoke of earlier is within your reach as long as you have the heart to achieve it. You can keep your heart vibrant and pumping full of life when you resolve yourself to live every second of every day in an uncompromised state of mental focus. That means in every situation, whether you're alone in a quiet room or in a crowd full of noisy people, make the smart choice to keep your wits about you so you can *turn your foot from evil*.

Keep in mind, however, that even the best of men are men at best. No one is perfect. Every man, even great men like David and Solomon, make mistakes from time to time. When those times come, don't let your failures get the best of you.

Listen carefully to me here. I'm not telling you to ignore your sins like some kind of sociopath. Nor am I instructing you to wallow like a weakling in the tepid murk of self-pity. What I'm saying is: Don't let failure become a way of life. When you stumble and fall, own up to your error. Seek God's forgiveness. Repent of your sin. Get back on your feet. Clean up your mess. Make things right. Then learn from your blunders and move forward a stronger and wiser man.[10]

Don't let missteps stop you from achieving the destiny God has set before you. *Don't turn to the right or to the left* in an attempt to wimp out and find an easier path. Instead, prove yourself a man of strength and determination—a man of true heart—and keep your feet planted firmly on the way of wisdom.

---

10. David's behavior in the aftermath of his sin with Bathsheba serves as a good example how a man owns up to his mistake, accepts his discipline, and rebounds from a moral failure (2 Sam 11–12).

No matter how rocky that uphill path may get, God will *establish all your steps* as long as you have the heart to keep your aim high and keep your feet moving forward.

Son, God has given you a job to do—a destiny to fulfill.

The only way you will achieve your destiny is to grow into the man he created you to be. A man of wisdom and determination. A man of true heart.

It's your responsibility to do all the work necessary to become that man. But it's my job to help you get there. So if you ever find yourself in need of some support as you walk in the way of wisdom—if your legs ever get weak or your heart ever gets heavy—just keep your eyes and your ears on me. Pay attention to my example. Follow in my footsteps. Honor my teachings. Stick to the straight path of God's wisdom. I'll always be right there beside you to help you in every way that I can. And together you and I will climb that upright path.

We'll do it as a team. As father and son.

With every step you take, I want you to work hard and give God your very best effort. Protect your body and your mind. Prove yourself to be a man God can rely on to meet his responsibilities, and he will reward your effort with those sweet words every man wants to hear: "Well done, good and faithful servant. You have been faithful over a little; I will set you over much. Enter into the joy of your master" (Matt 25:21 ESV).

And when God blesses you with your greatest earthly responsibility—when he blesses you with a family of your own—you can pass these teachings on to your children and perpetuate our family's multi-generational tradition of living lives of godly wisdom.

Love,
Dad

Letter 9

Let's Have A Rational Talk About Sex

Prov 5:1–14; 6:20–35; 7:1–27; 9:13–18

"... *the right woman will open your heart to all that is good, while the wrong woman will tear your heart to shreds.*"

Son, you've reached the age where we can start having a reasonable talk about sex.

I want us to begin our talk by recognizing these two simple truths: Sex is a meaningful activity; therefore, sex is a good activity.

I say this with all confidence for two reasons:

1. God made all things, including sex. And everything God made exists to accomplish a specific purpose.
2. All that he made was *very good* in its original form (Gen 1:31). And everything remains *very good*—that is, *righteous* and *beneficial*—as long as it's done in accord with its original God-given purpose.

Sex as God designed it, therefore, is a healthy and necessary aspect of romantic human harmony. In fact, I would go so far as to say that sex is one of God's greatest gifts to humanity. But if we really want to make the most of this special gift, we must understand how to use it responsibly—that is, according to its purpose.

To understand its purpose, however, we must briefly discuss the basics of human nature. And once again, we'll use Adam and Eve as our example.

In the beginning, God formed Adam's body from the dust of the earth, like a potter fashions clay. He then breathed into Adam the divine *breath of life*, which installed the spirit, the life force, within the flesh and made the man a conscious being, "a living soul" (Gen 2:7 KJV).[1] God went on to fashion Eve from the body of the man and gave her life in the same way. Thus man and woman both function in the image of God as a partnership of flesh and spirit, of dust and the divine (Gen 1:27).

God designed men and women to fit together. To *complement* one another. Thus he built within us a certain physical and spiritual chemistry that fosters a natural desire for intimacy with each other. One of the natural ways men and women express that desire is through sexual intercourse (Gen 1:28; 2:24; Matt 19:5-6).[2]

God designed mankind as a whole to interact with each other in all kinds of healthy and organized ways. He instituted three specific social institutions to facilitate wide-ranging human harmony: the family, civil government, and the church. All three of these institutions fulfill a specified purpose within the created order. But for the purposes of this letter, I will focus only on the function of the family—specifically marriage and God's design for marriage and sex.

And make no mistake: Marriage and sex go hand-in-hand. God designed sexual intercourse to take place *exclusively* within the parameters of the marriage union. Any violation of this standard is an immoral violation of God's created order (Heb 13:4).[3]

Once again, I'll refer back to Adam and Eve to prove my point.

God instituted the family back in the garden of Eden when he joined the man and the woman together in the covenant of marriage:

> "[21]So the LORD God caused a deep sleep to fall upon the man, and he slept; then He took one of his ribs and closed up the flesh at that place. [22]The LORD God fashioned into a woman the rib which He had taken from the man, and brought her to the

---

1. The Hebrew word *rûaḥ* can mean both *breath*—as in air—and *spirit*—as in that which animates or gives life to the body. Mounce, *Complete Expository Dictionary*, 675-76.

2. As conscious and rational beings, men and women have a more dynamic sense of interpersonal relationships than any other creature—including spiritual beings (angels), seemingly, who are not given in marriage (Matt 22:30).

3. Solomon and I will examine this topic further in letter 10.

man. ²³The man said, 'This is now bone of my bones, and flesh of my flesh; she shall be called Woman, because she was taken out of Man.' ²⁴For this reason a man shall leave his father and his mother, and *be joined to his wife; and they shall become one flesh.* ²⁵And the man and his wife were both naked and were not ashamed.... ²⁷God created man in His own image, in the image of God He created him; male and female He created them. ²⁸God blessed them; and God said to them, '*Be fruitful and multiply*, and fill the earth, and subdue it; and rule over the fish of the sea and over the birds of the sky and over every living thing that moves on the earth.'" (Gen 2:21–25; 1:27–28, emphasis added)

Notice that it was only *after* God married Adam and Eve—after the man was *joined to his wife*—that he commanded them to have sex, to become *one flesh* and *reproduce*. Sex is morally good and productive, therefore, when it's performed in its proper context, which is within the God-ordained covenant of marriage between one man and one woman.

We also see from these verses that God designed sex to achieve two purposes within the marriage:

1. To create an intimate one-flesh union between husband and wife (Gen 2:24).
2. To facilitate the procreation of humanity (Gen 1:28).

Let's talk briefly about these two purposes in a bit more detail.

- *One-flesh union.* Marriage between one man and one woman is the most intimate relationship two people can share. Their mutual love for each other facilitates a *spiritual* union, while the physical act of sex creates a *bodily* union. Remember, God designed men and women to *complement* each other, to fit together in a spiritual and physical manner and thus form one complete and cohesive entity (Eph 5:28).[4] Sex is the means by which the man and woman unite in a physical way so as to consummate their spiritual union (Gen 2:24; Matt 19:6; Eph 5:31).

- *Procreation.* The other purpose for sex is the physical and spiritual *continuation* of humanity.[5] After God married Adam and Eve, he

---

4. Homosexuality is contrary to God's natural design and is thus sinful. Two people of the same gender do not complement each other spiritually or physically. And no matter how hard two men or two women may try, they will never form a proper one-flesh union because God did not design them to join together in a sexual way.

5. Once again, homosexuality cannot accomplish this purpose for marriage, as homosexual couples cannot naturally procreate. As for heterosexual couples who cannot conceive, the Bible tells us that God controls the womb (Gen 4:1; 29:31; 1 Sam 1:5; Job 31:15; Ps 127:3; 139:13–16). Thus their inability to conceive is a result of God's

blessed them and instructed them: "Be fruitful and multiply, and fill the earth, and subdue it" (Gen 1:28). The sexual union is, of course, the means by which children are conceived: The husband and wife join together as one flesh and produce offspring. But procreation has a deeper meaning than the mere physical perpetuation of humanity. Jesus has commissioned his followers to go forth and make disciples. To be fruitful and multiply *spiritually* as well as physically. The family unit is the most natural starting point for fulfilling that command. God has called husbands and wives to serve as fathers and mothers to the children they bear. Parents meet their responsibility to *be fruitful and multiply* on a spiritual level when they ground their children in biblical instruction and raise them up as disciples of Jesus Christ (Deut 6:4–9; Matt 28:19–20).

As you can see, God's design for sex is good and beneficial because it serves a *rational twofold purpose*. Fallen humanity, however, has a knack for perverting all that God made to be good. Sex is no exception.

Since Adam and Eve introduced the corruption of sin into God's *very good* world, men and women have developed a depraved sexual instinct, one that at times operates in direct opposition to God's created intention. With minds and bodies bent toward rebellion, humanity has a bad habit of taking God's original design for sex and stripping it of its benefit and purpose. The result is a perverted paradigm of human sexuality.

Son, as you make your way in the world, you're going to hear a lot of distorted ideas about sex. With the next two letters, Solomon and I will work to cut through the confusion and help you understand the responsible way—the biblical way—to think about sex.

In this letter, we'll show you that the best way to handle sexual temptation is to use your mind, not your body, to discern right from wrong in a romantic context. And as Solomon will explain in the following section, an active mind is the most effective weapon you can wield to combat the onslaught of sexual temptations.

---

sovereign decision for that individual couple, not the result of a mismatched anatomy.

WISDOM IS A MAN'S BEST WEAPON AGAINST SEXUAL TEMPTATION

Prov 5:1–2; 6:20–24; 7:1–5

Son, here's an old saying you should take to heart: Any man who thinks himself beyond sexual temptation considers himself more righteous than David, wiser than Solomon, and stronger than Samson.

As these three men unfortunately proved, even the best and wisest and strongest among us can fall victim to sexual sin.[6] That's because sensuality is a unique type of desire, one that has the ability to impair the better judgment of any man, no matter how grounded he is in his faith. Solomon knew this to be true. He *personally* understood how easily wisdom can be forgotten or brushed off, especially when it comes to physical attraction and romantic situations.

There's going to come a point when every father will have to sit down and have *the talk* with his son about sex. In Proverbs chapters 5, 6, and 7, Solomon has his own version of *the talk* with his son. And he starts it off by repeating a lesson that's as powerful as it is familiar: *Son, if you want to learn the truth about sex, don't listen to perverts and fools. Instead, listen to the two people who care about you the most: your parents. And be sure to take our words of wisdom with you wherever you go.*

Here are his words:

> "¹My son, give attention to my wisdom, incline your ear to my understanding; ²that you may observe discretion and your lips may reserve knowledge. . . . ²⁰My son, observe the commandment of your father and do not forsake the teaching of your mother; ²¹bind them continually on your heart; tie them around your neck. ²²When you walk about, they will guide you; when you sleep, they will watch over you; and when you awake, they will talk to you. ²³For the commandment is a lamp and the teaching is light; and reproofs for discipline are the way of life ²⁴to keep you from the evil woman, from the smooth tongue of the adulteress." (5:1–2; 6:20–24)

In these verses, Solomon instructs his son to take three specific actions to achieve victory in the battle against sexual temptation:

- *Observe discretion.* In every situation—but especially in romantic situations—you should always work hard to keep your wits about you. Use

---

6. Read about David's failure in 2 Sam 11–12, Solomon's failure in 1 Kgs 11, and Samson's failure in Judg 16.

that one-of-a-kind mind God gave you to make rational moral judgments. Let the wisdom of your mind, not the desires of your body, determine right from wrong.

- *Reserve knowledge.* Remember everything your mother and I have taught you. No matter where you are or who you're with, do the smart thing and *honor the commands of your father* and *never forsake the teachings of your mother.*

- *Bind our instructions continually on your heart.* Take your homegrown convictions wherever you go because "When you walk about, they will guide you; when you sleep, they will watch over you; and when you awake, they will talk to you" and keep your feet firmly planted on the right path (6:22).

In short, Solomon is calling on his son to remain true to the biblical convictions and values that have come to define his life. He reiterates this familiar lesson once again because he understood that any man who wants to protect his integrity must keep his priorities in order. And to do that, he must *always be thinking.* Foolishness can ruin a man and even cost him his life. That's why Solomon commands his son to utilize God's wisdom as his sword and his father's words as his shield to keep him safe from the *smooth tongue* of *the forbidden woman.*

Son, no man can fight the battle against temptation alone. Solomon affirmed this truth in Eccl 4:9–12, where he advocated the wise concept of *safety in numbers.* "Two are better than one, because they have a good reward for their toil. For if they fall, one will lift up his fellow. But woe to him who is alone when he falls and has not another to lift him up! Again, if two lie together, they keep warm, but how can one keep warm alone? And though a man might prevail against one who is alone, two will withstand him—a threefold cord is not quickly broken" (ESV).

Son, as I mentioned earlier, God made humans to be relational, not loners. The only way you will stand strong in those moments of temptation is if you have a reliable companion to watch your back. This makes the wise counsel of accountability partners a valuable asset in your life.

Remember, you can always count on my support. But I can't physically follow you around everywhere you go. There are going to be times when you will have to go out into the world alone, with only your wits and your convictions to guide your steps. In those moments, I encourage you, as Solomon does with his son, to rely on your most constant source of companionship for support: the ever-faithful (and ever-present) Lady Wisdom.

In Prov 7, Solomon promises his son that Lady Wisdom will accompany him wherever he goes. She will never abandon him. She will never fail him. And no matter the circumstance, she will always prove herself to be his most trustworthy source of support.

> "¹My son, keep my words and treasure up my commandments with you; ²keep my commandments and live; keep my teaching as the apple of your eye; ³bind them on your fingers; write them on the tablet of your heart. ⁴Say to wisdom, 'You are my sister,' and call insight your intimate friend, ⁵to keep you from the forbidden woman, from the adulteress with her smooth words." (7:1–5 ESV)

Son, like Solomon, I will encourage you again and again to join with Lady Wisdom and trust her to guide your behavior, especially when it comes to the more complex aspects of life like love and romance and sex.

Choosing the right woman is not a decision that should be made lightly. It requires a high level of discernment because the right woman will open your heart to all that is good, while the wrong woman will tear your heart to shreds. You must choose wisely, for the ramifications of your choice will spread deeply into the distant reaches of your future. The best way to differentiate the right woman from the wrong one is to judge each woman by her behavior and not just by her looks. That's why I'm instructing you, as Solomon does, to bond with Lady Wisdom. Grant her access to your mind. Give her control of your body. Allow her to help you judge between the sinful lust of a forbidden woman and the love of a godly wife.

We'll talk more about the godly wife in the next letter. For now, I want to teach you one of the most valuable lessons you will ever learn.

That lesson is: How to steer clear of the type of woman God says should remain off-limits.

AVOID THE FORBIDDEN WOMAN'S SEDUCTIVE SCAM

Prov 5:3–6; 9:13–18

Solomon has already warned his son against getting tangled up with the wrong kind of woman (2:16–19, letter 5).

But in Prov 5, he issues an even more explicit warning to his son to avoid the forbidden woman and her seductive scam.

> "³For the lips of an adulteress drip honey and smoother than oil is her speech; ⁴but in the end she is bitter as wormwood, sharp

as a two-edged sword. ⁵Her feet go down to death, her steps take hold of Sheol. ⁶She does not ponder the path of life; her ways are unstable, she does not know it." (5:3–6)

Remember when Solomon first mentioned this adulteress. He warned his son in Prov 2:17–19 to avoid the type of woman who "leaves the companion of her youth and forgets the covenant of her God; for her house sinks down to death and her tracks lead to the dead; none who go to her return again, nor do they reach the paths of life."

Just as Solomon uses Lady Wisdom as a literary device to personify God's wisdom, he likewise uses the forbidden woman, the *adulteress*, to personify temptation. Specifically sexual temptation. Notice how the forbidden woman stands in stark contrast to everything Lady Wisdom symbolizes. Lady Wisdom's demeanor is one of elegance and respect. Her companionship is designed to lift men up into the presence of God.

"A foolish woman," however, "is noisy." And unlike Lady Wisdom, "she is wanton and knows no shame . . .

> "¹⁴She sits at the door of her house, she takes a seat on the high places of the town, ¹⁵calling to those who pass by, who are going straight on their way, ¹⁶'Whoever is simple, let him turn in here!' And to him who is without sense she says, ¹⁷'Stolen water is sweet, and bread eaten in secret is pleasant.' ¹⁸But he does not know that the dead are there, that her guests are in the depths of Sheol." (9:13–18 RSV)

As Solomon makes clear in these verses, the forbidden woman is not someone you want to be around. Only men who *lack sense* cast their eyes in her direction and look to walk down the road to her house. She's a *noisy* seductress who *knows no shame*. To put it poetically, she's the type of woman who likes to sip *stolen water* in *secret* as she slow-dances with *dark spirits* in the *realm of the dead*. Every day God reaches out to her thirsty soul with an offer of mercy. To lift her up into the light. But every day she slaps his outstretched hand aside and instead pulls the cup of his wrath to her lips. Her lust for the cold touch of darkness has infected her spirit with a lingering madness, one that has caused her to mistake the pale shadows of the world for the shining light of paradise. In reality, the darkness is nothing but a gloomy cage. But to her, the gloom feels like home. It's become her world. Thus she possesses neither the will nor the desire to rid herself of its control.[7]

---

7. The book of Job describes this contradictory mindset in vivid detail: "Though evil is sweet in his mouth and he hides it under his tongue, though he desires it and will not let it go, but holds it in his mouth, yet his food in his stomach is changed to the venom

The three characteristics of the forbidden woman

Son this kind of woman doesn't exercise good judgment. She clearly doesn't respect herself. And if she doesn't respect herself, then she won't respect you either. The forbidden woman is a bad influence, plain and simple. And you must work extra hard to resist her seductive call. Such a woman, however, can oftentimes be difficult to spot. After all, no one can properly judge a person's character based exclusively on outward appearances.

Speaking of appearances, as I mentioned in letter 4, no other aspect of physical creation wields greater influence over a man's mind and body than the sight of an attractive woman. In romantic situations, the best way to tell if a woman is good for you or bad for you is to look beyond her pretty physical exterior and base your attraction on how she *acts*, not just on how she *looks*. Don't allow your eyes to settle upon her superficial flesh. Instead, look deeper. Observe her in total as body and spirit and judge her beauty by her behavior. Focus your gaze inward. Take a hard look at the intentions of her heart (and those of your own), because the aims of her heart will echo in her actions.[8]

Son, I won't lie to you. Looking beyond a woman's physical appearance is hard to do. But it can be done. In an effort to simplify this difficult process, Solomon took it upon himself to identify the three characteristics that define the forbidden woman's personality.

If you want to look beyond her external splendor and see her for who she truly is on the inside, then follow Solomon's instruction and keep an eye out for these three behavioral traits:

1. *The forbidden woman is untrustworthy*

Much like her appearance, the forbidden woman's words are shapely and smooth. Solomon says her lips *drip honey* and her speech is *smoother than*

---

of cobras within him. He swallows riches, but will vomit them up; God will expel them from his belly. He sucks the poison of cobras; the viper's tongue slays him. . . . Because he knew no quiet within him, he does not retain anything he desires. . . . When he fills his belly, God will send His fierce anger on him and will rain it on him while he is eating" (Job 20:12-23).

8. Examining the specific character traits of a godly woman would require its own separate volume. Here are just a few of the general behaviors to look for to discern a young woman's character: How healthy is her relationship with Jesus Christ? Does she treat her parents, her father in particular, with respect or ridicule? How does she treat children? Is she protective? Is she a hard worker? Does she love her church? Does she hold the word of God in high esteem? How does she treat people who are in need of grace? Who are the kinds of people she admires? How does she handle conflict with others? Etc.

oil. But behind those blood-red lips is a *bitter* tongue that's as sharp as any two-edged sword.

She may speak with sweet words and a flirty tone, but keep in mind that her tongue is a source of pain, not pleasure. And it's up to you to see beyond her empty affections and recognize that she is not who she makes herself out to be. Remember, she is an *adulteress*. Her heart belongs to the darkness. Thus her intentions for you are not love and respect, but the reckless indulgence of her darkest desires. She exists only to serve her own self-absorbed lusts, and she will say whatever she has to say to gratify them. And like the blade of a well-crafted dagger, the words she uses may appear clean and elegant, but they are also sharp and piercing and ultimately designed to draw blood and deal pain.

2. The forbidden woman is godless

The forbidden woman shows her disdain for the truth by betraying the covenant of her God (2:17). She has danced with the devil for so long that she has all but forgotten the warm touch of God's righteous hand. Her infatuation with depravity has ripped her conscience to shreds; and as a result, *she angles her feet toward death* and *her steps take hold of Sheol*.

No one in true fellowship with God walks on the downward path of the wicked. The forbidden woman's actions reveal that her relationship with God is phony. They prove that she does not respect God, herself, or the people she intends to manipulate. She may attempt to justify her actions by claiming to *follow her heart* or some other nonsensical rationale, but her heart is a haunted cavern that's aimed toward the realm of the dead. And as long as she follows her heart down that road to perdition, the spindly fingers of darkness will continue to tighten around her neck until they slowly choke the life out of her.

3. The forbidden woman acts on whims, not on principles

The forbidden woman doesn't think rationally. Like the bad influence that she is, she doesn't think ahead. And this makes her dangerous. She never takes the time to consider the direction her life is going. When Solomon said *she does not ponder the path of life*, he means she acts with no sense of rational judgment. She allows her emotional whims to govern her behavior. Thus if something, *anything*, pleases her—if it *feels* right—then, according to her cankered logic, it must be good.

Son, you must understand that whims are dangerous things. Whims are nothing more than superficial flights of fancy, arbitrary urges uncoupled from rationality or principle. Yet the forbidden woman allows her whims to function as her personal standard of morality.

Here is an example of her behavior: An impulse arises within her and spins her up with desire—but never does she pause to consider the cost of her behavior. She instead acts without thinking things through and suffers the obvious consequences of her bad choices. As a result, *her life is unstable and she doesn't know why.* Her soul is wayward. Her mind is adrift. And her behavior is erratic because she doesn't act with any long-range sense of purpose. Her only goal from moment to moment is *getting her way.* Thus she wanders from one bad situation to the next, from one man to the next, from one argument to the next, from one heartache to the next, and so on.

Her inconsistent lifestyle makes her spiritually unstable. And as long as she refuses to think beyond her own juvenile whims, she'll never figure out why her emotions are disordered and her life is overrun with chaos.

SENSELESSNESS AND SEDUCTION: A CAUTIONARY TALE

Prov 7:6–23

Solomon could impart such wisdom to his son regarding the inner workings of the forbidden woman because his keen eyes had witnessed her in action.

In Prov 7, Solomon recounts to his son a specific instance in which he observed a young man's senselessness and a forbidden woman's pattern of seduction. The story begins with Solomon standing at the window of his house one evening, watching a crowd of people on the street.

Until a certain young man caught his attention:

> "⁶For at the window of my house I looked out through my lattice, ⁷and I saw among the naive, and discerned among the youths a young man lacking sense, ⁸passing through the street near her corner; and he takes the way to her house, ⁹in the twilight, in the evening, in the middle of the night and in the darkness." (7:6–9)

Solomon watched the young man make his way toward *her* corner and take the road to *her* house. He saw him sneaking around under the fey cover of twilight, scrounging for someone *forbidden* to satisfy his sinful lust. It was at that point, when he saw where the young man was headed, that Solomon understood him to be *a young man lacking sense.*

He continues:

> "¹⁰And behold, a woman comes to meet him, dressed as a harlot and cunning of heart. ¹¹She is boisterous and rebellious, her feet do not remain at home; ¹²she is now in the streets, now in the squares, and lurks by every corner. ¹³So she seizes him and kisses him and with a brazen face she says to him: ¹⁴'I was due to offer peace offerings; today I have paid my vows. ¹⁵Therefore I have come out to meet you, to seek your presence earnestly, and I have found you. ¹⁶I have spread my couch with coverings, with colored linens of Egypt. ¹⁷I have sprinkled my bed with myrrh, aloes and cinnamon. ¹⁸Come, let us drink our fill of love until morning; let us delight ourselves with caresses. ¹⁹For my husband is not at home, he has gone on a long journey; ²⁰he has taken a bag of money with him, at the full moon he will come home.'" (7:10–20)

Solomon watched as the object of the young man's desire, a woman lacking self-respect and dressed like a prostitute, came out to meet the young man in the street. She was a married woman yet she grabbed the young man and kissed him there in the open street. With her smooth tongue she flattered his ego. And with her lips she enticed him into her bed.

> "²¹With much seductive speech she persuades him; with her smooth talk she compels him. ²²All at once he follows her, as an ox goes to the slaughter, or as a stag is caught fast ²³till an arrow pierces its liver; as a bird rushes into a snare; he does not know that it will cost him his life." (7:21–23 ESV)

Solomon said the woman was persistent in her pleading. After *much* seductive speech she persuaded the young man to come into her home. Perhaps the young man showed some hesitation because the notion of adultery pricked his conscience. Or more likely, he hesitated out of fear of her husband's vengeance should he ever find out. Whatever the case, after much flattering talk the young man made the conscious choice to indulge his whimsical urges and follow this forbidden woman inside, like a mindless beast heading to the slaughter.

Son, let's go over the details of this story and analyze the behavior of both people involved. Let's take a close look at the behavior of this forbidden woman and see how she acts in a real-world situation. We'll also take a hard look at the actions of the young man—because sometimes learning *what not to do* is just as important as learning *the right thing to do*.

As we do this, I want you to recall Solomon's three characteristics of the forbidden woman. Notice how this particular woman is the literal embodiment of those three characteristics.

1. This woman is untrustworthy

The woman's smooth words dripped like honey from her lips when she spoke to the young man as if he actually *meant something* to her: "I have come out to meet *you*, to seek *your* presence earnestly, and I have found *you*" (7:15, emphasis added).

Notice how many times she said the word *you* in that verse, how she stroked his ego and puffed up his self-esteem and thereby lowered his defenses. Such soft words are indeed appealing to a man's ears. But despite her alluring tone, any rational person can see that the young man ultimately means nothing to her. Her words are empty and *untrustworthy*. She doesn't love him. She loves the darkness. She loves her lusts. And she desires the young man only as long as she can use him to gratify her own emotional and physical whims.

Notice how she masks her sinister intentions with tender speech—she spoke of emotional and physical *love* in v. 18. But her words are nothing more than a clever disguise to cover her adulterous intentions. She is a married woman, yet *her feet do not remain at home*. Once upon a time she undoubtedly spoke with similar tenderness to her husband and made vows to forsake all others and remain loyal only to him. Yet here she is, betraying those vows and seeking out the affections of another man as soon as her husband has gone away *on a long journey*.

Son, a virtuous woman is trustworthy. She doesn't pierce her man's heart and bleed him dry. Nor does she manipulate his affections in an effort to use him like an object. The forbidden woman, however, does all of those things. And when she speaks her lies, she reveals her true self. She proves herself to be a woman whose only affection is for the dark cravings within her own wayward soul.

The young man is just as dishonest. He is hardly an innocent victim. Rather, he is an eager participant in this duet of deception. He has his own lies to tell—only the main target of his dishonesty is not a significant other. It's *his own mind*. He has tricked himself into believing two specific lies: (1) that fooling around with a married woman is a smart thing to do and (2) that he won't get caught, that he'll magically walk away from this illicit rendezvous without facing any consequences. The young man feasts on his self-deceptions until his mind grows bloated with delusion, to the point that he is no longer able to think clearly enough to weigh the cost of his actions.

2. This woman is godless

Remember Solomon's initial description of the forbidden woman. She is an adulteress who speaks smooth words. She forsakes the companion of her youth (in this case, her husband) and forgets the covenant of her God (2:17). After this forbidden woman came out to greet the young man with kisses and an embrace, she said *with a bold face*, "I was due to offer peace offerings; today I have paid my vows" (7:14).

The forbidden woman's reference to *offerings* and *paying her vows* shows that religion is a part of her life. But her devotion to God is insincere, as she uses her religion not as a means of worship, but as a way to accomplish her own self-centered goals (to manipulate appearances, to puff up her reputation, to take the edge off her guilt, etc.). Whatever her motives, she goes through the motions of faith; but in reality, her faith is a fraud and her relationship with God is all an act. She knows information about God, but she doesn't *know* God, nor is she *known* by God.[9] She's aware of God's commands, yet she makes the conscious choice to rebel. At some point she probably taste-tested the truth of his word. But the truth created such a rancid taste that she held God in contempt and vomited his wisdom from her mouth.

She's made the choice to remain hidebound in her *godlessness*. Yet she still invokes the name of God when it's convenient for her. To her, the name of God is just another card to play, another *thing* she can manipulate to *get her way* in any given circumstance. In this particular situation, this woman is willing to say whatever she has to say about *offerings* and *vows* to rationalize her immorality and convince herself and the young man that their mutual sin of adultery is justifiable.

Son, when it comes to romance and relationships, you'll learn quickly that talk is cheap. But God's grace is not. Jesus Christ is merciful and forgiving. But he will not be mocked. I am warning you: Never take God's mercy for granted and never use his hard-earned grace as an excuse to sin. Beware: Just because an attractive girl says she believes in God and goes to such-and-such church doesn't mean she has an authentic relationship with Jesus Christ. Nor does it mean her intentions for you are pure. Don't let physical desire cloud your spiritual judgment. Faith without works is a dead faith (Jas

---

9. See letter 2 for analysis of what it means to truly *know* God and to *be known* by God.

2:26). So judge the sincerity of a woman's heart for God and for you by her actions, not her words.

The young man is just as godless. Solomon doesn't make mention of the young man's attitude toward God, but his description of his behavior tells us all we need to know. The young man is too self-absorbed in his lust to even take God into consideration. Like the woman, any devotion he may claim for God is formless and void.

Notice how this fool is sneaking around and using the cover of darkness to camouflage his sin. Look at this poor soul: He's putting his faith in a delusion that tells him he can do whatever he wants and somehow get away with it. He actually seems to think he can keep his sin a secret from God and thus avoid his judgment. But what he doesn't realize is that his consequence-free notion of life is the real fantasy. On the flipside of that fantasy is an active reality in which God reigns supreme on an eternal throne of justice and righteousness. And when that Reality comes knocking, the young man will finally wake from his dreamlike state with a start and realize that his nighttime fantasies have morphed into a living nightmare.

3. This woman acts on whims, not on principles

Solomon describes this particular woman as *cunning of heart*, meaning that she operates with ulterior motives and uses deception to get what she wants out of people. Simply put, she doesn't take the time to stop, think, and make sound judgements. She makes bad choices because she allows her emotions, her *whims*, to govern her behavior. As Solomon says, she doesn't think ahead: "She does not ponder the path of life; her ways are unstable, she does not know it" (5:6).

Her refusal to stop and think makes her reckless. It fills her life with disarray. Just look at her irresponsible behavior here: She runs into a public street in a loud manner dressed like a prostitute, hugging and kissing on a man who is not her husband, in an attempt to lure him into having sex with her in the bed she shares with her husband who just happens to be out of town.

These are not the actions of a rational woman. Instead her actions prove that she has abandoned all sense of absolute truth and has instead adopted an attitude of moral relativism: *Wisdom is whatever works for me,* she seems to think. *I decide what's true. And my truth is whatever helps me get what I want when I want it.*

If deception facilitates her pleasure, then her lie is just as valid as any truth. If a superficial adherence to religious practices helps her sleep at night, then consider her well-rested. According to her subjective mentality, what's right or wrong changes with her whims. Her code of ethics is fluid, with *the good* being whatever satisfies her desire *at that moment*. And so long as she seeks validation in the reckless indulgence of her sinful lusts, chaos (and the frustration that comes with it) will be the only absolute in her life.

The young man is just as thoughtless. Rather than taking the time to stop and judge his own behavior, the young man likewise acts on the whims of his sinful lust. He knows exactly what his body wants to do. He knows just the type of woman he wants to do it with. He knows the particular woman he has his eye on is married. He knows her husband is away. And he knows precisely what his motives are as he's passing along the street near her corner, taking the road to her house. His mind is active—he's making willful choices—yet he is not really *thinking*. He has suspended his conscious mind and allowed the physical desires of his body to take control.

The woman's shallow flatteries have spun him up with desire. So he follows her willingly but mindlessly, "as an ox goes to the slaughter, or as a stag is caught fast till an arrow pierces its liver; as a bird rushes into a snare; he does not know that it will cost him his life" (7:22–23 ESV).

Just like an animal walking into an ambush, the young man thinks he has everything under control—that is, until the deathblow comes swiftly and quietly, unexpectedly yet assuredly.

LEAVE LUST IN THE DUST AND LET YOUR MIND TAKE THE LEAD

Prov 5:7–14; 6:25–35; 7:24–27

Son, as Solomon's story proves, people get into trouble when they don't think.

If you want to defeat sexual temptation, you need to keep your mind in charge of your body. An active mind makes wise choices. It cuts through all the phony posing people do and sees them for who they are. Not who they try to portray themselves to be and not who we want them to be, but for *who they truly are*.

Yes, the forbidden woman's outward appearance may be appealing. But on the inside, her spirit is corrosive, like acid. This combination makes her dangerous and deadly. Throughout these verses, Solomon has portrayed the forbidden woman as a devouring huntress looking to feast on the flesh of her prey. Any man in his right mind can see the need to stay away from such a woman, no matter how pretty she is. But, as is always the case with good-looking women, staying away from them is easier said than done.

The sensual sight and the delicate sounds of a forbidden woman, whether in person or on some screen, can easily overwhelm a man's senses and render his body a raging inferno of desire. And son, once your flesh is enflamed with passion, letting your mind take the lead is nearly an impossible task.

That fact applies to every man. *Every* man is susceptible to the power of sexual temptation. Remember David, Solomon, and Samson—no matter how righteous or wise or strong a man may be, sinful lust is a devilish flame that can consume even the mightiest of men and reduce his integrity to a pile of ashes.

Son, be aware that in spite of our *spiritual* rebirth in Jesus Christ, the *flesh* of all men still bears the curse of sin. The fallen blood of Adam still flows in our veins. And sexual passion is perhaps the one bodily appetite most corrupted by the fall of mankind. It is a persistent urge that must be constantly bridled, tamed, and channeled in the proper direction. And the best way to keep your physical desire in check is to keep your body and mind in sync.

Never disassociate your mind from your body—that is, never betray with your actions what you know with your mind to be true and good. Any man who compromises his principles for the sake of something superficial like bodily pleasure starts to behave less like a man and more like a dumb and primitive beast. He allows his unbridled lust to lead him by the loins down into the more toxic depths of his fallen nature, where life is nothing more than a pale and shadowy imitation of the real thing.

And the longer he gives himself over to that shadow, the more conditioned his mind becomes to the darkness that surrounds him.

Guard your integrity by getting out of there

Solomon says the best way to *stay out* of sexual trouble is to *stay away* from sexual trouble. Regarding the forbidden woman and the sexual temptation she personifies, Solomon issues another stern warning:

> "⁷Now then, my sons, listen to me and do not depart from the words of my mouth. ⁸*Keep your way far from her and do not go near the door of her house.* . . . ²⁴Now therefore, my sons, listen to me, and pay attention to the words of my mouth. ²⁵*Do not let your heart turn aside to her ways, do not stray into her paths.* ²⁶For many are the victims she has cast down, and numerous are all her slain. ²⁷Her house is the way to Sheol, descending to the chambers of death." (5:7–8; 7:24–27, emphasis added)

Son, as radical as it may sound, total avoidance—abstinence—is a simple yet powerful lust-deterring strategy that works every time. If you want to control your physical urges—if you want to keep your mind free and clear and keep your integrity intact—then stay far away from every form of sexual temptation: pornography, the wrong woman, and even the right woman in the wrong situation. Staying away from trouble keeps your mind (and not your libido) in charge. If you want to stay out of trouble, then follow Solomon's instruction and stay away from trouble.

Solomon was not the first man to advocate *abstinence* as a strategy. This tried and true method is as old as time itself. To prove my point, let's take a look back to the book of Genesis, the very first book of the Bible, and see how a wise young man named Joseph put this age-old principle of abstinence into practice.

In the land of Canaan, seventeen-year-old Joseph was his father's favorite son.[10] His older brothers grew jealous of Joseph and attacked him and sold him into slavery. He eventually ended up in Egypt as a slave to a man named Potiphar, an officer of the Pharaoh.

Even during his time as a slave, Joseph worked hard to maintain his integrity and his relationship with God. As a result: "The LORD was with Joseph, so he became a successful man. And he was in the house of his master, the Egyptian. Now his master saw that the LORD was with him and how the LORD caused all that he did to prosper in his hand. So Joseph found favor in his sight and became his personal servant; and he made him overseer over his house, and all that he owned he put in his charge. It came about that from the time he made him overseer in his house and over all that he owned, the LORD blessed the Egyptian's house on account of Joseph; thus the LORD's blessing was upon all that he owned, in the house and in the field" (Gen 39:2–5).

The Bible tells us that Joseph was a handsome man; and after a while of serving in Potiphar's house, his master's wife "looked with desire at Joseph" and tried to seduce him (Gen 39:7). She threw herself at him many times. Yet each time Joseph rebuffed her advances: "How then could I do this great evil and sin against God?" he would say to her (Gen 39:9). Yet she persisted in her seduction. Day after day she would plead with Joseph to have sex with her. And day after day, the virtuous Joseph answered with a resounding *NO!*

One day when Joseph went into Potiphar's house alone to do his work, Potiphar's wife "caught him by his garment, saying, 'Lie with me!' And he left his garment in her hand and *fled*, and went outside" (Gen 39:11–12, emphasis added).

---

10. See Gen 37–50 to read the full and fascinating story of Joseph.

Like the forbidden woman Solomon spoke of earlier, Potiphar's wife was loud and cunning with her adulterous intentions. She grabbed Joseph in the fullness of daylight and pleaded with him, her employee, to sleep with her in the house she shared with her husband. Unlike the young man in Solomon's scenario, however, Joseph's mind overruled his loins and he did what all men should do in those moments of sexual temptation.

He got out of there. And he did it quickly.

Son, I want you to understand this hard truth: A man has a limited amount of willpower. No matter how righteous or how wise or how strong he may be, sooner or later every man will give in to temptation if he relies solely on a finite resource like willpower.

Joseph was indeed a righteous man. But even he didn't put his trust in his willpower. Potiphar's wife approached Joseph when he was alone in an empty house and tried her best to seduce him. Her advances undoubtedly caught Joseph off guard. But notice how he handled himself. He didn't trust in his willpower. He didn't allow himself just a little touch or a little taste of this forbidden woman's fruit. He didn't waste time debating the pros and cons of sexual sin and adultery. He didn't worry about her feelings or his own coat.

He left his garment in her hand and fled out of the house, as the Bible says.

Joseph's story is a textbook example of how a wise young man can keep his head (and not his loins) in charge in a difficult sexual situation. Joseph followed his convictions rather than the desires of his flesh: "How then could I do this great evil and sin against God?" he said as Potiphar's wife attempted to seduce him.

He knew adultery was an evil practice. He understood that sleeping with his master's wife would result in all kinds of trouble, both with God and with his boss. So he stayed away from her. Even when Joseph was minding his own business and she followed him into the house and threw herself at him when he didn't expect it, he didn't give in. He didn't negotiate. He didn't compromise. He didn't rely on willpower. He just left. Quickly.

Son, removing yourself from a tempting situation removes the temptation. Plain and simple. So whenever you're tempted to go farther physically with a girl than you know you should, whenever you are tempted to look at something degrading, or whenever your mind starts to wander toward those darker corners of desire, think back on Solomon's instruction and Joseph's example.

Don't give in.

Don't negotiate.

Don't compromise.

Don't rely on willpower.

Just leave.

The simple act of removing yourself from the situation accomplishes two purposes:

Leaving frees your mind to think clearly

Son, lust is like a dense fog. Once it settles in over a man's mind, it clouds his judgment, imposes tunnel vision, and motivates him to use his hands to feel his way around. A mind that's stuck in the fog of sinful lust will never be able to make good choices. That's why Solomon warns his son regarding the forbidden woman: "Do not desire her beauty in your heart, and do not let her capture you with her eyelashes" (6:25 ESV).

His instruction here is twofold in its approach:

- Don't lust in your heart for her beauty. Learn to exercise self-control over your own body and its lustful urges. Pursue healthy desires and meaningful relationships, not harmful ones.
- Don't let her captivate you with her eyes. Don't be foolish enough to put yourself in a situation where you fall victim to the forbidden woman's seduction.

Solomon, the wisest of all men, understood the power lust wields over the mind of men. It hinders a man's ability to think. It darkens his view of reality and deforms his view of people—specifically women, as it strips them of their dignity and degrades them as objects that exist only to satisfy sexual desires. Such a mindset is destructive and dangerous. So heed Solomon's warning and keep your mind free from the fog of lust.

Remember, you are not a slave to the whims of your body. You are not an animal. You are a man with a mind unlike anything else on this planet—so use it. God has empowered your mind to overcome the more noxious urges of your sinful nature. Removing yourself from a tempting situation puts some distance between you and the source of your temptation. It gives you the space you need to think clearly and pay attention to the warnings coming from your *conscience*—that is, the homegrown voice of wisdom that divides right from wrong.

Son, in those moments of temptation, your conscience will act as a reliable watchman perched on the walls of your spirit, one that's ready to sound the alarm and take up arms when evil sets its siege. Your conscience will bring to mind my instructions and the truth of God's word. It will remind you of the convictions that govern your life and keep you faithful to the bond you share with Lady Wisdom.

Son, a clear mind is an invaluable weapon in the battle against temptation. So do whatever you need to do to remove yourself from a dangerous situation. To clear the fog of lust and let your brain, not your body, call the shots.

Leaving helps you to keep the consequences in mind

Son, understand this truth: Nothing—*nothing*—in life is free. Everything comes at a price.

And, according to Solomon, the cost of sexual sin is always steep:

> "[26][F]or a harlot may be hired for a loaf of bread, but an adulteress stalks a man's very life. [27]Can a man carry fire in his bosom and his clothes not be burned? [28]Or can one walk upon hot coals and his feet not be scorched? [29]So is he who goes in to his neighbor's wife; none who touches her will go unpunished." (6:26–29 RSV)

As Solomon points out, the cost may seem cheap on the surface—as cheap as a loaf of bread. But sexual sin always carries a heavier price than a man expects. Rest assured, a sexually immoral man will *always* pay a stiff price for his stupidity. In the heat of the moment, however, it's easy to push the thought of *consequences* out of your mind. It's only once you've removed yourself from the situation that you can more easily consider the dangers of sexual sin.

Son, there is no reward in toying around with the dark flame of lust. Whether it's with the mind using pornography or with the body of a forbidden woman, Solomon says there will always be consequences to sexual sin that result in disgrace and danger.

> "[30]Men do not despise a thief if he steals to satisfy himself when he is hungry; [31]but when he is found, he must repay sevenfold; he must give all the substance of his house. [32]The one who commits adultery with a woman is lacking sense; he who would destroy himself does it. [33]Wounds and disgrace he will find, and his reproach will not be blotted out. [34]For jealousy enrages a man, and he will not spare in the day of vengeance. [35]He will not accept any ransom, nor will he be satisfied though you give many gifts." (6:30–35)

This is Solomon's point: A man who steals food because he's starving is still a thief. No matter the reason, he broke the law and should pay the price for his crime. That being said, his crime, while indefensible, is somewhat understandable. The man was starving. He stole so he could eat and survive.

There is no understandable reason, however, to commit a sexual sin like adultery. There is no sympathy to be had for a man who fools around with another man's wife. "He who commits adultery has no sense," as Solomon says; "he who does it destroys himself" (6:32 RSV).

The thief stole food because a man needs to eat in order to live. In contrast—and I know this next statement is a sharp diversion from the sex-crazed mindset of our modern culture—a man does not need sex to live. Hunger and sexual desire are indeed both powerful physical urges. But only starvation will kill a man. Sexual starvation, on the other hand, may actually be good for some people.

A little bit of restraint never hurt anybody. But unchecked sexual urges always get men into trouble. As Solomon observes of the man who fools around with forbidden women: "Wounds and disgrace he will find, and his reproach will not be blotted out" (6:33).

There is no dignity for an adulterer. There is only scorn. And when—not *if*, but *when*—the woman's husband finds out, public scorn will be nothing compared to an enraged husband looking for revenge.

Son, the dangers involved with sexual sin are very, very real. Sinful lust is a spiritual blade that's sharp enough to carve out deep wounds within your heart. By his grace God can heal those wounds. But the scars of sexual sin will remain for a long time afterward as lingering reminders that yesterday's wounds were real and so was the pain that caused them.

Remember: Every choice has a consequence. Giving in to short-term sin always results in long-term pain.

Always.

So temper your lust and save yourself some heartache by keeping the cost of your actions in mind.

Son, your mind and your body belong to God.

So give the best of who you are to him—and not to people who don't care about you. Don't "give your vigor to others and your years to the cruel one." If you do, then "strangers will be filled with your strength and your hard-earned goods will go to the house of an alien; and you groan at your final end, when your flesh and body are consumed; and you say, 'How I have hated instruction! And my heart spurned reproof! I have not listened to the voice of my teachers, nor inclined my ear to my instructors! I was almost in utter ruin in the midst of the assembly and congregation'" (5:9–14).

Solomon's message here is simple: Don't waste your time and your effort on people who only want to bleed you dry.

Bad romances are like vampires. They clothe themselves in darkness and utilize seductive speech in an effort to satisfy their wicked lusts. But their smooth approach is nothing more than an elegant façade; and if you give these forbidden creatures of the night access to your mind and body, all you will be able to do is groan in agony as they slowly but surely drain the life out of you. And the most frightening part is: you won't even know it's happening.

Solomon repeatedly warns his son against getting involved with bad influences.[11] And I will reinforce his warning to you: If you choose to involve yourself with the forbidden woman, the *baddest* of bad influences, be prepared to get hurt. And no, those fleeting moments of bodily pleasure will never outshine the spiritual scars that she will most definitely leave behind. She *will* use you for all your worth; and when she's done with you, you'll be much worse off than you were before you met her. As you groan in pain, the only person you'll have to blame for your condition is yourself. And all you'll be able to do is ask yourself *How did I end up here, on the brink of utter ruin?*

Solomon did not want this future for his son and I do not want this future for you. Guard your integrity and stay away from the forbidden woman, son.

Stay far, far away.

Love,

Dad

---

11. We discuss the topic of bad influences in letters 3, 5, 8, and 10.

Letter 10

Earn Your Own Self-Respect on a Daily Basis

Prov 5:15–23; 6:1–19; 8:12–16; 9:1–9, 11–12

> "Son, a man also has just as much of a responsibility to treat himself with respect as he does other people."

Son, you are an *individual*, a living soul—and that fact alone means that you and your life are *valuable*.

To put it simply, your life is valuable because God himself values your life. He is your Creator and the source of all that is *you*. He made you to exist as a part of his world. He fearfully and wonderfully formed your inner parts and knitted you together in your mother's womb. But before he formed you on a physical level, he *knew* you on an intellectual level. From eternity past you existed in his mind; and before your conception, he had already consecrated your life with a divinely ordained destiny (Ps 139:13–16; Jer 1:5).

In short, God created you because he has a plan for you. Based on his own independent sovereignty—by his own *free choice*, not out of compulsion or need, but with authentic desire—God has called you forth for a purpose. And he forever solidified his decree when he created you to live as a reflection of his divine image. In his infinite wisdom, God, the ultimate Individual, shared his image, his *individuality*, with you.[1]

Son, you share my genetics, but it's your Heavenly Father's image that defines who you are. You and I are physically bound by blood, but you and he are unified in Spirit, and it's *that* eternal bond that motivates him to involve himself in every area of your life. From the moment of your conception until you draw your last breath on this physical plane, from the moment you enter the heavenly kingdom to the endless days of life everlasting, you are and forever will be precious in his sight.[2]

At the same time, however, it's my responsibility to remind you that while you are valuable, you are not *special*. You are a single individual in a world full of individuals. You bear the image of God in the same way every other human being does. Your life has the same intrinsic value (no more, no less) as everyone else. You have the same rights (no more, no fewer) as everyone else. Therefore, the same rules for living apply to you as they apply to everyone else. I tell you this not to discourage you, but to help you maintain a healthy perspective. That's one of my jobs as your father: to help you understand and appreciate your God-given value as an individual. Not so you can puff yourself up with self-absorbed vanity, but so you can take your life seriously and do the job God has put you on this earth to do. So you can achieve your destiny. So you can live with a proper sense of perspective, knowing that God Almighty has chosen you as his man for this time and this place.

Son, as we discussed in letter 7, God expects you to use the time he's given you on this earth to live a valuable life—a life worthy of bearing his

---

1. Bearing God's image is both an honor and a responsibility. His image bestows upon you the inviolate right to life—the right to achieve your God-given destiny and the right to live your life as a celebration of his glory. But it's also a job description. Bearing God's image means we are God's representatives on earth. According to biblical scholar Michael Heiser: "To be human is to image God. This is why Genesis 1:26–27 is followed by what theologians call the 'dominion mandate' in verse 28. The verse informs us that God intends us to be him on this planet. We are to create more imagers ('be fruitful and multiply . . . fill') in order to oversee the earth by stewarding its resources and harnessing them for the benefit of all human imagers ('subdue . . . rule over')." God, in his authority, issues decrees. Our job as his human imagers is to follow God's direction and make those decrees happen. To once again quote Michael Heiser, God "tells us what his will is and commands his loyal children to get the job done" (*The Unseen Realm*, 43, 52). Whatever our individual jobs may be, God has called all humans to do those jobs in a way that properly reflects his image—that is, his character.

2. Son, if you ever doubt God's affection for you, then cast your eyes no farther than the blood-stained cross of Christ. Look upon its gore and its glory and observe the depths of his love. Gaze upon that violent symbol of God's hard-earned victory over sin, death, and the devil. Then hopefully you will understand how uncompromising your God is in his devotion to preserving all that he deems valuable.

image. He has equipped you with everything you need to do your job. But in order to do your job well, there's one final character lesson you need to learn: You must know how to value yourself and your life as much as God does.

That is, you must learn how to properly *respect* yourself.

Self-respect is essential for achieving your God-given destiny. But like anything else of real and lasting value, if you want self-respect, you have to go out and earn it. With this final letter, Solomon and I will teach you how to go out into the world and earn self-respect.

Just as a man gets up and goes to work every day to earn a living, so you must likewise get up out of bed, walk out the door like a man, and earn your own self-respect on a daily basis.

And according to Solomon, the best way to do that is to develop three specific *self-oriented* character qualities.

THE THREE SELF-ORIENTED CHARACTER TRAITS OF A SELF-RESPECTING MAN

Prov 5:15–23; 6:1–19; 8:14–16; 9:1–12

A self-respecting man is self-controlled

Solomon spent the first half of Prov 5 warning his son to avoid the forbidden woman.[3] But in the second half of that chapter, he calls on his son to hold tight with all his heart, soul, mind, and strength to the most important woman he will ever love: the wife of his youth.

Here are his words:

> "[15]Drink water from your own cistern, flowing water from your own well. [16]Should your springs be scattered abroad, streams of water in the streets? [17]Let them be for yourself alone, and not for strangers with you. [18]Let your fountain be blessed, and rejoice in the wife of your youth, [19]a lovely deer, a graceful doe. Let her breasts fill you at all times with delight; be intoxicated always in her love." (5:15–19 ESV)

Solomon was a poetic kind of guy. He frequently used analogies and artistic devices in his writings to get his points across. In these verses, which serve as a good example of his poetic sensibilities, Solomon commands his son to "Drink water from your own cistern, flowing water from your own well" (5:15 ESV).

---

3. See letter 9.

A *cistern* is a container used to protect and preserve a supply of water. In this analogy, the cistern is a symbol of a husband's relationship with his wife and the blessed covenant of marriage they share. The cistern is significant as a symbol because it represents a sacred space designed to preserve and protect the waters of their love from the corruption of the outside world. The *springs of fresh and flowing water* within the cistern symbolize the intellectual, emotional, and physical affections a husband and wife show exclusively for each other. The purity of the water is a reference to the innocence of their romance, while the flowing motion indicates an active and vibrant love. This mutual love is the fountainhead of their marriage covenant—and if their relationship is to last, their love must remain undefiled. They must keep it *contained* within the boundaries of the cistern. After all, "Should your springs be scattered abroad, streams of water in the streets?" (5:16). In other words, Solomon asks his son a powerful question: *Is it wise to scatter your romantic affections throughout the dirty streets? Is it wise to surrender the purity of your heart, mind, and body to any random person who just happens to be wandering around in the public squares?*

The implied answer is obviously: *No*. Solomon makes clear to his son that the springs of his intimate affections are to be reserved solely for one special woman: the wife of his youth. "Drink water from *your own* cistern," he says, "flowing water from *your own* well. . . . Let them be *for yourself alone*, and *not for strangers* with you. Let your fountain be blessed, and rejoice *in the wife of your youth*, a lovely deer, a graceful doe. Let her breasts fill you at all times with delight; be intoxicated always in her love" (5:15–19 ESV, emphasis added).[4]

Son, as I mentioned in my previous letter, the sexual union is the most intimate connection a man and a woman can share. It is a taste of heaven. A special gift from God. Therefore, it must be "held in honor among all, and the marriage bed is to be *undefiled*; for fornicators and adulterers God will judge" (Heb 13:4, emphasis added).

---

4. As we discussed in letter 9, the husband and wife join together in body and in spirit—they become one flesh—through marriage. The husband, therefore, must love his wife just as he loves his own body because she is now in fact a part of his body. His affections for his wife are *his own* because, as Paul said, she is actually a part of him. "So husbands ought also to love their own wives as their own bodies. He who loves his own wife loves himself; for no one ever hated his own flesh, but nourishes and cherishes it, just as Christ also does the church, because we are members of His body. 'For this reason a man shall leave his father and mother and shall be joined to his wife, and the two shall become one flesh.' This mystery is great; but I am speaking with reference to Christ and the church. Nevertheless, each individual among you also is to love his own wife even as himself, and the wife must see to it that she respects her husband" (Eph 5:28–33).

Even as an unmarried man, you can maintain the purity of your marriage bed by saving your sexual affections for the wife of your youth. Your (future) marriage bed is a sacred space that God has entrusted to your care. It's your job as a man to guard its integrity and protect it from intruders, even during this pre-marital stage of your life. Don't invite the filth and the chaos of the city streets into your bed. Hold fast instead to your wife, even if you don't know her yet. Wait for God to bring her to you. And then, just like Adam and Eve in Eden, the two of you will come together as one flesh, naked and unashamed. God will reward your patience with a love that flows like a pure and mighty stream, and the fountains of your love will be forever blessed.

I know saving yourself for marriage seems like a tall order. But you can do it if you learn to master the art of self-control. The road to self-respect is paved with stones of self-control. And two aspects of your daily life that demand the strictest sense of self-control are the areas of romance and sexuality.

If you want God to bless your relational fountains, then you need to heed Solomon's words and learn how to let your mind control your body (and not vice-versa).

Let your mind, not your body, call the shots

Son, at the time of this writing you are a boy still somewhat tender in years and naive in outlook. But I must admit: You are quickly growing into a young man. Perhaps even more quickly than you realize. You are maturing in mind and body and you will soon develop all the natural inclinations that come along with manhood—including an appreciation for lovely women.

Don't worry. You're not guilty of any crime just because you think a woman is pretty. As I said in letters 4 and 9, that attraction is natural and good. God designed men to be attracted to women. A wise man, however, will exercise authority over his attractions, and he'll do so by allowing his mind, not his body, to guide his behavior.

A self-controlled man doesn't just *feel* his desires. He *thinks* about them rationally. He takes the time to understand *why* he's feeling what he's feeling. He considers his emotions with a sense of wisdom and thereby learns to recognize the difference between a healthy sexual attraction and the harm of sinful lust.[5]

---

5. I specify "sinful lust" because the Greek word often translated as "lust," *epithymeō*, can have both negative and positive connotations. According to Mounce, in its positive sense, *epithymeō* denotes the earnest longing for good things, like the desire of the prophets to see the messianic fulfillment of Jesus' ministry (Matt 13:17). Or Jesus' eager desire to eat the Passover with his disciples (Luke 22:15). As we'll see later on in this section, Matt

Let me explain the difference between the two. Sinful lust is a strong desire to take something (or someone) that does not belong to you. In the sexual sense, it's an unprincipled urge of the flesh that seeks to use a woman (one who is not your own) as a mere object of pleasure. A healthy attraction, on the other hand, reflects a man's rational and controlled appreciation of a woman's natural majesty—yet he never corrupts his appreciation by striving to partake of that which does not belong to him.

The man who asserts mental control over his bodily urges will learn to differentiate between love and sinful lust. And in the process, he will also learn to recognize the difference between a physically good-looking woman and a woman of true beauty.

Son, you must understand this fact: Plenty of women are good-looking. But not all women are beautiful. A forbidden woman can have an enticing appearance; but as we learned in letter 9, her looks are just a tantalizing veil that masks her corrosive spirit.

A woman of true beauty, however, is as lovely on the inside as she is on the outside. She's a balance of body and spirit—a melody of loveliness, integrity, strength, and grace. You'll know such a woman when you see her. Her physical beauty will catch your eye, but her spiritual beauty will take hold of your heart; and *together*, you will develop a sacred bond that is unique only to the two of you. When your relationship reaches maturity, she will share in your life (and you in hers) through marriage as the wife of your youth. You will cleave to her and the two of you will become one flesh. In her alone you will find the true meaning of pleasure as you spend your years exploring the vast labyrinth of her love. Her spirit and body will never fail to satisfy you. And in her, above all others, you will find lasting fulfillment all the days of your life.

The difference between the two is as simple as it is profound: Forbidden women come and go, but a godly wife is a gift from God that lasts forever (Prov 18:22; 19:14; 31:10–31).

Son, as you're reading this, I want you to understand that this woman, your future wife, is somewhere out there in the world right now.[6] But until

---

5:28 is an instance of the negative use of *epithymeō*. In that verse, Jesus is using *epithymeō* to denote sinful lust or covetousness—that is, desiring to have someone who is not your own. Mounce points out Paul's use of the term to highlight the difference between good desire and bad desire: "In Gal. 5:17, the term takes on a more refined theological meaning as Paul teaches the Galatians about the struggle between the flesh and the Spirit, explaining that the flesh 'lusts' (KJV) against or desires what is contrary to the Spirit, and the Spirit desires what is contrary to the flesh" (*Complete Expository Dictionary*, 172–73). I have used "sinful lust" throughout this letter to specify the negative connotation.

6. That is unless God has destined you to remain single. Marriage is most definitely one of God's greatest gifts to mankind. God has called on some people, however, to remain single and celibate. Those people who possess this gift are happy and productive

God decides you are ready to receive her, you must commit yourself to controlling your romantic urges.

As you get older, those urges will come on stronger and more often than you'd like. But you must stand firm and overcome their temptation because your future wife deserves *the best* of who you are, not the hollowed-out leftovers of some shell of a man. She is worth waiting for, worth *saving yourself* for, so don't make the mistake of giving your body over to some forbidden woman who only wants to kick your heart around in the dirt. As Solomon asks his son: Why temporarily embrace the breast of a stranger when you can live forever, heart-to-heart and skin-to-skin, with a dignified woman who will set your life on high?

That being said, as an unmarried man you must be prepared to wait for the right woman to come along. Believe me, I understand how lonely the romantic scene can be for a young man. Loneliness is a tough emotion to deal with. Most people, even the most cantankerous curmudgeons, want someone to connect with on a romantic level.[7] Such feelings are natural and God-given. But son, no matter how intense those relational urges get, you must never compromise your integrity in an attempt to satisfy them.

When it comes to finding the right woman, be sure to avoid the short-sighted cycle of destructive dating. Destructive dating is an irrational process, one designed to find a woman to meet your lusts, not share your love.

In practice it looks something like this:

- A romantic desire arises within a man.[8]
- A man lacking self-control will seek to satisfy his desire in the quickest and most convenient way possible.
- He'll then go body-shopping for some woman (any woman, usually the first one available, even one on a two-dimensional screen) who can best satisfy his sinful lust.
- When he gets what he wants from her, he'll toss her aside and move on to the next woman and repeat the cycle.

Sinful lust is indeed a powerful urge. It's like a spiritual narcotic that promises the highest of highs; but if you indulge it, it will do what any illicit drug does: poison your body, corrupt your mind, and destroy your life. Any

---

in their singleness. The Apostle Paul addresses this topic in 1 Cor 7.

7. I say *most people* because, again, God has called some people to singleness. See the previous footnote.

8. Both men and women are capable of being motivated by physical and emotional lust. But since you are a male, I have chosen to address this topic from a male-centered perspective.

man, even a professed believer, who's tripping on sinful lust will eventually come to act as if God and his moral standards are non-existent in the areas of romance and sexuality—rendering him, in effect, a sexual atheist.

Son, God is very real, and his authority extends into every area of your life, even the most intimate ones like love, romance, and sexuality. If you want a healthy and productive love-life, then learn to exercise self-control over your romantic feelings.

Remember, when it comes to romance, you should drink from your own cistern, not the town water fountain. That means you don't go out with any ol' girl just to be going out with someone. Don't settle for the first girl who's willing or available just to avoid loneliness or to have someone to hook up with. Don't yoke yourself to spiritual strangers and don't get emotionally invested in a relationship with a woman who doesn't share your godly values or live by biblical principles.[9]

The destructive dating process (as outlined above) will only serve to waste your time—and even worse, break your heart. Don't toss your heart into the streets where strangers can trample on it and kick it around like dirt. Use some of that good moral judgment we talked about in letter 9 and be discerning with your affections. When it comes to your romantic attractions, think rationally and understand *why* you're attracted to a certain girl. Are you only interested in using her body to satisfy sinful desires? Or are you interested in connecting with her on a physical *and* a spiritual level in a way that honors God and keeps your integrity intact?

Be careful when it comes to sharing your physical affections. God gave them to *you* to share with the wife of your youth and none other. He expects you to keep them clean and use them wisely. You can do that by dedicating yourself to living in-step with God's commands and trusting in him to bring a wise and beautiful woman across your path when the time is right. Even if it means exercising great self-control, you need to stand firm in your conviction to share your heart and your body with a godly woman—not with strangers who don't share your moral values.

I want you also to be aware that the battle against lust is not just a physical one. Sinful lust has more layers than just physical sex with real-world forbidden women. There's also a mental element to sinful lust, so you're going to have to learn to control your mind as well as your body. Jesus said

---

9. A Christian has no business engaging in a romantic relationship with a non-Christian. Heed Paul's warning: "Do not be bound together with unbelievers;" especially in a romantic sense, "for what partnership have righteousness and lawlessness, or what fellowship has light with darkness? Or what harmony has Christ with Belial, or what has a believer in common with an unbeliever? Or what agreement has the temple of God with idols?" (2 Cor 6:14–16). The implied answer to all of these questions is: *none*.

any man "who looks at a woman with lust for her has already committed adultery with her in his heart" (Matt 5:28). Here Jesus is not condemning a man for being naturally attracted to a pretty woman. He's speaking out against the man with an undisciplined mind, one that's overrun with covetous intentions to partake of someone who is not his own.

Solomon likewise warns his son to keep his affections pure by keeping his mind out of the gutter:

> "[20]For why should you, my son, be exhilarated with an adulteress and embrace the bosom of a foreigner? [21]For the ways of a man are before the eyes of the LORD, and He watches all his paths. [22]His own iniquities will capture the wicked, and he will be held with the cords of his sin. [23]He will die for lack of instruction, *and in the greatness of his folly* he will go astray." (5:20-23, emphasis added)

The man who fails to exercise discipline over his own mind is a man destined to commit *great folly*. Simply put, an undisciplined mind leads to stupid behavior. And stupid behavior always gets a man in trouble. Like Solomon says, a foolish and undisciplined man will eventually find himself trapped in the cords of his own stupidity—like a hapless fly who's gotten himself twisted up in a black widow's silky web of horror.

Sexual foolishness (like looking at pornography, for instance) facilitates this mental imprisonment, so don't poison your mind with the venom of empty smut. Don't disrespect yourself by getting high on the lust of your flesh. And don't disrespect women by treating them as props to populate your own self-centered illusions of pleasure. Again, you're not wrong or weird for being sexually attracted to girls. But a gentleman must not allow himself to desire a woman's body at the expense of her spirit. And no man can gratify his sinful flesh without corroding a tiny part of his own soul in the process.

As I mentioned in letter 9, the fallen world promotes a distorted form of sexuality. So be mindful about what you allow to pass before your eyes. The battle against lust begins in the mind. Be careful of the ideas and the images you allow into your head.[10] If you learn to control the direction of your thoughts, you will gain more control over the urges of your body.

And you will earn self-respect in the process.

---

10. The father in Cormac McCarthy's novel, *The Road*, summed this idea up best: "'Just remember that the things you put into your head are there forever,' he said (to his son). 'You might want to think about that.' 'You forget some things, don't you?' (the son replied). 'Yes. You forget what you want to remember and you remember what you want to forget.'" As a writer, McCarthy is notorious for using very few marks of punctuation. I added them in this quote so as to establish the context and keep the speakers distinct (*The Road*, 11).

A self-respecting man is self-interested

Son, a man also has just as much of a responsibility to treat himself with respect as he does other people. In Prov 6, Solomon reiterates that point by teaching his son the following lesson: A man earns self-respect when he works hard to preserve the sanctity of his own self-interest.

> "¹My son, if you have put up security for your neighbor, have given your pledge for a stranger, ²if you are snared in the words of your mouth, caught in the words of your mouth, ³then do this, my son, and save yourself, for you have come into the hand of your neighbor: go, hasten, and plead urgently with your neighbor. ⁴Give your eyes no sleep and your eyelids no slumber; ⁵save yourself like a gazelle from the hand of the hunter, like a bird from the hand of the fowler." (6:1–5 ESV)

Here, Solomon warns his son against two self-defeating practices:

- *Putting up security for a neighbor.* That is, promising to pay a friend's debts.
- *Making a pledge to a stranger.* That is, obligating himself financially (or otherwise) to someone he doesn't know.

Regarding these practices, he instructs his son in this way: *Son, if you have agreed to help your neighbor, or if you have entered into an agreement with a stranger, if you are snared in the words of your mouth, then you are bound by your word. You must fulfill your end of the contract. Give your eyes no sleep, however, and do not rest until you have kept your end of the bargain and freed yourself from all your debts and obligations.*

Son, the deep waters of debt can be tricky to navigate, even for the smartest of people. I suggest you avoid them as much as possible. But if you find yourself in a position where you have given your word or pledged your services to someone, be it your friend or a stranger, the best thing to do is see the job through to completion. Do not rest until you have followed through on your promises and fulfilled all your obligations. Keep Solomon's instruction and do not harm people by violating your contractual commitments. Be a man of your word and earn a trustworthy reputation as someone who honors his responsibilities.

But Solomon's instruction does not end here—in fact, he's just getting started. A deeper reading of these verses reveals Solomon's advocacy of the concept of *rational self-interest*, which refers to a man's rational regard for his own personal responsibilities. A man of rational self-interest understands that he alone is responsible for living his life. Such a man earns self-respect when he acts with self-reliance—when he meets his responsibilities with dignity and sustains his life by his own mind and his own work.

In these verses, while Solomon encourages his son to pay off his debts in full, his deeper lesson is to avoid indebtedness altogether.[11] Notice the grave tone Solomon takes at the idea of his son subordinating himself unnecessarily to someone else: if you have been "*snared* in the words of your mouth . . . *save* yourself . . . Give your eyes *no sleep* . . . *save yourself* like a gazelle from the hand of the *hunter*, like a bird from the hand of the *fowler*" (6:2–5 ESV, emphasis added).

He compares the man who takes on unwise obligations to an animal trapped in the merciless snare of a hunter. Thus he portrays foolish debt as a first step on the dangerous path toward moral compromise, since a man in debt must sacrifice his own needs and his own effort in order to produce for someone else.

Son, I will warn you as Solomon did his son: Give neither a friend nor a stranger undue authority over you and the fruits of your labor. I'll also encourage you to heed the words of another wise man, the Apostle Paul: "Owe nothing to anyone except to love one another; for he who loves his neighbor has fulfilled the law" (Rom 13:8).

God commands you to *love* your neighbor, not to subordinate yourself to him. You do not have a moral duty to jeopardize your own rational self-interest for anyone else's benefit. So don't unwisely put yourself on the hook for someone else. Be wise and be discerning to whom you pledge your time and your effort and your money.

Don't misunderstand me. There's nothing wrong with sharing or helping someone who legitimately needs help. In fact, God said a wise man will "look not only to his own interests, but also to the interests of others" (Phil 2:4 ESV). But a wise man cannot serve God if he refuses to be accountable with his own life. Nor can he be a helpful friend if he isn't first responsible with his own interests.

As Solomon will explain, God has called on you, son, to be wise first for yourself and for the benefit of your own household. After all, you can't properly interact with your neighbor and fulfill God's law until you've put your own home in order first. If you want to keep the two greatest commands to love God first and foremost and love your neighbor as you love yourself, then you must maintain your own self-interests. You must first nurture and protect your own life as well as those people and things God has put under your authority.

---

11. Regarding the danger of debt, Solomon issues this warning in Prov 22:7: "The rich rules over the poor, and the borrower becomes the lender's slave."

Acting rationally on behalf of your own self-interest and for your own benefit is not greed—it's *morally responsible* behavior. A self-respecting man *must* be a self-interested man. He has a moral obligation to value his own life just as much as God does. He must support his own life by his own effort and trust in others to do the same for themselves.

To highlight this point, Solomon points his son back to the example of Lady Wisdom.

> "¹Wisdom has built her house, she has hewn out her seven pillars; ²she has prepared her food, she has mixed her wine; she has also set her table; ³she has sent out her maidens, she calls from the tops of the heights of the city: ⁴'Whoever is naive, let him turn in here!' To him who lacks understanding she says, ⁵'Come, eat of my food and drink of the wine I have mixed. ⁶Forsake your folly and live, and proceed in the way of understanding.' ⁷He who corrects a scoffer gets dishonor for himself, and he who reproves a wicked man gets insults for himself. ⁸Do not reprove a scoffer, or he will hate you, reprove a wise man and he will love you. ⁹Give instruction to a wise man and he will be still wiser, teach a righteous man and he will increase his learning. ¹⁰The fear of the LORD is the beginning of wisdom, and the knowledge of the Holy One is understanding. ¹¹For by me your days will be multiplied, and years of life will be added to you. ¹²*If you are wise, you are wise for yourself, and if you scoff, you alone will bear it.*" (9:1–12, emphasis added)

In these verses Solomon portrays Lady Wisdom as a self-reliant woman. Rather than waiting around for someone else to do her work for her, she meets her own responsibilities by the skill of her mind and the sweat of her brow. Notice how she takes care of her self-interests—her own home—in full *before* she extends help to her neighbors. First, she builds her own house. She prepares her own meat. She mixes her own drink. And she sets her own table. *Then* she invites others to "Come, eat of my food and drink the wine I have mixed" (9:5).

Like Lady Wisdom, a wise man will also strive to be self-reliant.[12] He will work hard to meet his own needs and establish his own home first and in full before he involves himself in the lives of others.

He is not one of the immature men, the mockers, or the wicked men that Lady Wisdom speaks out against in vv. 4–8. These are the types of men who scoff at Wisdom's call for personal responsibility. They are schemers and deadbeats who shirk their responsibilities. As we'll see later on in this

---

12. See letter 7 for my analysis of what it means to be self-reliant.

letter, they are the type of people Solomon refers to as *worthless* men. Rather than work hard to meet their personal responsibilities, these moochers choose instead to value comfort and relaxation over self-respect. And as we discussed in letters 4 and 7, God will recompense their laziness with the one single wage they have managed to earn: the just penalties that come with living idle and meaningless lives.

We'll discuss the pitfalls of laziness in the next section. Right now, I want you to understand this point: You have the right to freely associate with any person you choose. Likewise, you are free to avoid anyone or any situation you judge to be harmful. Trade value for value with men and women you trust and respect. Don't waste your time with worthless people, with looters who pervert the concept of justice or moochers who scoff at the notion of self-respect. Once you involve yourself with such people, they will only serve to squander your effort and your time and your resources.

Always remember that you are under no moral obligation to harm your personal integrity for your neighbor's sake. God has not called on you to compromise your self-respect for the sake of someone else. He has, however, called on you to gain insight, to get wisdom and reap her rewards: "If you are wise, you are wise *for yourself*, and if you scoff" at the idea of meeting your own responsibilities, "*you alone* will bear it" (9:12, emphasis added).

Son, Solomon and I are calling on you to be a man of rational self-interest. Give of yourself for the right reasons—for virtuous endeavors that bring about good and worthwhile rewards for everyone. Including you. Before you pledge your support to anyone, take your own self-interests into consideration. Follow Solomon's instruction and *be wise for yourself*. Take your values, your principles, your relationships, your responsibilities, your reputation, and your possessions into consideration before you obligate yourself to anyone. God has given you many blessings with the expectation that you will be a good steward over all he has given you.

Remember: You don't exist for the sake of your neighbor. Your life belongs to God and you exist primarily to love and serve him. One of the best ways to serve God is to *love yourself just as much as* you love your neighbor (Mark 12:31).

That means you never compromise your rational self-interest for the sake of your neighbor. Nor do you act as a bad influence and ask your neighbor to compromise his rational self-interest for your sake.

A self-respecting man is self-governing

In this next section of verses, Solomon warns his son against the pitfalls of laziness. He points him to the example of the ant, one of the hardest-working members of the insect kingdom, to teach him about the daily benefits of a self-governing work ethic.

> "⁶Go to the ant, O sluggard, observe her ways and be wise, ⁷which, having no chief, officer or ruler, ⁸prepares her food in the summer and gathers her provisions in the harvest. ⁹How long will you lie down, O sluggard? When will you arise from your sleep? ¹⁰'A little sleep, a little slumber, a little folding of the hands to rest'— ¹¹your poverty will come in like a vagabond and your need like an armed man." (6:6–11)

Notice the ant's behavior and contrast her wisdom with the sluggard's foolishness. The ant has no need for a supervisor to direct her actions because she is *self-governing*. And although she is part of a colony, she works independently, without the oversight of a superior to tell her what she needs to do. On her own initiative, she prepares her provisions in the summer and gathers her food in the harvest.

The ant is an insect with a brain that's far inferior to the human mind. Yet even she instinctively understands that it's her responsibility to provide for herself. Like we discussed in letter 7, she lives a focused and goal-oriented lifestyle; and by her self-reliant work, she sustains her life and fulfills her God-given function as an ant.

The sluggard, meanwhile, is a man who has his own set of responsibilities—yet he refuses to put forth the effort to meet them in full. He is a lazy man who spends the better part of his day lying around rather than working for a living. Solomon says this guy's top priorities are *a little sleep, a little slumber, a little folding of the hands to rest*. Unlike the ant, he refuses to get up and do the things necessary to even meet his own needs. And in this way, he acts with self-contempt rather than self-respect.

The sluggard has the ability to work, but he lacks the grit to be self-reliant. He lacks the fortitude to produce and provide. He would rather subordinate himself to the cold chains of poverty than go out and get a productive job and make something of himself. He has made the conscious choice to evade his daily God-given call to sustain his existence and actually live his life—to think, to grow, to work, and to produce. As a result of his foolish choices, *want* and *need* will come upon him like armed bandits and rob him of what little he has managed to accumulate.

Son, your life belongs to your Creator. You and your life are the effect of God's productive work. But in his sovereignty and wisdom, God has given you volitional control over your mind and your body. He has entrusted the responsibility of governing your life to you—and the most effective way to make the most of your life is to govern yourself according to the counsel of Lady Wisdom.

> "^{14}Counsel is mine and sound wisdom," she says. "I am understanding, power is mine. ^{15}By me kings reign, and rulers decree justice. ^{16}By me princes rule, and nobles, all who judge rightly."
> (8:14–16)

Son, if Lady Wisdom empowers kings and judges to govern with justice and righteousness, she will likewise provide you with all the understanding you need to govern yourself. God has furnished you with all the mental and physical tools you need to not only sustain your life but to excel at life. It's never your neighbor's responsibility to live your life for you, so never outsource your God-given daily responsibilities to others. Such laziness is demeaning and destructive to your spirit and to your reputation.

You are responsible for your own well-being. That means it's up to you to govern yourself and to meet your own daily needs. Be a man and earn your keep. Use the skill of your mind and the sweat of your brow to work hard to keep the two greatest commands. Honor God by working with integrity. Love your neighbor by producing useful services. And respect yourself by being self-reliant and providing for your family like a real man.

Son, if you live your life this way—as a self-controlled, self-interested, and self-governing man—you will most certainly create a meaningful life for yourself. Just as we discussed in letter 7, you will savor the sweet taste of genuine pride on a daily basis when you do the work necessary to fulfill your God-given destiny.

Be aware, though, that not every man will taste that kind of success. The sad truth is, some men aren't willing to do the work necessary to put their lives to good use. These are men who'd rather shirk their responsibilities than put in a hard day's work, men who'd rather waste their time chasing phantom pleasures than achieving their God-given destinies. Solomon describes these kinds of men as *worthless* because they don't strive to achieve anything of real value. They just wander around from one place to the next mooching off the goodwill of others and making trouble—that is, until God decides he's had enough of their wanton rebellion and brings them face-to-face with the consequences of their own bad choices.

In the next section, Solomon and I will examine the behavior of the worthless man in greater detail. And in so doing, we'll use him as an example of the kind of man you *don't* want to be.

DON'T LIVE A WORTHLESS LIFE

Prov 6:12–19; 8:12–13

Son, understand that God designed every aspect of creation to achieve a specific purpose.

He structured the universe and its inhabitants to operate in an orderly manner, with the expectation that all creation would function in a way that is consistent with the character of our Creator: ordered, productive, righteous, and just.

As we discussed earlier, God has given mankind the privilege of bearing his image. He's given us dominion over his creation and the authority to rule as he does—as his holy regents on the earth (Gen 1:26–31). That means in everything that we do, we are to reflect the character of God. We are to be holy as he is holy, to be perfect as our Heavenly Father is perfect (Lev 19:2; Matt 5:48).

To properly carry out our divine duties, God has given us the ability to think far above every other earthly creature. He has equipped us with minds capable of observing the natural world and understanding the natural law that governs it. It's our God-given ability to think, to *reason*, that enables us to understand the objective difference between *good behavior*—behavior that's natural and prosperous—and *bad behavior*—behavior that's unnatural and unproductive.

Remember: God acted of his own free will when he breathed life into humanity. He acted with wisdom when he put good rules in place and gave us a good purpose to serve.[13] He expects us as his image bearers to follow his lead. He expects us to use our God-given free will to reject *the bad* and act in accord with *the good*—that is, to live productive lives by operating within the rules that govern the reality in which we live.[14] To act on *the good* is to do

---

13. The rules are good not just because they're the rules. They're good because they reflect the good character of God.

14. Scholar Michael Heiser also makes the following noteworthy point regarding free will and its relation to bearing the image of God: Humanity's God-given directive "was to multiply, steward the creation, and govern on God's behalf. The goal was to care for the earth and harness its gifts for the betterment of fellow human imagers, all the while enjoying the presence of God." Heiser goes on to note that humans reflect the image of God "by means of a spectrum of abilities we have as humans. These abilities are

our job successfully, which is to reflect the image of our Creator and thus accomplish our created purpose. To act in accord with our created purpose is to act with righteousness. To fail to achieve this purpose—to *miss the target*, in a literal sense—is to sin.[15] Such rebellion introduces unrighteousness and corruption into God's "very good" creation. It also introduces disorder and trouble into our own personal lives.

God has armed his imagers with all the tools we need to carry out his decrees. Some men, however, use their God-given free will to reject their Creator.[16] They want no part of God or his commands, so they ignore the call to reflect his character. They reject their created purpose. They abandon their God-given responsibilities. They turn their backs on their destinies and leave them to wither. Thus their lives are devoid of meaning because they accomplish no real goals; and as a result, God curses them with a disordered and frustrating existence. One that's empty and doomed for failure.

Solomon has a specific word he uses to describe these kinds of men and the behaviors that define their lives.

His adjective of choice is: *worthless*.

> "[12]A worthless person, a wicked man, is the one who walks with a perverse mouth, [13]who winks with his eyes, who signals with his feet, who points with his fingers; [14]who with perversity in his

---

part of our being like God. They are attributes we share with God, such as intelligence and creativity. The attributes God shared with us are the means to imaging, not the image status itself.... One of these attributes is freedom—free will that reveals itself in decision making. If humanity had not been created with genuine freedom, representation of God would have been impossible. Humans would not mirror their Maker. They could not accurately *image* him. God is no robot. We are reflections of a free Being, not a cosmic automaton.... Representation of God as his imagers and possession of free will are inextricably related" (*The Unseen Realm*, 59).

15. According to Mounce, the literal definition of sin is *to miss the mark*, or *to fail to achieve an established goal* (*Complete Expository Dictionary*, 655–56).

16. The apocryphal book of 2 Esdras effectively describes the rebellious nature of wicked men and the divine justice that awaits them: "Let many perish who are now living, rather than that the law of God which is set before them be disregarded! For God strictly commanded those who came into the world, when they came, what they should do to live, and what they should observe to avoid punishment. Nevertheless they were not obedient, and spoke against him; they devised for themselves vain thoughts, and proposed to themselves wicked frauds; they even declared that the Most High does not exist, and they ignored his ways! They scorned his law, and denied his covenants; they have been unfaithful to his statutes, and have not performed his works. Therefore, Ezra, *empty things are for the empty, and full things are for the full*" (2 Esd 7:20–24 RSV, emphasis added). Also see Wis 15:10–11 regarding the fate of the worthless man: "His heart is ashes, his hope is cheaper than dirt, and his life is of less worth than clay, because he failed to know the one who formed him and inspired him with an active soul and breathed into him a living spirit" (RSV).

heart continually devises evil, who spreads strife. ¹⁵Therefore his calamity will come suddenly; instantly he will be broken and there will be no healing." (6:12–15)

To be clear: Solomon is not describing a man with a godly heart who tries to accomplish good but stumbles in his effort. Rather, Solomon identifies a man as *worthless* based on the empty behavior that has come to define his life. And he is correct in his judgement. Such actions are of no value—they serve no rational purpose in the structure of God's world. The logical destiny for any man who acts this way is failure. As David said, "the worthless, every one of them will be thrust away like thorns, because they cannot be taken in hand *[because they outright refuse to be productive]*; but the man who touches them must be armed with iron and the shaft of a spear, and they will be completely burned with fire in their place" (2 Sam 23:6–7, emphasis added).

Solomon, like his father before him, warns his son to avoid the destructive path of the worthless man. Like the forbidden woman, the worthless man is easy to spot, as he dedicates nearly every member of his body to perpetual wickedness. As Solomon pointed out in the verses above, the worthless man speaks crooked perversions with his *mouth*. He winks with his *eyes*, signals with his *feet*, and gestures with his *fingers* in an effort to entice or intimidate others into following in his wicked footsteps.

In his arrogance, the worthless man disrespects Lady Wisdom. He mocks her virtue and scoffs at her promises. Her ways are of no appeal to him because, like the forbidden woman, his heart lusts for the cold touch of spiritual darkness.

Lady Wisdom, as we learned in letter 4, offers him nothing in return but a tone of righteous contempt:

> "¹²I, wisdom, dwell with prudence, and I find knowledge and discretion. ¹³The fear of the LORD is to hate evil; pride and arrogance and the evil way and the perverted mouth, I hate." (8:12–13)

Son, every choice comes with a consequence. As we discussed in the first half of this letter, the man who is self-controlled, self-interested, and self-governing will reap the real-life rewards of his wise choices. The worthless man's fate, however, lies in stark opposition to that of the wise man.

Once again, think back to letter 4: Every man who ignores Wisdom's call will bring suffering upon himself. The worthless man is no exception. His rude rejection of Lady Wisdom brings about harsh consequences. And as a result, the worthless man's self-induced *calamity will come suddenly*, when he least expects it, and "instantly he will be broken and there will be no healing" (6:15).

The seven character traits of a worthless man

In Prov 6:16-19, Solomon delves deeper into his study of the worthless man's personality. He begins his analysis by informing his son of the seven wicked character traits that God despises in every human being:

> "^{16}There are six things which the LORD hates, yes, seven which are an abomination to Him: ^{17}haughty eyes, a lying tongue, and hands that shed innocent blood, ^{18}a heart that devises wicked plans, feet that run rapidly to evil, ^{19}a false witness who utters lies, and one who spreads strife among brothers." (6:16-19)

Son, refer back to Solomon's description of the worthless man's behavior in 6:12-15. Notice how he is the literal embodiment of these seven hateful abominations:

1. *Haughty eyes*

The worthless man idolizes attention and approval. He wants to be seen as great in the eyes of others, so he *winks his eyes* (6:13) in an effort to sell this inflated image of himself to the public at large. He acts with a haughty attitude because he has a bone-deep need to feel superior to the people around him. But his puffed-up view of himself actually betrays an underlying insecurity that constantly gnaws away at his soul. He is not a man of personal excellence—and he knows it. He works hard to tell everyone how awesome he thinks he is because in reality he is a puny man with limited ability. His big talk is a sham. And for all his bravado, he's nothing more than a sad sack of hot air trying to conceal the truth about his mediocrity.

2. *A lying tongue*

Crooked speech (6:12) is the worthless man's calling card. He'll claim to be a good guy, but he's not. He'll say he's your friend, but he's not. He'll tell you that he'll be there when you need him, but he won't. He'll shake your hand and smile to your face—but as soon as you turn your back, he'll unsheathe his knife and slide it between your ribs. Remember our discussion in letter 3 about bad influences. They'll pretend to be your friends so long as you serve their purposes. Then when they don't need you anymore, they'll throw you under the bus at the first opportunity. The worthless man is the epitome of a bad influence. He is not your friend. He's a con-man who'll say whatever he has to say to advance himself at your expense.

3. Hands that shed innocent blood

If manipulation and deceit don't work, Solomon says the worthless man won't hesitate to *use his fingers* and *his hands* to start trouble and *shed innocent blood* (6:13–14). Remember what we learned in letter 7: A wise man doesn't initiate force against his neighbor. The worthless man, on the other hand, utilizes force and bully tactics on a regular basis. Whether he's behind a keyboard trying to sound tough by typing with the Caps Lock on, or whether he's physically attacking someone who has the audacity to disagree with him, he's always angling for a fight. He's so quick to resort to violence because he's a thug who would rather use his hands as instruments of destruction than as tools of righteousness and justice.

4. A heart that devises wicked plans

The worthless man feeds on negative emotion. He seeks out conflict because without it, his life is boring. He's one of those lazy guys that we discussed in the previous section. He ignores his responsibilities and therefore has nothing better to think about. He has nothing to occupy his mind except the nagging feelings of failure, envy, and resentment that accompany an empty life. Rather than watching over his own heart with all diligence as Solomon suggests in Prov 4:23 (letter 8), he leaves his heart unattended and vulnerable to these negative emotions. And rather than taking responsibility for his own bad choices, he shifts the blame to others and spends his time *devising wicked plans* (6:14) against those people he (wrongly) feels are the cause of his suffering.

5. Feet that run rapidly to evil

The worthless man is a good liar. But you can see through all the calculated posing he does by watching his feet, which Solomon says *signal toward trouble* (6:13). Remember what I said in letter 3: You can identify a bad influence by observing what excites him. Like the bad influence that he is, the worthless man's *feet run rapidly to evil*. They *hasten to shed blood* because he's a troublemaker who's attracted to antisocial behavior (Prov 1:16). Think back once again to letter 7, when we discussed the three general principles of successful social relationships: (1) A wise man will trade good for good with the people around him, (2) he won't initiate harm against his neighbor, (3) nor will he copy bad behavior just to get ahead (Prov 3:27–35). The worthless man acts in stark opposition to these principles. He doesn't trade good for good with the people around him. Instead, he takes advantage of others by exploiting their weaknesses and manipulating their emotions. The worthless man does not seek to live at peace with his neighbors. Instead, he uses controlling or violent behavior in his dealings with them. He acts this way because he does not fear God, nor does he respect Lady Wisdom. Instead, he aims his admiration toward wicked men and his feet are quick to follow in their footsteps.

6. A false witness who utters lies

Solomon yet again brings up the worthless man's penchant for dishonesty. He says the worthless man *goes around breathing out lies* (6:12, 19 RSV), meaning that deception is more than just a bad habit for the worthless man—it's his way of life. Dishonesty is such a fundamental aspect of his character that telling lies has become an instinctive behavior, like breathing or blinking. He has embraced the identity of a false witness full on. And in doing so, he's allowed untrustworthiness to settle in as the predominant characteristic that defines him as a man.

7. One who spreads strife among brothers.

Of all the bad things the worthless man does—manipulation, lying, devising evil, and committing violence—Solomon points out that they're all done to accomplish one wicked purpose: to spread strife (6:14). The worthless man is a miserable man who's not content to keep his misery to himself. He has a desperate need to take his frustrations out on the people around him. So he employs deception and violence as a means of *spreading conflict among brothers*. The worthless man spends a large portion of his time arguing and tearing others down because, like we discussed just three paragraphs earlier, he has nothing but negative emotions to occupy his thoughts. Notice how he won't put the same amount of time and effort into cultivating positive relationships and earning self-respect. He's a sluggard who doesn't want to do the work necessary to put his life to good use. His life is empty and lacks meaning. This makes him a bitter man who won't rest until he can share his pain and misery with the people around him.

Son, as you can clearly see, the worthless man is not the kind of guy you need to be around.

His actions go beyond disrespect. All his wicked thoughts, his wicked words, and his wicked deeds—they all spring forth from a hateful heart that beats in rebellion to God. The Lord is patient with sinners. But remember:

He will not be mocked. If the worthless man chooses to continue in his rebellion, God will most assuredly whip the cords of justice across his back. God will rain the consequences of his own bad choices down upon his head and the worthless man will have no one to blame but himself—and as long as he refuses to repent of his worthless ways, his life will stay saturated with pain and failure.

Son, if you want to avoid God's judgment, then avoid the worthless man. He is not your friend. He isn't funny or cool. He is *the* primary male bad influence you will encounter in your life. Solomon has gone into great detail on how to identify him, so heed his warnings and steer clear of the worthless man just as you would the forbidden woman.

Only a self-controlled, self-interested, and self-governing man is capable of ignoring the peer pressure of fools and standing firm against the threats of bullies. Such a man stands strong on his principles and works hard day in and day out to reflect God's image, accomplish his created purpose, and achieve his destiny.

And it's in this way that he *earns* his self-respect.

Son, we've made it to the end of Solomon's discourse.

But your journey into manhood is just beginning. I've done my job as your father up to this point. With these letters, I've provided you with the basic tools you need to walk out the door and start building a beautiful life. The next step is up to you.

You can be the kind of man who honors God, provides for his family, and earns his own self-respect when you choose to walk in the way of wisdom. Remember what I said back in letter 1: Wisdom is a choice—it's *your* choice. I have chosen to follow the path of wisdom by honoring my fatherly responsibilities and instructing you with the words of God.

It's your responsibility to choose what you will do with these words.

My prayer is that you will do the wise thing and put this knowledge to work in the real world. I want you to remember my words and use them to achieve your destiny and create a good life for yourself.

A life lived in God's presence.

A life defined by heroism and strength.

A life filled with meaningful relationships and significant accomplishments.

A life rich in love and happiness and genuine pride.

In essence, the life of a real man.

Love,

Dad

Bibliography

Ace of Spades HQ. "An Observation of the Decay of Learned Restraint." Last modified August 9, 2018. Accessed August 10, 2018. http://ace.mu.nu/archives/376502.php#376502.

Anselm. *Monologion and Proslogion: with the replies of Gaunilo and Anselm*. Translated by Thomas Williams. Indianapolis: Hackett, 1995.

Brunton, Jacob. "Athens & Jerusalem: General and Specific Revelation." *For the New Christian Intellectual*, September 10, 2013. Accessed March 11, 2020. https://medium.com/christian-intellectual/athens-jerusalem-general-and-specific-revelation-31f6622d7e67.

———. "Revelation and Responsibility." *For the New Christian Intellectual*. Accessed March 11, 2020. https://christianintellectual.com/revelation-and-responsibility/.

———. "The Wisdom of the World." *For the New Christian Intellectual*. Accessed March 11, 2020. https://christianintellectual.com/the-wisdom-of-the-world/.

Calvin, John. *Institutes of the Christian Religion*. Vol. 1. Louisville: Westminster John Knox, 2006.

Campbell, Joseph. *The Hero With A Thousand Faces*. Collected Works of Joseph Campbell. 1949. Reprint, Novato, CA: New World Library, 2008.

Garrett, Duane. *The New American Commentary*. Vol. 14, *Proverbs, Ecclesiastes, Song of Songs*. Nashville: Broadman & Holman, 1993.

Heiser, Michael H. "Jesus and Wisdom." *The Divine Council*. Accessed June 18, 2019. https://www.thedivinecouncil.com/JesusandWisdom.pdf.

———. "The New Testament Writers Had the Apocrypha and Pseudepigrapha in their Heads." *Dr. Michael S. Heiser*, January 12, 2016. Accessed January 21, 2020. https://drmsh.com/the-new-testament-writers-had-the-apocrypha-and-pseudepigrapha-in-their-heads/.

———. *The Unseen Realm: Rediscovering the Supernatural Worldview of the Bible*. Bellingham, WA: Lexham, 2015.

Hill, Andrew E., and John H. Walton. *A Survey of the Old Testament*. 3rd ed. Grand Rapids: Zondervan, 2009.

Kahl, Jeffrey. "In Defense of Leisure." *For the New Christian Intellectual*. Accessed May 23, 2019. https://christianintellectual.com/leisure/.

Keil, Carl F., and Franz Delitzsch. *Minor Prophets*. Vol. 10, *Commentary on the Old Testament*. 3rd ed. Peabody, MA: Hendrickson, 2011.

———. *The Pentateuch*. Vol. 1, *Commentary on the Old Testament*. 3rd ed. Peabody, MA: Hendrickson, 2011.

———. *Proverbs, Ecclesiastes, Song of Songs*. Vol. 6, *Commentary on the Old Testament*. 3rd ed. Peabody, MA: Hendrickson, 2011.

———. *Psalms*. Vol. 5, *Commentary on the Old Testament*. 3rd ed. Peabody, MA: Hendrickson, 2011.

Köestenberger, Andreas. *God, Marriage, and Family: Rebuilding the Biblical Foundation*. Wheaton, IL: Crossway, 2004.

Lewis, C. S. *The Chronicles of Narnia*. New York: Harper, 2008.

———. *On Stories: And Other Essays on Literature*. San Diego: Harcourt, 1982.

Libolt, Cody. "Ayn Rand and Christianity?" *For the New Christian Intellectual*. Accessed January 29, 2020. https://christianintellectual.com/ayn-rand/.

Loeb, Jeph. *Batman: Hush*. Illustrated by Jim Lee. Burbank, CA: DC Comics, 2009.

McCarthy, Cormac. *The Road*. London: Picador, 2006.

Miller, Frank. *Batman: The Dark Knight Returns*. Illustrated by Lynn Varley and Klaus Janson. Burbank, CA: DC Comics, 2016.

Moore, Robert, and Douglas Gillette. *King Warrior Magician Lover: Rediscovering the Archetypes of the Mature Masculine*. San Francisco: HarperOne, 1990.

Morse, Jennifer Roback. *Love and Economics: Why the Laissez-Faire Family Doesn't Work*. Dallas: Spence, 2003.

Mounce, William D., ed. *Mounce's Complete Expository Dictionary of Old & New Testament Words*. Grand Rapids: Zondervan, 2006.

Peterson, Jordan B. *12 Rules for Life: An Antidote to Chaos*. Toronto: Random House Canada, 2018.

———. "Maps of Meaning: The Architecture of Belief, Lecture 2: Marionettes and Individuals 02 (Part 1)." Video lecture, University of Toronto, Canada, January 25, 2017. Accessed November 11, 2019. www.youtube.com/watch?v=EN2lyN7rM4E.

Rand, Ayn. *The Art of Fiction: A Guide for Writers and Readers*. New York: Plume, 2000.

———. *Philosophy: Who Needs It*. New York: Signet, 1984.

———. *The Virtue of Selfishness: A New Concept of Egoism*. New York: Signet, 1964.

Ryken, Leland, et al., eds. *Dictionary of Biblical Imagery*. Downers Grove, IL: InterVarsity, 1998.

Sproul, R. C., et al. *Classical Apologetics: A Rational Defense of the Christian Faith and a Critique of Presuppositional Apologetics*. Grand Rapids: Zondervan, 1984.

Taylor, Richard. *Restoring Pride: The Lost Virtue of Our Age*. Amherst, MA: Prometheus, 1996.

Van Leeuwen, Raymond C. *Introduction to Wisdom Literature, Proverbs, Ecclesiastes, Song of Solomon, Wisdom, Sirach*. Vol. 5, *The New Interpreter's Bible: A Commentary in Twelve Volumes*. Nashville: Abingdon, 1997.

Walton, John H. *Ancient Near Eastern Thought and the Old Testament: Introducing the Conceptual World of the Hebrew Bible*. Grand Rapids: Baker Academic, 2006.

www.ingramcontent.com/pod-product-compliance
Lightning Source LLC
Chambersburg PA
CBHW051927160426
43198CB00012B/2070